# More Advance Praise for
## *A World Gone Social*

"Welcome to the 'Age of Influence,' where anyone can build an audience and effect change, advocate brands, build relationships, and make a difference. If your brand is not making the effort, you will be overtaken by those who do. So critical to follow the advice and leadership of Ted Coiné and Mark Babbitt . . . do not risk being left behind!"

—**Ted Rubin**, author of *Return on Relationship*

"A fascinating read! Two of the best minds in the business provide a valuable perspective on the Social Age and a practical roadmap to achieving success."

—**Frank Sonnenberg**, former National Director Marketing, Ernst & Young Management Consulting Group, and author of *Managing with a Conscience*

"*A World Gone Social* is an essential roadmap for today's fast-changing business environment. If you really want to understand how to reach and build relationships with customers in the Social Era, read this book now."

—**Dorie Clark**, author of *Reinventing You: Define Your Brand, Imagine Your Future* and adjunct professor, Duke University Fuqua School of Business

"Ted Coiné and Mark Babbitt are two of the surprisingly few who truly understand social media's deeper power to transform leadership and management, not just marketing. Now that the Social Age has become permanent, *A World Gone Social* is a must-read for leaders at all levels who want to thrive."

—**Jamie Notter**, Partner at Culture That Works and coauthor of *Humanize: How People-Centric Organizations Succeed in a Social World*

"*A World Gone Social* makes the compelling case that the Social Age isn't a fad that will go away but a revolution in how we do business. The pages are packed with thought-provoking insights and ideas for how to translate this new way of working into your organization. A must-read for any business professional!"

—**Patti Johnson**, CEO and Founder of PeopleResults and author of *Make Waves: Be the One to Start Change at Work and in Life*

"*A World Gone Social* provides an extraordinary vision and script for leaders and organizations alike to not just survive but thrive in the new Social Era. My sincerest gratitude to authors Ted Coiné and Mark Babbitt for their work as true 'Blue Unicorns' of our generation."

—**Mark Fernandes**, Chief Leadership Officer at the Luck Companies

"The connectedness brought by the Social Age has fundamentally shifted the playing field for business. Ted and Mark have provided the essential guidebook to help business leaders understand, navigate, and prosper in 'A World Gone Social.'"

—**Lisa Shelley**, Founder of Essentia Limited

"Ted and Mark have the distinct ability to see around the corner of business and accurately describe the future. How do I know this? Because I'm living in the future as a nano entrepreneur and this book depicts my world better than I could."

—**Bronson Taylor**, GrowthHackerTV

"Engage, persuade, and build your brand online—here's how to make it happen. *A World Gone Social* is a vital resource for navigating the maze of social media, from two of the top leaders in the space. Highly recommended."

—**Chris Westfall**, author of *BulletProof Branding* and *The NEW Elevator Pitch*

"To understand how to survive and thrive the social era, where we must move fast and adapt quickly, *A World Gone Social* is a must-read."

—**David Houle**, author of *Entering the Shift Age*

"*A World Gone Social* makes the point that social is so much more than a medium; social is the catalyst for cultural change in an organization. For leaders keen to transform their organizations, I recommend this insightful book as the place to start."

—**John Richard Bell**, former CEO of Jacob Suchard

"Today 'social' is a buzzword that's almost meaningless. Mark and Ted cut through the jargon and hype to teach us what social really is—and isn't. Social is about being human—and how to make your business a truly social business. Read, Learn, Apply, and Share."

—**Deb Mills-Scofield**, Partner at Glengary LLC, a Venture Capital Firm, and Visiting Scholar at Brown University

"Who better to guide you through this brave new social world than the guys who discovered that without the human side, businesses lose their edge. Leaders, future leaders, entrepreneurs: This is what you need to know to thrive in the world where connection is everything."

—**Dr. Janice Presser**, The Gabriel Institute

"In every aspect of our lives, from early education to established corporations, social media has had a tremendous impact. How we think, learn, and create has changed. *A World Gone Social* is our guide through this change . . . and a must-read for every social leader in the 21st Century."

—**Angela Maiers**, author of *Habitudes*

"Finally! A book that puts 'social' in context. This broad yet practical and engaging read adds much-needed perspective to the social revolution. Pay attention—this could be the blueprint for your company's next transformation."

—**Dr. Todd Dewett, Ph.D.**, author of *The Little Black Book of Leadership*

"Get ready for social disruption! Ted and Mark's *A World Gone Social* is a powerful learn, do, share model to change how you think about and use social media. If you haven't put the human piece into social yet, these guys will show you how."

—**Roy Saunderson**, Chief Learning Officer at Rideau's Recognition Management Institute

"*A World Gone Social* is a master playbook for what social means to any manager, leader, or strategist—smart, comprehensive, irreverent. I picked up enough action items to know this isn't a theory book; it's about getting social done and done right."

—**Ron Ricci**, Vice President, Cisco

"Ted and Mark have captured a critical handbook for change based on practical ideas rather than theory. Don't be intimidated if it sounds like too much. Read the book and ask yourself (a) where am I already doing this? and (b) what needs to be different? then (c) start taking small steps right away. Remember William James's line 'The art of being wise is knowing what to overlook.' Overlook your doubts and give the ideas a try. The results won't be what you expected (handing the power over to your customers results in many surprises!), but they will be remarkable."

—**Alan Kay**, Solution Focused Change Leader and author of *Fry the Monkeys*

"This book is packed full of radical thinking, innovative insight, and real-world experience to give each of us an arsenal of tactics and a powerful compass in this era of unprecedented social change and influence. Will those companies unwilling to change cease to exist in the social age? One cannot help but think a little differently after reading *A World Gone Social*."

—**Mark Lukens,** Founding Partner at Method3 and Chairman of the Board, Behavioral Health Services North

"*A World Gone Social* is the ultimate wake-up call for companies to embrace the human side of business, or face extinction. Offering a brilliant blend of visionary, thought-provoking, and actionable ideas, Ted and Mark call on the business world to turn serendipity from being social into business-as-usual. Their book offers a wealth of inspiration to transform leadership, people and culture management, marketing, sales, and operations to the rules of the Social Age. A must-read to survive and thrive!"

—**Kristof De Wulf,** CEO at @InSites

"In *A World Gone Social*, Ted and Mark provide an in-depth overview of how social media has begun to transform, and will continue to revolutionize, the way successful businesses operate. As formal, structured organizations give way to fluid, dynamic, informal collaborations, the ability to build meaningful relationships with respect, appreciation, and gratitude opens up even more possibilities and becomes critical to success. Ted and Mark offer excellent perspective and insights both for those who have social media savvy and those who are social media novices."

—**Margie Bressler,** Founder of Moving Messages

"In *A World Gone Social*, Coiné and Babbitt deftly deconstruct the tectonic impact that social media has had on nearly every aspect of our lives. But this isn't only a book about social media; it's also a handbook for understanding how the principles of social media can ignite profitable transformation in your organization. At its heart, this is a book about the gentle revolution of 'open,' the ironic power of the listening leader, and the cultural need for more rebel heretics."

—**Josh Allan Dykstra,** author of *Igniting the Invisible Tribe: Designing an Organization That Doesn't Suck*

"A dynamic and insightful read, *A World Gone Social* manages to emulate the pace and experience of the social world in a book! Bringing the kind of insight typically only available in hindsight into current view, the authors do a brilliant job of illuminating the implications of the Social Age on the way we do business. And, perhaps most importantly, they guide us in making the mind shifts essential to engage and leverage the extraordinary opportunities a social world creates."

—**Susan Mazza,** CEO of Clarus Works

# A World Gone Social

## How Companies Must Adapt to Survive

Ted Coiné

Mark Babbitt

### American Management Association

New York · Atlanta · Brussels · Chicago · Mexico City · San Francisco
Shanghai · Tokyo · Toronto · Washington, D.C.

Bulk discounts available. For details visit:
www.amacombooks.org/go/specialsales
Or contact special sales:
Phone: 800–250–5308
Email: specialsls@amanet.org
View all the AMACOM titles at: www.amacombooks.org
American Management Association: www.amanet.org

This publication is designed to provide accurate and authoritative information in regard to the subject matter covered. It is sold with the understanding that the publisher is not engaged in rendering legal, accounting, or other professional service. If legal advice or other expert assistance is required, the services of a competent professional person should be sought.

Library of Congress Cataloging-in-Publication Data

Coiné, Ted.
    A world gone social : how companies must adapt to survive / Ted Coiné and Mark Babbitt.
        pages cm
    Includes index.
    ISBN 978-0-8144-3326-3 (hardcover)—ISBN 0-8144-3326-X (hardcover)
1. Social networks. 2. Strategic planning. 3. Success in business. I. Babbitt, Mark. II. Title.
    HM741.C63 2014
    302.30285—dc23
                                2014015350

**About AMA**
American Management Association (www.amanet.org) is a world leader in talent development, advancing the skills of individuals to drive business success. Our mission is to support the goals of individuals and organizations through a complete range of products and services, including classroom and virtual seminars, webcasts, webinars, podcasts, conferences, corporate and government solutions, business books, and research. AMA's approach to improving performance combines experiential learning—learning through doing—with opportunities for ongoing professional growth at every step of one's career journey.

Printing number

10 9 8 7 6 5 4 3 2 1

# Contents

# Foreword

I would rather engage in a Twitter conversation with a single customer than see our company attempt to attract the attention of millions in a coveted Super Bowl commercial.

Why? Because having people discuss your brand directly with you, actually connecting one-on-one, is far more valuable—not to mention far cheaper!

But if you think this position is about social media, you're wrong. As you'll come to see in this book, this is less about media and more about understanding what it means to lead in the Social Age—less to do with campaigning and more to do with engaging.

It is, in fact, about a better way to do business.

But my point of view is not a popular one. The business world still struggles— with a great deal of resistance— to see the true value of the Social Age. Many are still saddled with old-school best practice perspectives that do not serve today's leadership well.

That is why the Social Age is a vital and relevant topic to cover. The business world *must* prioritize this issue.

As recently as eighteen months ago, executives had so-called control. They defined the rules of the game for consumers: "To do business with us, here's what we offer, and here's how you do it." Propaganda shaped advertising. Consumers lost trust.

But times have changed and roles have shifted.

Consumers want to discuss what they like, the companies they support, and the organizations and leaders they resent. They want a community. They want to be heard.

Consumers now demand that business becomes a compelling experience, which moves the power from the executive boardroom (where decisions used to be made) to the living rooms of everyday consumers.

This is not entirely different from what employees now demand, too. Both consumers and employees are telling us how, where, and when they want to work with us. They are better informed, they expect more, and they certainly have the voice to make a strong impact.

The Social Age is a revolution, one that affects all parts of the business model. The way an organization creates, delivers, and captures value. The way a business talks with employees, customers, communities, even regulators and government. And certainly the way leaders lead and behave.

So we face a big challenge. But it certainly is not Facebook, Twitter, or the latest social media platform. The biggest challenge the world has seen since the Industrial Age is not social media. It is transparency.

You already know, change is not easy. Many run away from the challenge. But businesses must see the Social Age as an opportunity to authentically reconnect with their employees and consumers. Forget price, products, and services. Trust is the new competitive advantage. Adapt, or you may not survive.

The Social Age implies—to a certain degree—that the walls between our offices have been torn down. And we have let the world look inside, read our e-mails, and sit in on our meetings. It suggests that our employees have a real ability to shape their own careers, demand work that matters, change their working conditions, and get direct access to the executive teams, or their CEOs.

*Imagine that!*

I can see how scary that would be for most. But this is the future. And it is certainly the better way. Better for your business, your employees, your customers, and guess what? It is far better for your shareholders as well.

We have a choice to passively listen to what employees and customers—and potential customers—think about us and our businesses. Or we can choose to be a part of the conversation. We can, by choice, help inform, educate, and teach people about what we do, what the business stands for, and how we plan to change their lives in a positive way.

We have the opportunity to reveal who we truly are.

And better yet, if we engage employees, customers, and prospective customers in meaningful dialogue about their lives, challenges, interests, and concerns, we can build a community of trust, loyalty, and—possibly over time—help them become advocates and champions for the brand.

That is the type of brand evangelism shareholders, until recently, could only dream of!

Some companies are already being run differently. Some have figured out how to navigate the Social Age and are in fact thriving. But some haven't—and they will soon find their backs against the wall.

I am thrilled that Ted Coiné and Mark Babbitt have the courage to address this much-needed topic of change in the business world. I imagine it would be interesting for you to know that I first met Ted and Mark on Twitter! Also interesting is that Ted and Mark met on Twitter.

I have followed their valuable insight for years, and I am convinced that there is no one better suited to address this topic.

Their relentless focus to drive a better way to do business is undeniable, and admirable. The common denominators in all the writings I have been exposed to from both Ted and Mark are simple:

*Less jargon, more sincerity . . . Less propaganda, more value . . . Less process, more humanity.*

We live in a hyperconnected world. For those of us who engage in it well, for those of us who choose to see the significance of change, we stand a better chance to establish real value, for our customers, colleagues, the world, and ourselves. In a world gone social, we have chosen the human side of business.

Happy reading!

*Peter Aceto, CEO, Tangerine*

# Introduction

The Industrial Age is dead.

Welcome to the Social Age.

Social media has proven to be an insurmountable market force, changing how we innovate, collaborate, serve our customers, hire and develop team members, motivate others toward a common mission, communicate with stakeholders, display our character, and demonstrate accountability. This isn't change for the sake of change. Neither is this change to fine-tune the status quo, as we saw in the twentieth century with Six Sigma, Total Quality Management, and the Lean movement, which simply helped bureaucracies function at a more efficient, profitable level. This is real, systemic change.

Human change.

Which isn't easy.

We two authors—ourselves successful veterans of the social revolution—will help you initiate that change. By discussing the next major era in business, *A World Gone Social* will enable you to adapt quickly, so you can thrive in the Social Age:

- ► We'll help you, your company, and your industry get out in front of the social revolution.

- ► We'll ensure you have the voice, influence, and power to lead engaged, innovative teams.

- ► We'll help you learn from the successes and failures of the early adopters and companies that have already taken to social (some in a good way, and others that have made community-killing mistakes).

- ► We'll discuss the power of OPEN, where ordinary people intersect to form extraordinary networks.

- ► We'll introduce you to some of the fascinating change makers, innovators, and mistake makers in the vanguard of the Social Age.

- ► And, along the way, you'll learn our secret to social: *More social. Less media.*

In Section I of *A World Gone Social,* we'll talk about the surface changes currently under way—business issues that have caught much attention. We'll discuss how some old-school leaders seem dimly aware of the new era upon us and so are left grasping in the dark, while others remain unconvinced of the power of social, so they fail to take action. We'll also take on those who resist for another reason: the "if it ain't broke, don't fix it" crowd, oblivious to the imminent change—and the turf protectors who perhaps have a vested personal interest in resisting social's influence.

We'll then delve deeper into those seismic changes that have already occurred in the Social Age: how the balance of power has shifted from message-controlling corporations to customers and employees who can now voice their opinions—both good and bad—through social. We'll show how one customer, or employee, can disrupt operations and the focus of an entire corporation based on one seemingly simple decision. And we'll discuss how those voices are amplified, and create real impact, through social.

Next, we'll demonstrate how social has already disrupted critical aspects of every business: the very way we'll build our teams moving forward, how we'll engage *with* (rather than broadcast *at*) stakeholders, and how five-star, 100 percent transparent customer service will lead to a community of evangelists organically supporting your brand.

In Section II, we'll take on the "death of large" and show how even the biggest enterprises need to get—or at least think and act—small to survive and that nimble, engaging, focused teams are how business will succeed in the Social Age. We'll ask if "flat" is the new black—a trend that, as social management takes root and grows exponentially, will become our "new" form of collaborative leadership (even though its roots are decades old). Finally, we'll introduce OPEN (Ordinary People | Extraordinary Network) not just as a method of building lifelong personal relationships but as the foundation of organizational success and as a catalyst for entire business models. Along the way, we'll introduce you to some people and companies that have already jumped into social, with varying degrees of success.

In Section III, we'll turn to how you can lead your organization to success in a world gone social. You will discover how to objectively assess the fitness of your organization's culture and social presence and how to improve every aspect that might be failing while leveraging what works well. We'll discuss the best possible approach to building socially enabled teams, turning customers into ambassadors, and cultivating passionate advocates and champions for your brand. And, with a world-class collaborative team and customer-centric culture in place, we'll dive into the dynamics at play in digital marketing—and how best to position your company in a world gone social.

In Section IV, we take a look at the future of social business and discuss how we might measure return on investment (ROI) on what is likely to remain more art than science. Finally, we'll look at what might be next steps for social media in general and for you as a leader in our new, socially driven economy.

In fact, that's our primary goal throughout this book: to enable you to lead your organization confidently and successfully through the Social Age.

We're sure you'll enjoy what you are about to read. After all, we have a passion for the subject that goes beyond social— to personal. As admirably as it served the first-world economy, we want the Industrial Age—and the autocratic leadership practices and soul-sucking working conditions that came with that era—to die. We want organizations to become more transparent, more accountable. We want teams to continuously innovate and collaborate, rather than be throttled by hundred-year-old "best practices."

In a world gone social, we want business *to become more human.*

*Let's get started . . .*

CHAPTER 1

# Welcome to the Social Age

*Change happens only as the result of insurmountable market pressure.*
*—Law of Change*

Finally (*finally!*) organizations—probably yours, too—are dabbling in social media. Most are playing catch-up, trying to seize the comet before the once-in-a-lifetime opportunity to lead (rather than follow) quickly passes overhead.

The Facebook fan page is established; the Twitter feed is blasting away. Human Resources is recruiting on LinkedIn, and their memberships at Glassdoor are in good standing. Interns are pinning on Pinterest, and C-level execs are blogging (or at least reading blog posts). Marketing budgets now have line items for digital media and something called "engagement." CFOs scramble to measure ROI and, so far, aren't impressed.

Still . . .

Although we can brag about our "presence" on social media, there's a deep and swift undercurrent of discontent. Especially among enterprise leaders, the sentiment seems to be: "Social is all hype" and "Social isn't working for us."

## THEY'RE MISSING SOMETHING. SOMETHING BIG.

The resistance seems to come from several different camps:

► Those rooted in the belief that social is a fad and will go the way of the Rolodex, fax machine, and VHS.

► Those living in a comfortable state of ignorance: "If I don't know it, it can't be that big a deal."

► Those who view social from a "sales have never been better; our quarterly report was great; why change now?" mentality.

► Those who are afraid to lose the control they have now as leaders (and our experience shows there are more old-schoolers in this camp than we'd like to admit). They don't want change, because it effectively means the end of their power.

Regardless of the reason why, with those enterprise leaders who resist the onrushing Social Age we share this display of stubbornness—dare we say a daring display of arrogance—that allegedly occurred in October 1998 off the coast of Kerry, Ireland:

> *Irish: Please divert your course 15 degrees to the south, to avoid a collision.*
> *British: Recommend you divert your course 15 degrees to the north to avoid a collision.*
> *Irish: Negative. Divert your course 15 degrees to the south to avoid a collision.*
> *British: This is the captain of a British navy ship. I say again, divert YOUR course.*
> *Irish: Negative. I say again, you will have to divert YOUR course.*
> *British: This is the aircraft carrier HMS Britannia! We are the second largest ship in the British Atlantic fleet. We are accompanied by three destroyers, three cruisers, and numerous support vessels. I demand that you change your course 15 degrees north. I say again, that is 15 degrees north, or countermeasures will be undertaken to ensure the safety of this ship and her crew.*
> *Irish: We are a lighthouse. Your call.*

## THE SOCIAL LEADER

*A World Gone Social: How Companies Must Adapt to Survive* is, in part, a book about social media. More precisely, though, the book encourages you to fully embrace the Social Age, to lead your organization, department, or team in this entirely new era of business, with a workforce that fundamentally thinks differently about work.

Especially among the digital natives, the Millennials who now make up the majority of the workforce, the workforce thinks *much* differently.

In today's workforce, many of us trust each other and communicate more, and in turn, we're more authentic and open to input and criticism. Many of us invite collaboration from all sources—even from our competition, when mutually beneficial. More than anything else, we're more cooperative, and more social.

As organizations and leaders, we must adapt to this social, collaborative, open environment—or we simply won't survive. For many organizations still entrenched in old-fashioned Industrial Age–style management practices, it may be too late.

While these antiquated businesses are busy chasing what appears to be a shiny new comet, they fail to realize that the big ball of light isn't actually a comet but more like that giant asteroid that slammed into Earth 65 million years ago—and killed all the dinosaurs.

In today's business climate, social media represents the asteroid, the change agent. Those who don't embrace social media—and fail to realize the monumental impact social has on their customers, employees, and collaborative partnerships, as well as their bottom line, are the dinosaurs.

Stubbornly, they look up at the sky and say, "That big fiery ball won't hurt us. We're safe behind our brick-and-mortar fortresses."

They are wrong. Dead wrong. And they will learn, perhaps the hard way, that the Industrial Age is behind us already.

## WELCOME TO THE SOCIAL AGE

Already, old-school leaders, companies, and industries—including newspapers, magazines, broadcast television, the U.S. Postal Service, and many legacy retailers—have been walking down a path of self-inflicted ignorance. Burdened by a failure to adapt to this new environment, many have lost their footholds in the new business climate; some are already nearing extinction. Others are already gone.

Other industries, such as music and movies, have seen a massive shift in how their products are marketed and consumed. While there was a time *Rolling Stone* was considered a trendsetter and barometer of what would be hot next, chances are now that whatever new band *Rolling Stone* is talking about blew up in the blogosphere six months ago. Movie studios, to create organic buzz about a new release, send review copies to bloggers and digital influencers most of us have never heard of, sometimes before far more famous and traditional reviewers—Peter Travers of *Rolling Stone* or Janet Maslin of *The New York Times,* for instance—receive them.

Meanwhile, enabled by social, the human side of business grows exponentially:

► In the form of solopreneurs, freelancers, and nano corps (which we'll discuss in Chapter 7), competition in our new economy sprouts up at will. With little or no infrastructure, minuscule start-up costs, and next-to-nothing monthly expenses, they launch in a matter of days—and gain immense traction, even when competing against corporate giants—through social media.

► Customers, no longer beholden to marketing departments or advertising agencies for guidance or input, confer with each other; they compare notes, thoughts, and experiences about the companies with which they and their vast networks do business.

- ▶ One person, with a Twitter account and a lot of passion, can hobble corporate titans, media outlets, politicians, and others with less-than-honorable ambitions.

- ▶ Expertise has become democratic; in less than an hour and for zero dollars, anyone can establish him- or herself as an expert—or an expert critic—in any industry.

- ▶ Without corporate consent (or even knowledge), employees collaborate with each other, as well as with vendors, with customers, and even with competitors.

- ▶ Job seekers ask current employees (as well as past employees, vendors, customers, partners, public forums, and personal networking contacts) what working at the company is *really* like; in the process, they mute the canned, inauthentic messages of recruiters and public relations departments.

- ▶ Highly competitive human resources departments—those effectively attracting, hiring, and retaining top talent in our new economy—are becoming *human* again (the rest are accelerating their companies' collective plunge toward extinction).

- ▶ Through digital self-learning, knowledge is everywhere.

- ▶ The "powers that be"—those previously able to hoard knowledge—are now impotent rulers, the "powers that were."

The way we did business in the twentieth century worked great—in the twentieth century! Frederick Taylor's scientific management theories on industrial efficiency *did* work to tame the chaos of production. By measuring every little aspect of production in the industrialized world, managers were able to squeeze inefficiencies out of business, drive prices down to previously unimaginable levels, and build whole infrastructures of prosperity. In less than a generation, this efficiency killed the cottage industry dead. Among countless examples is Andrew Carnegie's father, a prosperous hand-weaver in Scotland. Within ten years, inexpensive factory production of fine cloth put Carnegie's father (as well as most of his peers; in fact, an entire community) out of business. Young Andrew took the lesson to heart. In large part, he established his fortune by relentlessly investing in technological advancements.

Along those lines, enormous factories and massive enterprises were built; staggering bureaucracies were then formed to run them. From the 1870s until the present day, we've been living in this system—which your authors have unimaginatively labeled "old-school" management. While the nature of work, and of the goods produced, has steadily become more complex over time, the fundamentals have not changed.

## INDUSTRIAL AGE VS. SOCIAL AGE

In the old-school system:

► Top-down, command-and-control management was highly efficient.

► Massive bureaucracies to support this hierarchy made sense.

► Profit margins (and generally expanding economies) enabled "too many chiefs" management teams.

► Silos, caused by specialization of roles and internal protectionism, were a necessary evil of the system.

► Knowledge (and with it, power) was jealously guarded by those atop the corporate pyramid.

► Advertisers, marketers, PR departments, recruiters, and sales teams were able to spin their version of the truth relatively free of fact-checking (or reality).

► Disillusioned customers, employees, vendors, and communities had little recourse.

Yes, some remarkable companies were run in enlightened fashion: more openly, creatively, democratically, and better principled. W. L. Gore & Associates, most recognized for its Gore-Tex line of clothing and accessories, and Morning Star, the well-studied tomato processor, are widely known for their flat management styles without a chain of command or prescribed communication channels and are regarded as standard-bearers. And, yes, even among the old-school organizations, some were run as more benevolent dictatorships than others.

Yet even then we did not like being commanded. Or controlled.

We did not thrive—as employees, consumers, team leaders, or innovators— when ruled by autocrats. We wanted to bring our whole brains to work. We wanted to know that our opinions, our insight—our *genius*—mattered. We lacked a voice. We lacked influence. We lacked power.

Then social media happened. And everything changed.

The old way of doing things, of course, sputters on to this day. Yet that model is no longer competitive. Closed, hierarchical cultures do not prosper. Less-than-authentic business practices do not go unrevealed. Orders are not so easily barked to subordinates behind closed doors with an evil laugh, because there seem to be lurkers behind every partially open door. Less and less gets past those socially enabled workers every day. They are more aware; we are held more accountable.

In a world gone social, this is how business is done—and at a comet's speed.

## SOCIAL ISN'T ALL ROSES AND RAINBOWS

Of course, social media isn't all roses, rainbows, and Disney princesses singing in perfect tune with their animal friends. Social, as many have discovered, can amplify a bad idea to the point that a misinformed campaign—or even a single comment by a CEO that goes viral on social media—can at least momentarily hobble an entire organization.

Chip Wilson, founder of Lululemon, said this when asked about the perception of poor quality of his company's yoga pants (specifically, that they "pilled" and "sheered" when worn): "Well, some women's bodies just don't work for it."

In the Industrial Age, Wilson's comments would have been restricted to an audience of some industry insiders, perhaps a fashion tabloid or two, and a handful of angry customers. In the Social Age, the comment—as well as the insincere apology that followed—went viral. By the company's own estimate, this error in judgment cost Lululemon over $80 million. Wilson eventually resigned, leaving his replacement to admit that the company's PR issues had a hugely negative impact on the brand.

Also from the fashion world, Abercrombie & Fitch CEO Mike Jeffries learned there is apparently no statute of limitations on being stupid and insensitive. Comments he made in a 2006 interview—well before Facebook was in every home, and about the same time Twitter was launched—resurfaced on social media in 2013. Jeffries said: "In every school there are the cool kids and popular kids, and then there are the not-so-cool kids. . . . Candidly, we go after the cool kids."

Seven years later, those supporting the #FitchtheHomeless hashtag campaign purchased used A&F clothing by whatever means possible and donated it to the homeless, a tactic aimed at making the clothes-for-cool-kids manufacturer rue the highbrow remark. After another less-than-authentic apology, seven consecutive quarters of dwindling same-store sales, and a precipitous drop in stock price, Jeffries and A&F backtracked. In 2014, A&F would once again feature different "sizes, colors, and fits" in its stores. The move did not help Jeffries, however. Under intense pressure from influential shareholders, he lost his role as chairman and was being asked to find a buyer for the flailing company.

In the old days, Jeffries would have been seen as no more than yet another elitist, arrogant CEO. In the Social Age, which demands fair-minded leadership and purpose-driven commerce, Jeffries is considered an *über*villain.

Of course, social media's pillorying of idiocy isn't limited to the fashion industry. A radio interview with Barilla's CEO, Guido Barilla, in which he said that homosexuals do not represent a "sacred family" so therefore could never be featured in his company's ads, launched the pasta maker into intense and long-term damage-control mode. Specifically on Twitter, the hashtag #biocottabarilla ("Boycott Barilla") caused a huge uproar that forced the company and the CEO to issue many versions of the same apology.

While the financial and brand impact of Barilla's unenlightened comments is not yet known, there is no doubt about the role social media played in the firestorm: In the old days (think five years ago), this damage would have most likely been limited to the conservative audience of a little radio station in Italy. Today, Barilla still fights an international uproar.

For every instance of social brand bashing (some may call it digital bullying), however, there are hundreds of stories that show how getting noticed on social media—for all the right reasons—means nothing but good for the companies getting in front of the impact. For them, that asteroid doesn't mean destruction. Instead, it means a fresh beginning with customers in larger numbers than ever imagined.

## STAN PHELPS'S PURPLE GOLDFISH

A good friend of ours, Stan Phelps, is an amazing marketer. Stan is also the author of *What's Your Purple Goldfish? How to Win Customers and Influence Word of Mouth.* Stan talks eloquently about the power of *lagniappe*, whereby a merchant provides the customer with a small "extra" gift at the time of purchase. In his book, he refers to the most impactful of these small yet infinitely appreciated tokens as "purple goldfish"—something tiny that sets a business apart from all the gold-colored goldfish out there.

One of Stan's favorite purple goldfish stories involves a grandma with cancer, a grandson named Brandon Cook, and clam chowder from Panera, the bakery/café with great coffee (and, for some of us who contribute virtually and can work from anywhere, even better wi-fi).

Here is the text from Brandon's post on Facebook:

*My grandmother is passing soon with cancer. I visited her the other day and she was telling me about how she really wanted soup, but not hospital soup because she said it tasted "awful"[;] she went on about how she really would like some clam chowder from Panera. Unfortunately Panera only sells clam chowder on Friday. I called the manager, Sue, and told them the situation. I wasn't looking for anything special just a bowl of clam chowder. Without hesitation she said absolutely she would make her some clam chowder. When I went to pick it up they wound up giving me a box of cookies as well. It's not that big of a deal to most, but to my grandma it meant a lot. I really want to thank Sue and the rest of the staff from Panera in Nashua NH just for making my grandmother happy.*

*Thank you so much!*

To show her appreciation to Panera, Brandon's mother shared that post directly on their Facebook page. That little post—within just a few days—received *over a half-million* likes on the Panera page. To date, that number has climbed to over 800,000. The post has received nearly 35,000 comments praising the Panera brand.

As reported in an article in *AdWeek*, Brandon said: "If my grandma even knew what a Facebook page was, I'd show her. My grandma's biggest fear was dying with no friends. I wish I could show her how many 'friends' she has out there, and how many prayers people are saying for her."

What did this mean for Panera? How did this little story about a dying grandma, clam chowder, a customer-focused manager, and a grateful grandson impact the company's bottom line?

The next quarter, Panera's same-store sales increased 28 percent. The quarter after, same store sales were up 34 percent. Sure, there's no way of proving that this was all a direct result of the Facebook post, but the rapidly spreading goodwill generated by one person performing one moment of kindness, amplified nearly a million times over, certainly had a significant effect. That is the impact of the Social Age.

Yet too many of us are resistant to embrace the Social Age. Seemingly in direct proportion to the number of white hairs (or lack of hair) on our heads, we blow off social as a passing fad or "something for the kids" (as one executive told us while we were doing research for this book).

Ironic, isn't it? These old-school dinosaurs are the same people who, during their childhood and young adulthood, welcomed Elvis Presley as a sign that their generation could show some personality, that they could be deliberately different. Who accepted the Beatles as a welcome diversion after the JFK assassination? Who beamed with pride when we landed on the moon and when Ronald Reagan metaphorically knocked down the decades-old walls of the Cold War?

Who—perhaps as younger versions of themselves—demanded social, political, and economic change.

Wasn't change good then?

Didn't we accept that change with open arms and minds?

Social is not change for change's sake. *It is a monumental shift in how we think, work, and live.* Social is global change for good. It is how business is done. And it works for one simple reason: We humans, at our core, are *social* creatures.

Social media enables us to be more . . . "us."

Yes, as with all things human, both the good and the bad are magnified; for every story of good-gone-social it seems there are a thousand social sharks and trolls ready to feed on the bad.

Your role—as a leader challenged with taking your organization into the Social

Age—is to place your company square in the path of good. To enable those around you to do right by the customers, employees, vendors, and communities you serve. To build teams that understand the important role social plays in today's new economy. To build a culture where giving gets noticed. And to be fully accountable just after something goes bad—but before it gets much worse.

In a world gone social, this is how business is done.

Welcome to the Social Age.

Next, we'll begin to introduce the stakeholders most impacted by the Social Age, starting with those who now find themselves with a unified—and influential, even amplified—voice: the customers.

# CHAPTER 2

# The Customer Holds All the Cards

What would the world look like if customers had all the power?

The fact is, in the Social Age, they already do. And they're coming to realize it. Business will never be the same—certainly not as we knew it in the Industrial Age.

## A PRECEDENT SET: UNITED BREAKS GUITARS

In the early days of the Social Age, an example of social media cluelessness occurred that set an example for all customers who felt wronged—and all companies that fail to understand the power of social media. The story, which set off a media frenzy that still rears its ugly head five years later, goes something like this . . .

Imagine you're in a plane waiting for your flight to take off, when suddenly you hear the woman beside you say, "Oh my God! They're throwing guitars!"

This actually happened to a man named Dave Carroll. Guess whose guitar United Airlines baggage handlers were tossing around? There he was, trapped inside the plane on the tarmac in Chicago, watching in disbelieving horror as United staff played "Samsonite Gorilla" with his Taylor guitar. Sure enough, when the plane landed and he opened the case, the guitar was destroyed beyond repair.

Carroll attempted to work with United to resolve the situation. However, no matter who he talked to, they told him no compensation was coming; they weren't going to pay for a new guitar. Why? Because he failed to report the problem within the mandated twenty-four-hour window as required by United.

Who is Dave Carroll? Just some guy—a not-at-all-famous (at that point, anyway) professional musician. In that way, he was exactly like most of United's other passengers: unremarkable by himself. But as a part of a community, he is eminently important to United's reputation.

Knowing this depends on many variables; this figure may be laughably low or impossibly high, but so the math doesn't make any of our heads hurt let's say that for every $100 you spend on advertising, you earn one new customer.

Then, let's factor in the Industrial Age conventional wisdom that tells us that every time a company angers us with bad service or a faulty product, we're likely to inform ten friends, relatives, or colleagues of our dissatisfaction. In this case, one bad experience multiplied by ten friends wipes out $1,000 of advertising.

Big deal, right? All your old-school company—or United—need do is spend $1,000 *more* on advertising to undo the damage. This is the way we've done business for generations; it's often cheaper to buy more ads than to address customer complaints in a fair and proactive manner.

Don't get us wrong: It was never *smarter*. Just cheaper.

In Dave Carroll's case, a new guitar would have cost United about $3,500. Using United's calculus and infinite ability to rationalize the company's decision, it was more economical to alienate this customer and ten of his friends than to pay for a new guitar.

Only, here's the thing . . .

In the Social Age, wisdom is anything but "conventional." Conventional is a relic of the last century.

Ten friends? If you're a completely obscure singer/guitarist with an ax to grind, you can reach nearly 14 *million* people with a homemade video on YouTube—perhaps a video you name, appropriately, "United Breaks Guitars."

That's 14,000,000 . . . with six zeros. Just in the two years since we first thought to include "United Breaks Guitars" in this book, that number has climbed by about 3,000,000 views. Much to the dismay of United, this drag on its brand just won't go away.

Have you seen the video? If not, you owe yourself the pleasure—it's very funny. The tune is catchy and tells an entertaining story about an industry many have learned to despise.

Despite his best efforts, Carroll couldn't get financial satisfaction. Instead, he sought out emotional satisfaction.

He wrote a song, lined up some volunteer actors, and recorded a video about the experience. The video went "viral"—which is to say that one person told his closest 200 friends, who told their closest 200 friends, and so on, and so on. Today, not only have those 14 million YouTubers gotten a chuckle at United's expense, there has been a book, a speaking tour, and a few quasi-lame sequels to the song.

Some might even say the best thing that ever happened to Dave Carroll's music career was United breaking his guitar.

Yes, Carroll is an engaging presenter on the speaking circuit. He's gone from struggling musician to customer service rock star —literally a rock star in his case. Really, that's his job: He badmouths United Airlines for a living, to audiences around the world eager to listen to his little-guy-wins story.

And United?

Of course, it's still in business; you may be on one of its flights as you read this. And despite an urban legend (or bad accounting on the part of United's detractors), the airline did not lose $180 million all because of the little ditty by Carroll.

Still, it's hard to imagine the staggering amount of advertising money spent and opportunity cost United must have incurred to counter Carroll's negative advertising—which, let's remember, was nearly free for him to produce. Other than perhaps some elbow grease Carroll spent next to nothing to launch his video, the centerpiece of his revenge campaign.

Is this an exceptional case? Is this perhaps the best-known example of a cause going viral on social? Absolutely. It may even be one of the first, and it is certainly one of the best-documented.

Videos go truly viral once in a great while; those that do usually include a talking dog, a cute kitten or baby (sometimes both), or the newest reality television show star in an "oops" moment. Videos based on poor customer service? Those are much less likely than most to reach millions of viewers. Chances are, your complaint of bad service won't reach 14 million pairs of eyeballs no matter how much effort you put into emotional revenge.

But let's not lose sight of a very important issue: To create real impact in the Social Age, your video doesn't need to go viral; you don't need to become famous yourself or be famous to get started. You only need a Robin Hood–style just cause, a heartbreaking moment, or a moral outrage—and you're on your way.

You can tell your story as easily as talking to the video camera built into your computer or phone. You can write a post on your blog. You can share your complaint with friends on Facebook and with your colleagues, past and present, on LinkedIn. Pin it on Pinterest, and give it a +1 on Google+. Even document the exact moment of hurt in beautifully framed, full-color evidence on Instagram.

Or you can try your author's social tool of choice and tweet. Maybe you aren't a Twitter "Power Influencer" with 25,000 or 250,000 followers of your own, but there's an excellent chance you're following someone who is. When picked up by a Twitter heavy hitter, a brief line of text or a Twitter photo can span the globe in seconds. Others read and retweet to their followers, where it will get picked up again and again. Social media precedent shows it isn't too hard for something entertaining or interesting—or infuriating—to earn tens of thousands, even millions, of impressions in no time. And, in almost all cases, faster than your organization can react.

Even five years into the Social Age, customers are just beginning to grasp this shift in power; they are only just now understanding how their voices can be amplified. Companies are even slower to catch on. Still, a few (like United) have already lived this firsthand, one painful note at a time, played on a brand-new guitar they should have paid for without hesitation.

## BURNING MONEY

Before we move on to a wholly positive outcome of the social media revolution (there are so many, and we've got a few for you coming up soon), we'll dive a bit deeper into the perils of old-school leadership in this very social environment.

We don't mean to pick on United Airlines—at least, we don't want to give the other airlines a free pass by focusing exclusively on one bad apple among so many. But to continue the conversation from a positive perspective, we must talk about Southwest Airlines, the "Low Fare Airline." Yes, cheap is so central to this company's business that its *tagline* flaunts its commitment to cheap prices.

Yet knitted into the fabric of this company is an almost slavish drive to please the customer. No, Southwest hasn't begun offering first-class seats; it doesn't even *try* to provide five-star service to the pampered traveler. But when comparing apples to apples (in this case, coach seats to coach seats), most who've flown Southwest would agree there's something fundamentally different about the way it treats its customers.

Despite the pedestal it is often placed on by consumers, however, Southwest isn't immune to being called out on social.

## TOO FAT TO FLY SOUTHWEST

While the "United Breaks Guitars" video was still flexing its social muscles, film director, producer, and actor Kevin Smith was kicked off a Southwest flight by the crew for being . . . too fat. Again, a precedent was set: This time, the "good guy" (or at least the party that was given credit for handling the situation well) was the megacorporation.

On a Saturday morning, Smith tweeted to his 1 million Twitter followers from his @ThatKevinSmith handle:

*Dear @SouthwestAir—I know I'm fat, but was Captain Leysath really justified in throwing me off a flight for which I was already seated?*

The Twitter tirade went on:

*I'm way fat . . . But I'm not THERE just yet.*

*But if I am, why wait til my bag is up, and I'm seated WITH ARM RESTS DOWN. In front of a packed plane with a bunch of folks who'd already I.d.ed me . . .*

Many sometimes colorful tweets later, Kevin Smith's hurt and embarrassment was well known. Despite being on the next available plane, Smith continued his social attack:

*The @SouthwestAir Diet. How it works: you're publicly shamed into a slimmer figure. Crying the weight right off has never been easier!*

*Hey @SouthwestAir! I've landed in Burbank. Don't worry: wall of the plane was opened & I was airlifted out while Richard Simmons supervised.*

Before the weekend was over, the tweets were picked up by mainstream media; *USA Today,* the *Wall Street Journal,* CNN, and the major television networks had all run the story. Digital media, led by Mashable and Huffington Post, also jumped into the fray.

No doubt: This could have been a public relations nightmare for Southwest. Only it wasn't.

And here is where a long-term ethic of customer devotion can save a brand. Southwest Airlines has a history of listening to customers. And there was no reason to think that wouldn't continue, even in the dawning hours of the Social Age. Boasting nearly 1 million Twitter followers at the time, Southwest jumped into action. Tweets, which started rolling out that same day and continued through the weekend, included:

*@ThatKevinSmith hey Kevin! I'm so sorry for your experience tonight! Hopefully we can make things right, please follow so we may DM!*

*Hey folks—trust me, I saw the tweets from @ThatKevinSmith I'll get all the details and handle accordingly! Thanks for your concerns!*

*I read every single tweet that comes into this account, and take every tweet seriously. We'll handle @thatkevinsmith issue asap*

*I've read the tweets all night from @thatkevinsmith—He'll be getting a call at home from our Customer Relations VP tonight.*

*@ThatKevinSmith Ok, I'll be sure to check it out. Hopefully you received our voicemail earlier this evening.*

*@ThatKevinSmith Again, I'm very sorry for the experience you had tonight. Please let me know if there is anything else I can do.*

*@ThatKevinSmith We called you on the number you had on file in your reservation. If you prefer a different number, please DM me. Thanks!*

*Our apology to @ThatKevinSmith and more details regarding the events from last night—http://cot.ag/96KHC7 #Southwest*

In the Social world, that last tweet is very important. Note the URL (http://cot.ag/96KHC7) contained in the tweet. Not only did Southwest take the digital high road on Twitter, the company proactively posted a blog to calmly and professionally address the situation. And it did this knowing full well that all the Smith sympathizers would flock to the blog to defend the public figure and tell their personal stories around being what Southwest calls a "Customer of Size."

Sure enough, the blog post received several thousand comments—many of which blasted Southwest, on its own site. None of the comments were removed. All were allowed to tell their story and express their frustrations.

Brave. Very brave.

And the exact right thing to do—in a world gone social.

Instead of waiting until Monday morning for the PR and legal teams to generate a message-controlled response and quasi-apology (as would have been done by most major corporations in the old-school days), Southwest placed itself—and its reputation for excellent customer experience—in the virtual crosshairs. It was the proverbial sitting duck—like its competitor United just a few months before.

With much different results.

So let's take United on the one hand and Southwest on the other. They compete on price. Margins are incredibly slim. Both buy plenty of advertising. Both, within a few short months of each other, were deeply entrenched in a social firestorm.

▶ United—with one broken guitar and plenty of arrogance—wiped out years of advertising investment. It rose to the occasion only when its version of the firestorm forced it to. (As we opened the book and will discuss more in

Chapter 8, change happens only under insurmountable market pressure.) United's advertising spend over the next several quarters was designed in part to replace the customers lost; the overall negative impact is likely in the tens of millions.

► Southwest—by deliberately becoming an early adopter of social and taking on a challenge with humble confidence—retained its brand's reputation and perhaps even solidified its place in the customer experience hall of fame. It generates revenue from new customers (some of whom may have finally deserted a certain "full service" airline after hearing a catchy tune) while retaining its existing champion-for-life customers. Over time, the positive impact is likely in the billions of dollars.

Two very different airlines. Two polar-opposite approaches to a social media mess. Two corporate reputations going in two very different directions.

Over the long term, with years of positive tweets, +1s, likes, Yelp reviews, and blog posts in its favor, Southwest is likely to continue to thrive. United, with years of negatives in all those categories, will be required to spend more and more—*and more*—on traditional advertising to balance out those negatives. Market share—and that Holy Grail of the boardroom, stock price—is at stake.

Check back with us in five to ten years, but our guess is that, in the Social Age, Southwest will remain a customer-centric company that really gets the importance of being socially aware. Meanwhile, United will still be playing social catch-up . . . and we'll still be listening to that catchy tune.

## THE AMPLIFIER ONLY GETS LOUDER

Do you have a smartphone? Do you access social media on that device?

Your authors have, for years (if you follow us on Twitter, you certainly have some idea of how often—how compulsively—we access social via our smartphones). For us and others with the same OCD-like connection habits, it's hard to wrap our heads around the notion that only a relatively small percentage of the world's population—typically those under 30 years old—has yet to "smarten" their smartphones. As a worldwide community, we simply haven't started using social sites like Twitter or Facebook via mobile devices, as shown here:

► According to the Pew Internet Project from January 2014, just 58 percent of Americans have these pocketsize communication devices.

► BI Intelligence reports that worldwide just one in five cell phone customers uses a smartphone.

► Gartner estimates that in 2014 sales of tablets like the iPad, Kindle, and Surface will increase year to year by 46 percent.

► In January 2014, the opinion engine Twitter reported active users numbering 645 million—less than 9 percent of the world's population.

► Facebook now boasts over 1 billion users. (If Facebook were a country, in terms of population it would be in the top three of all the countries in the world.)

► Pinterest, Instagram, and Foursquare continue to grow rapidly.

► Together, these major social networks and LinkedIn have over 2 billion registered and active users.

In other words, if you're a global brand—or a brand considering a global presence—the social party has just started. While not everyone on the planet will have access to the Internet or a smartphone, amplification of opinion, worldwide, will grow exponentially.

If a guy with a broken guitar posts something on social media and gets nearly 14 million views from 2009 to 2014, what will be the result of a similar situation when nearly the entire world has gone social by 2030?

We'll tell you what will happen to the brands that don't adapt: trouble. Like what happened to Bank of America.

## NOT SO FAST . . .

*They'll understand what we're doing—they understand we have a right to make a profit.*

What do customers do when one of the world's largest companies imposes a random fee just because it can? From the dawn of commerce until the dawn of the Social Age, the options were few:

► Complain to a few friends and move on with your life

► Write a letter to the company's president or to the local paper

► Take your business to a competitor—that would inevitably impose those same fees once they saw the coast was clear

Social offers no place to hide, however. The change caught one company in the light like a late-night cockroach in the kitchen.

Still smarting in late 2011 from the recent financial crisis, Bank of America made a regrettable decision and then made the situation much worse by maintaining what many believed to be an arrogant corporate—almost a "let them eat cake"—public stance.

For years, it has been the practice of banks large and small to offer *free* checking and *free* debit card use as a way to entice the general public to become customers. The strategy: Cast the widest net possible, gather retail bank customers; then (once part of the "family") the bank entices them with more profitable mortgages, brokerage accounts, retirement investment plans—all the products that generate hefty profits for the retail arm of a company like Bank of America.

In addition to bringing in customers who can afford the high-end products, this practice also brings in plenty who are not wealthy; many are not even considered middle class; some are the most economically vulnerable among our society.

Despite the tragic effect the Great Recession had just had on so many people, Bank of America, on September 29, 2011, made an announcement it likely still regrets today: It declared that with the 2012 New Year would come new fees for all of its customers who used its debit cards but did not also have mortgages (or other high-profit products) with the bank. The charge for Bank of America customers—for the *privilege* of accessing *their own money* through use of debit cards—would be $5 per month, or $60 per year, per customer, for what historically had been free. Those customers who could least afford this new fee, those who suffered the most in the three-year-long economic downturn, were also the most likely to be hit hard by this new fee.

In years past—in the era when bank leaders cut their teeth—we consumers had very little power. From that perspective, this was a safe move for those decision makers at Bank of America headquarters.

However, by 2011—just a few years into the Social Age—things had changed. We were not just online by then. We were "connected consumers"—connected to each other by the hundreds of millions on Facebook, Twitter, review sites, public forums, Q&A sites like Quora, and in so many other ways. The cataclysmic shift in connectivity—and collective power—was well under way, and we were just looking for a powerful test case where we could flex our collective digital muscle.

Bank of America became the target of these customers. *The* target.

And the fired-up crowd was relentless. One in particular.

When Bank of America announced its $5 fee, a customer—twenty-two-year-old Molly Katchpole, a recent college grad living in Washington, D.C.—started a petition in protest. Mind you, not just a paper-and-pencil petition gathering real-life signatures outside the grocery store, like when our parents were kids. Not even close. Instead, Molly created an online petition on a then-newish nonprofit website established in part to protest bonehead decisions made by out-of-touch CEOs—a site called Change.org.

The first day the petition was live, Molly gathered just 100 signatures. Big deal, right? The next day, however, the number of supporters shot up past 3,000. The following day, once the cause went seriously viral, the petition passed 75,000 signatures. In less than a week, Molly had 150,000 signatures. She printed them all, stuck them in a brown box, and delivered them to her Bank of America branch as she closed her account. She didn't really have a plan besides that. She just wanted to demonstrate to the bank how she—and 150,000 others—felt about the new fee.

Even after she delivered her point in person, her digital friends—her influence—kept rolling in. In a few more days, Molly's protest had eclipsed 300,000 signatures.

Prior to the Social Age, imagine one person standing outside her grocery store. Cold and lonely, asking one person at a time to sign her homemade petition. The cause was just, but that earlier offline version of Molly wouldn't have had much impact on Bank of America; her shouts would not have been heard.

Now, creating social awareness quickly is not just possible—it's easy.

Incredibly easy.

And wickedly fast.

Change.org is just one consumer-enabling website. There are plenty more venues for online organizing, and disgruntled customers can also create their own websites, protest blogs, Facebook campaigns, YouTube videos, tweets—and a combination of all of the above. Once momentum is gained, these causes easily bleed into traditional media, as happened in Molly's case: The story was picked up by the *Washington Post* and NPR. And all the while, Bank of America stood firm; defended by precedent, its executives stood secure in their ivory tower.

Yet Bank of America was facing extraordinary consumer backlash, for which it was completely unprepared because, let's face it, who saw this coming? (Well, we early-adopter social media geeks probably did. But who else? Certainly not the dinosaurs enjoying their Cobb salads in the penthouse executive dining room.)

In the middle of this PR nightmare, exactly when he should have been his most contrite and apologetic, Bank of America CEO Brian Moynihan managed to evade the public relations handlers. Those hired to keep him from saying something stupid—and repeatable—failed. He actually said that delicious "let them eat cake" line you read at the start of this section:

> *They'll understand what we're doing—they understand we have a right to make a profit.*

Whatever his motive, no matter how misguided, you've got to give him high marks for transparency—for saying publically *exactly* what was on his mind.

The backlash and negative press took about a month to create real impact. By November, however, Bank of America had announced it would not launch the planned $5 fee after all. A smart decision . . . made about thirty days too late and in a manner that not only failed to show empathy for those affected but showed Bank of America in a far-less-than-sympathetic light.

## LESSON LEARNED, THANK YOU, BofA

Not two months after the Bank of America fiasco, what does Verizon Wireless do? It unveils a remarkably similar fee. This time, however, the corporation listened . . . and a customer outrage was averted.

Right after Christmas 2011, Verizon unveiled a $2 "convenience fee" to be charged to any customer who opted for a onetime online bill payment. Sign up for automatic, recurring online payments, the company said, and the fee doesn't apply. But if you want to review your bill (and possibly challenge any parts you find suspect *before* you pay your invoice), Verizon would tack on an extra $2 for the privilege.

Ted first heard about this on the radio on the way to the office. He followed the story throughout the day on Twitter. By the time he was commuting home, Verizon had reversed itself and canceled the planned fee. In less than a normal business day, the Twittersphere had shot it down.

Verizon's position: We made a mistake. We listened. We fixed it. We're sorry. Here's what Brianna Cotter of Change.org had to say about the fiasco:

*Companies used to think they could get away with putting out unpopular policies. Today, hundreds of thousands of people can mobilize and change policies in a matter of hours. That's what we're seeing with Verizon.*

Using the exact opposite approach as Bank of America did, Verizon earned not only the respect of its customers but the admiration of influencers, bloggers, potential customers, and the mainstream press.

Admirable indeed.

They weren't the only competitive listeners lurking about. Citibank, noting the public sentiment, used social and more traditional delivery methods (e-mail, direct mail, print campaigns, and press releases) to send a message to its customers and potential customers (including those ready to leave Bank of America). That paraphrased message: We listen to our customers. We would never charge a fee you wouldn't understand. If you're concerned about your account with Citibank and the possibility of new fees, please contact us. We're here to help.

*Brilliant. Human. Approach.*

So did all this come about because we couldn't afford the fees? Was this about $2 or $5? Are we simply more cost-conscious these days than in years past?

No, not even close.

Rather, we humans have always had a passionate sense of fairness, what your authors refer to as a "Social Robin Hood Syndrome." We simply don't like it when the poor, sick, and vulnerable are victimized. And we fix it, even if that means indirectly "stealing" from the rich to save the poor.

Until the Social Age came along, though, we just didn't have the loud, unified voice to act on our moral outrage.

We do now.

To this day, it surprises us how many Robin Hoods are out there, waiting for a cause.

## HOW DO YOU USE THE SOCIAL MEDIA HAMMER?

Here's the thing. United is still in business, despite Dave Carroll's song. Despite its obtuse executive leadership, we expect even Bank of America will survive a while longer.

Social media is not going to kill a brand in a single tweet, or video, or blog post—not even in a sustained campaign of consumer outrage. Not going to happen. And it doesn't have to happen.

Over time, social can weaken a brand in "death by a thousand cuts" style. Marketing dollars that should be spent wooing new customers will instead be nullified by negative, even if nontraditional, press and public passion. Think of social complaints as an anchor, dragging your brand to a slow but inevitable stop. Each new public gaffe is another anchor thrown overboard, slowing your forward momentum further. If you're big and well funded, it may take years for the anchors to drag you down. Your company may never actually fail—but the hurt to your consumer, culture, and employer brand will be very real. The bottom line will feel the pain, too.

Are you willing to let that happen? Why would you, when—like Southwest and Verizon—you can use social influence and momentum to your advantage instead?

As we've discussed already, social is inherently neutral, like a hammer. It can smash your company's profitability when used as a tool of unrectified complaint. It can also build your brand, as a hammer helps build a house.

As a "Blue Unicorn"—the social leader we talk about a bit later in the book—the choice is entirely yours!

At this point, you may be tempted to jump ahead to Chapter 11, where we discuss how, in the Social Age, customer experience must come first. For now, though, turn to Chapter 3 and take a look at the next social subculture to be impacted: the employee.

# CHAPTER 3

# The Social Employee: Good, Bad, and Way Past Ugly

In Chapter 2, we discussed how the Social Age has turned the company-customer power dynamic on its head. This shift in power, of course, delights consumers. Leaders of companies with product, delivery, and ethics issues, on the other hand, are often caught with their well-tailored pants around their ankles.

In this chapter, we'll see how companies that fail to adapt to the Social Age are losing control with yet another group coming into power: employees.

In every possible aspect of employee relations—recruiting, retention, employer branding, training, knowledge, and much more—employers find that those employees helping accomplish the flowery words in their carefully crafted mission statement now do so while carrying a big stick.

That stick? It's social media. And employees use it to whack their employers over the head with responsibility, transparency, and accountability.

## THE GOOD: A NEW VOICE

*"Inhumane and inconsiderate."*

In the not-so-distant past, especially among members of the Greatest Generation (those born between 1901 and 1924), the Silent Generation (born 1925 to 1942), and early Baby Boomers (born 1943 to 1963), an employee might hold one job, maybe two, over an entire career. Many contemporary career experts refer to this as the "40–40–40 plan;" a person would work forty hours per week for the same company for forty years. Then, gold watch firmly clutched, the employee would retire with a pension that paid roughly 40 percent of what he or she made when working.

Back then, employees who worked for more than two companies their entire adult lives might be considered job hoppers. Even worse, they might be labeled malcontents—even unemployable.

Many referred to the mentality behind this long-term employment as "loyalty"—a trait in high demand by employers and recruiters, then and now. And, from the employees' perspective, it's a trait expected from employers. In many organizations, no matter their other faults, loyalty was a mutually advantageous "benefit"—and was mutually expected. The pension system developed during the Industrial Age was based on this simple truism: Do a good job, for an extended period of time, and we'll take care of you for a lifetime.

Looking back, however, the perception of loyalty was a positive spin on issues far darker: fear, repression, and employers who consistently motivated their workers with inspirational gems such as:

- ► "You're just lucky to have a job!"
- ► "Do you know how many people would kill to have this job? There are a million others who could replace you right now."
- ► "Is this really a good time to make waves? Just get the job done and go home."
- ► "You ought to pick your battles. Don't you want your pension?"

To an employee, what did this really mean?

You have no say. No opinion. No voice.

Then along came social media—the virtual watercooler—where employees' voices aren't just heard; not unlike the consumer's voice, they're amplified. In extreme cases the shouts may go viral, causing extensive (if short-term) damage to the employer's reputation—and the need for immediate damage control.

In one famous instance that occurred during the Christmas retail season of 2012, megaretailer Target was forced into a defensive stance in a nationwide public relations debacle known as Black Friday Creep started by part-time employee Casey St. Clair.

St. Clair's intention was to spend a traditional Thanksgiving dinner with her boyfriend, friends, and family. Instead, she was told her work schedule now included a shift on "Black Thursday"—she would have to work both Thanksgiving Day and night.

Respectfully (while even stating how much she loved her job and appreciated the time-and-a-half wages Target paid her during the holiday), she began a Change.org petition directed at Target CEO Gregg Steinhafel:

*To: Gregg W. Steinhafel, Target CEO*

*Return to Friday morning opening.*

*I'm not complaining about being a minimum wage worker. Target, as a company, does some good and maintains a commitment to charity. Thanksgiving, though, is one of the three days retail workers get off a year, a day most spend with family. The issue is not black Friday, though it's not exactly this country's shining moment. Every year the opening time gets pushed up more and more. Midnight last year was pushing it. How can you expect workers to spend time with family and then stay up all night? It's inhumane and inconsiderate. You are most likely tucked away in bed while workers are in the stores pushing back a rabid crowd of shoppers trying to get an iPod. A 9pm opening disgusts me and symbolizes everything that is wrong with this country. Give Thanksgiving back to families. The world won't end if people have [to] wait 7 more hours to buy useless junk that will be outdated in a year anyway.*

Some 375,000 signatures later, both St. Clair and Target found themselves mentioned on every national news show imaginable. After her campaign went viral, including hundreds of thousands of tweets and Facebook posts, dozens of similar petitions were filed on Change.org and other such sites, imploring Sears, Walmart, Kohl's, and many others to reverse this Black Friday Creep trend and stay closed for the national holiday. Boycotts were threatened. Retailers—almost universally beloved for their price slashing during the holiday season—were assigned a public persona similar to that of Ebenezer Scrooge.

Of course, in our new social world, we're often measured by how we respond to social chaos.

In this case, Target originally received high marks for a post on the store's own blog, "A Bullseye View":

*When we made the decision to open our doors at 9:00 p.m. on Thanksgiving, the first thing we did was reach out to all of our store leaders and ask them to have discussions with their team members and seek volunteers wanting to work. We had so many team members who wanted to work on Thursday that hundreds of our stores are now keeping lists of volunteers who want to work if shifts open up. Across the company, only one-third of Target's store team members are scheduled to work on Thanksgiving, and we continue to hear from store after store that there were more volunteers than shifts to fill.*

*—Tina Schiel, Executive Vice President Stores for Target*

Unfortunately for Target, the company also released this statement:

> *. . . there is no* **corporate** *policy mandating that people have to work on Thanksgiving or Black Friday. [Boldface added for emphasis.]*

This one sentence—specifically, that one word, *corporate*—left the door open for local stores to mandate that employees work on the Thanksgiving holiday, which only made the situation much worse for Target. This cemented the company's "Bah! Humbug!" reputation that season, when it was reinforced by none other than Casey St. Clair:

> *Up until a few days ago, there was a sign at my Target store listing "blackout dates" that employees couldn't request off, and Thanksgiving was one of them. If that's not a policy mandating people work on Thanksgiving, I don't know what is.*

Social chaos. All because of one respectful, yet vocal, part-time employee paid no more than minimum wage—and her use of social and digital media.

In the long run, no one is sure whether—or how—this chaos affected Target's, or any other retailer's, sales that holiday season. Yes, the story was picked up by every major news outlet. Yes, St. Clair's actions led to Thanksgiving protests at many major outlets. Even some of Target's major shareholders jumped into the fray.

Yet, fresh off a year impacted by a deep recession, no one really knew what to expect during the Christmas retail rush of 2012. Throughout the fall of that year, consumer confidence in the United States was at times crippled by worries about the fiscal cliff issue. And just as Christmas decorations had been perfectly placed in retail meccas in New York and surrounding areas, Superstorm Sandy hit, leaving tens of thousands homeless. Additionally, the tragedy of the Sandy Hook elementary school shooting shook the nation's psyche, pulling many away from any desire to celebrate the holidays in an exuberant fashion.

What we do know is that retail sales were far below expectations that year; according to many estimates, collective sales were the worst since the economic crisis began in 2008. However, we also know that Walmart, at the forefront of the Black Friday Creep movement, is believed to have been one of the retail winners of 2012. Many other stores—although they didn't do well in terms of same-store sales year to year—saw impressive gains in online sales as well.

We also know this: Neither the executive team at Target nor the management teams of other stores had planned to spend the happ-happ-happiest time of the year defending themselves from Change.org petitions, Scrooge references in the media, and protests that brought the Social Robin Hoods to their storefronts on Thanksgiving evening instead of having that extra piece of pumpkin pie.

Oops.

Run your company with bad karma; be prepared to reap what you sow.

Certainly, those companies survived; it takes a much larger army of socially armed elves to bring down the retail giants. And yet we have to wonder: How much did Casey St. Clair and the Christmas Outrage of 2012 affect future decisions made by these retailers? Are they more "accountable" now, compared to the old-school days? That answer seems obvious.

Welcome to the Social Age, in which every decision even *perceived* as not in the best interests of employees is publicly scrutinized—and where judge and jury come in the form of a Twitter handle.

## THE DEDICATED AMPLIFIERS

*"Shills."*

While Change.org is a social cause site (and not necessarily dedicated to strengthening the voice of disgruntled employees), there are other sites that deliberately amplify workers' opinions. Chief among them, Glassdoor.com—a site that is home to reviews of nearly 250,000 companies.

Launched in 2008, Glassdoor quickly became not only a sounding board for employees to vent about their experience at their current—or previous—employer but also exactly what its founder, Rich Barton (of Expedia and Zillow fame), intended: a crowd-sourced ratings bureau for employers. Want to know what it's *really* like to work for Amazon, IBM, or Ford Motor Company? Today, Glassdoor is well known among job seekers (themselves connected consumers who, in today's workforce, are looking for far more than just a paycheck) as a go-to resource for understanding the full culture of a company, including its core values and long-term prospects. For many, surprises and the potential for disappointment are averted because this all happens before the job seeker accepts the invitation for a job interview.

This is a perfect model for the Social Age: a free resource that provides true value to a community of job seekers. On the surface, this is digital utopia.

At least, that's the image Glassdoor wants to project.

More recently, however, Glassdoor has come under heavy criticism for filtering negative reviews that may impact the "scores" of their paying clients. The reviews on Yelp for Glassdoor are full of Glassdoor purists agonizing over the failure to support the popular "comments" feature on the site, as well as the rejection of reviews that might impact the standings of employers that pay Glassdoor a hefty annual fee to "monitor" their ratings.

According to detractors, many of the positive reviews left on the site are submitted by agencies ("shills," as one commenter remarked) contracted by the employers to upgrade their image on Glassdoor. These filters, besides causing some to question Glassdoor's credibility, can also create a false impression of the employers; in many cases, a job seeker simply must dig deeper than page one of the search results to see the big picture at a specific company.

Some social recruiters, however, disagree with speculation that the reviews are less than objective: The common belief seems to be that the reviews are all there; it is how they're ranked that makes assessing objectivity more difficult.

For some, the perception is that Glassdoor forces companies to become members or risk bad reviews surfacing more often: Otherwise, competitors can target an employer's primary page on Glassdoor and buy ads that sway potential employees away. If a bad review says, "Poor training and support by management" a competitor can place an ad that says: "Training and support important to your career? Come over to ABC Company."

Combine this with the consideration that many small businesses (that do not—or cannot—pay Glassdoor its fee) feel they are not allowed to effectively counter the musings of an angry ex-employee, and Glassdoor's pay-to-play model doesn't appear to serve the job seeker as well as intended, or expected.

With all these hints that Glassdoor may not be the objective resource it once was—or that it claims to be—can job seekers trust it as a neutral "review site"? Perhaps not. But with a salary calculator and a powerhouse blog meant to help job seekers greatly improve their chances of finding work, the site is listed on many "Top Resources for Job Seekers" lists, including an annual list three years running titled "Top 100 Twitter Accounts Job Seekers Must Follow" by one of this book's coauthors, Mark.

More important—and we can't stress this enough—any particular website or platform (Glassdoor, Indeed.com's review feature, or other review sites that will undoubtedly pop up in the coming years) is secondary to what the platform stands for: public accountability.

In Glassdoor's case, no matter what happens to that website in the long run, the genie is out of the bottle: Employers are being rated by their employees very publicly; other employees as well as candidates have a resource for what is perceived by many as objective, real-time information.

Meanwhile, corporate PR and recruiting departments have lost the ability to control the story. They can't hide behind press releases and carefully crafted employer branding. If the company is good, employees will say so. If not, they'll say that, too. In fact, a 2012 survey by Millennial-focused InternBridge found that 94 percent of young careerists will talk about their employers on social media. Our own more recent experience shows us that time and again, peers of any age are only too happy to provide their version of the truth, including in social forums.

Of course, once an employer hits a certain high-level status—say, that of megacorporations like United Airlines or Starbucks—ex-employees seem to find myriad ways to vocalize their displeasure. They don't need Glassdoor at all.

Untied.com and ihateStarbucks.com are examples of sites where the bitter and angry seem to have a never-ending supply of complaints and criticisms. Of course, the companies being attacked counter that these one-dimensional sites are less than objective—exactly the same complaint continually lobbed at Glassdoor.

What do vigilante-employee sites and amplifiers like Glassdoor really mean to employers?

For one, an entire industry has popped up that businesses must now consider in terms of their hiring strategy, budget, and personnel. Not only can ignoring these review sites cost them a good candidate once due diligence is performed (and after finding a hyper-negative review), but inaction can significantly hurt an employer's brand.

Perhaps the aspect of this discussion most critical to an employer's brand, however, is that no matter how "early" it is in the life cycle of employer review sites, who do you think a job seeker is more likely to believe? Yelp-like peers (100 percent objective or not) who take the time to write reviews for the company they work for now or worked for recently? Or a copywriter in your PR department tasked with making the company look good to potential employees?

Again, the final score might be obvious: Social Age 1, Corporations 0.

## TWEETS GONE BAD: BEWARE THE VIRTUAL LYNCH MOB

Of course, there is one more aspect of social that is decidedly bad for employees: the social lynch mob.

When it comes to being an employee, social isn't always our best friend. Social media holds incredible power. Social media can do immense good. And yet the dark side is strong; it has become a powerful force in swaying the court of public opinion against both employers *and* employees.

A far too common occurrence in this world gone social? Termination called for—and carried out by employers—because of posts on individuals' personal social media accounts.

In a well-publicized Facebook posting incident in 2012, a woman named Lindsey Stone was fired from her job after public uproar over a photo she posted to her personal Facebook account of herself at Arlington National Cemetery—a photo that seems to show Stone pretending to scream while giving the middle finger to a "Silence and Respect" sign located near the Tomb of the Unknown Soldier. The photo went viral, with thousands on Facebook—and then every major news outlet—calling her actions insensitive and inappropriate.

These digital citizens became so incensed, a virtual lynch mob formed ready to storm Frankenstein's castle. Soon after the Arlington story broke, a Facebook group (that grew to well over 5,000 likes in just forty-eight hours and to over 30,000 soon thereafter) was created calling for Stone's employer, who had paid for the trip to Arlington National, to dismiss her.

That employer—Living Independently Forever, Inc. (LIFE), a nonprofit organization in Hyannis, Massachusetts—had no choice but to respond:

> *This photograph in no way reflects the opinions or values of the LIFE organization, which holds our nation's veterans in the highest regard. We are proud to have veterans serving on our staff and board of trustees, and we value their service. The men and women who have selflessly fought and sacrificed their lives to protect the rights and lives of Americans deserve our utmost respect and gratitude. We are acutely aware that this photo has done a disservice to veterans and we are deeply saddened that it was taken and shared in a public medium.*

The company dismissed Stone, along with the supervisor who accompanied her that day and who took the photo.

The number of employees fired for less-than-appropriate Facebook posts alone is already in the thousands. In most of those cases, and this one, organizations like LIFE, regardless of how otherwise exemplary the employee is, have no choice but to terminate. To save face, and to avoid being dragged through the social media mud, companies bow to the will of the hashtagging masses. The employee must be sacrificed to the social lynch mob. Moving forward, more care must be taken to protect the company's hard-won reputation from poor decisions by internal team members—and attacks from external observers.

Such was the case for the highest-ranking public relations employee at IAC, owners of Match.com, The Daily Beast, and Dictionary.com, among many other popular websites.

While on a flight to Africa in late 2013, Justine Sacco, from her personal Twitter account, tweeted:

> *Going to Africa. Hope I don't get AIDS. Just kidding. I'm white!*

The social lynch mob wasted no time in condemning Sacco for her racially insensitive (let's face it: beyond stupid) comment. Before her plane had even landed in South Africa, IAC—which apparently had never checked the social media accounts of this high-ranking (and now high-profile) team member before—had already removed her from all responsibilities at the company:

> *The offensive comment does not reflect the views and values of IAC. We take this issue very seriously, and we have parted ways with the employee in question. There is no excuse for the hateful statements that have been made and we condemn them unequivocally. We hope, however, that time and action, and the forgiving human spirit, will not result in the wholesale condemnation of an individual who we have otherwise known to be a decent person at core.*

IAC officials went on to admit they hadn't even spoken to Sacco about the firing yet but were compelled to react:

> *Unfortunately, the employee in question is unreachable on an international flight, but this is a very serious matter and we are taking appropriate action.*

The tweet was removed. The Twitter account was suspended by Twitter. Shortly after, Sacco deleted her Facebook account—reportedly because her Facebook account contained other ill-advised posts such as "I can't get fired for things I say while intoxicated, right?"

Still, the social media uproar continued. The story was picked up by every major news outlet including Huffington Post, Mashable, and *The New York Times*. For a period of time in December 2013, according to VentureBeat, the hashtags #IAC and #HasJustineLandedYet were more popular than #Christmas.

Business Insider, which also picked up the Justine Sacco story, had just lived through a similarly embarrassing lynch mob moment itself. Pax Dickinson, the chief technology officer, had been fired just months before for what could only be considered beyond inappropriate and offensive tweets from his personal account:

> *[M]isogyny is "hatred of women." It is not misogyny to tell a sexist joke, or to fail to take a woman seriously, or enjoy <censored word female anatomy>:*

> *In The Passion Of The Christ 2, Jesus gets raped by a pack of <n-word>. It's his own fault for dressing like a whore . . .*

> *[A]w, you can't feed your family on minimum wage? well who told you to start a <expletive> family when your skills are only worth minimum wage?*

Business Insider didn't react as swiftly as IAC, enabling Pax Dickinson to go on the offensive with those he considered haters of his point of view. He was even so bold as to hint that his newfound fame might lead to a tongue-in-cheek career change:

*I gained 850 Twitter followers and +7 @klout in less than 24 hours. Now offering social media consulting services.*

Business Insider, eventually, had no choice; it did what should have been done months earlier—except it had no idea how offensive this C-level executive had become. The company fired him and issued the standard apology and disclaimer (an executive has made some comments . . . that do not reflect our values . . . no place in our company . . . executive has left the company . . . blah, blah, blah).

Wholly ineffective. Way too late. Business Insider is constantly reminded of the "Pax Effect" on its brand—and of how it could have avoided an ugly situation with just a little due diligence.

## HOW FAR IS TOO FAR?

When we discuss instances like these—and employees like Lindsay Stone, Justine Sacco, and Pax Dickinson—how far is too far? To what extent can an employer go to protect its brand? Don't employees have the right to a certain amount of privacy? Should there be a clear line of delineation between our personal and professional lives and behaviors?

No.

Not anymore.

As soon as we click that "Terms and Conditions" checkbox on social media sites, everything anyone does is fair game. In the Social Age, good or bad, we are all judged by that portion of our private lives that ends up in the public domain. And companies must protect themselves from what could be brand-damaging employees. This, of course, does not mean termination—or even light discipline. In most cases, a proactive stance can result in nothing more than cautionary counseling:

*What happens in Vegas may stay in Vegas . . . but not if you put it on Facebook.*

Most socially aware organizations believe that a proactive peek at the very public lives of employees on social is well worth the effort—and overrides the inevitable feelings that an invasion of privacy may be occurring. Unfortunately, this issue is magnified when the conversation that occurs next is parental or disciplinary in nature. The typical response:

*"You are spying on me?!"*

The key: Approach each of these instances from a mentoring point of view. Counsel, guide, and be respectful. In the end, done well, this sensitive approach has actually improved the perception of the employer—and solidified the company's culture as a great place to work.

## ROGUE TWEETERS: WAY PAST UGLY

There is another side to the employees-in-control scenario, one that has nothing to do with the tweets on personal accounts or during personal time.

Specifically, we're talking about what happens when the very people responsible for protecting your brand on social media turn on you—an area of the social employer-employee dynamic that, when it turns this toxic, we refer to as "way past ugly." Why? Because when this happens, an immediate need to implement damage control is necessary, since those currently *in control* are the ones causing the damage.

Case in point: You announce a massive layoff—perhaps brought on by a takeover, as was the case with a music retailer in 2012—and fail to think about how this might affect your company's social media team or take into account how they would react.

The result: a minute-by-minute report via Twitter of a "mass execution" of dedicated and loyal employees being fired. In the case of HMV, instead of tweeting authentic- and empathetic-seeming communications that carefully supported the official company line of caring messaging regarding the unfortunate layoff and the impact on the employees and their families, the company's social media team began "telling the world the truth" about HMV:

> *We're tweeting live from HR, where we'll [sic] all being fired! Exciting! #hmvXFactorFiring*

> *There are over 60 of us being fired at once. Mass execution of loyal employees who love the brand. #hmvXFactorFiring*

> *Sorry we've been quiet so long. Under contract, we've been unable to say a word, or—more importantly—tell the truth #hmvXFactorFiring*

At some point, the social team at HMV knew they had crossed the line. That didn't stop them. Before the marketing director could regain control of the @hmvtweets Twitter account, they added:

*Under normal circumstances we'd never dare do such a thing as this. However, when the company you love is being ruined . . .*

*. . . and those hard working individuals, who wanted to make hmv great again, have mostly been fired, there seemed no other choice.*

Way, way past ugly.

Those early adopters of social media learned an important lesson from @hmv tweets that day: When you open a branded Twitter account and trust employees to be 100 percent responsible for those accounts, there are huge risks. Especially when those employees control the accounts and passwords as word of the layoffs—or any other form of bad news—is being relayed internally. The social media team knew they maintained power, at least for the short term:

*Especially since these accounts were set up by an intern (unpaid . . . illegal) over two years ago.*

As HMV found out the hard way, attempting to delete tweets and posts that have already been sent can be a huge mistake. By the time HMV's marketing director realized the unhappy, brazen employees were hijacking the branded Twitter accounts (instead of venting from their personal accounts, as the unwritten rules of social media dictate), the reaction was less than helpful, prompting the rogue tweeters to add:

*Just overheard our Marketing Director (he's staying, folks) ask "How do I shut down Twitter?" #hmvXFactorFiring*

The presumably angry marketing director then took this epic fail to another level. Once he regained control of the Twitter accounts, he deleted all the tweets regarding the layoff.

By then, of course, the tweets had been seen by many of HMV's 65,000 followers; screen shots were being shared on Twitter and Reddit. The message had already spread; the damage had been done. Deleting tweets—a sure sign in the Social Age that you've done something worth hiding—only made support for the vigilante social media team grow.

Of course, a rogue tweet or post doesn't have to be precipitated by a major downsizing or corporate announcement.

Take this tweet by a previously-trusted-now-turned-loose-cannon employee of ticket seller StubHub:

*Thank <expletive-that-starts-with-F> it's Friday. Can't wait to get out of this stubsucking hell hole.*

Now, chances are good that if this tweet came from an employee—and the account wasn't hacked—the employee simply meant to use a personal account instead of StubHub's branded account, a fairly common mistake when using Tweet-Deck, HootSuite, or similar Twitter management tools (just ask KitchenAid, which had an employee use the @KitchenAidUSA handle, instead of his own as intended, to tweet a "joke" about President Obama's dead grandmother during a 2012 presidential debate).

Much more important, though, is something that goes way beyond the medium of Twitter or the company's social media team, for that matter: Why is this employee so disgruntled as to think of work as a "stubsucking hell hole"? In the twentieth century, maybe employee morale was a nice-to-have aspect of company culture. In the Social Age, that view just doesn't fly.

Sure, there will always be unhappy outliers. The truth is, though, it's far more rare to find a negative or inflammatory tweet from an employee of a truly beloved employer. An engaged, emotionally attached advocate—one who is tasked with serving as brand ambassador—would seldom even consider sending a tweet like that sent by the @StubHub employee, even if the wrong account was mistakenly used. To brand champions whose personal brand is tied to their day job, "treason" wouldn't even begin to describe the feeling one might sense when composing that tweet.

We would also be less-than-thorough if we didn't say that it is entirely possible that the account was hijacked, a fairly rare side effect of social media (despite what Anthony Weiner and Donald Trump would like us to believe). Regardless, the tweet remained live for over an hour before StubHub corporate was made aware, pulled the tweet, and issued a fact-and-tact apology:

*We've deleted an unauthorized tweet made from this Twitter handle. We apologize to all of our followers for the inappropriate language used.*

Again, not the end of the world—and the company reacted swiftly and well. But this is one of a thousand cuts that must heal before a brand can regain its previous status.

In Chapter 11, we'll talk in great detail about creating a world-class team—including internal advocates, ambassadors, and champions—and how they are an integral component of survival in the Social Age. For now, the lessons learned from "way past ugly" for social leaders: Control your social media accounts, passwords, and scheduled tweets/posts. Oh, and again, monitor your social media accounts (and those of your team members)—often.

Throughout the examples discussed here in Chapter 3 one thing is clear: A frenzied, mostly anonymous, not-so-well informed virtual lynch mob isn't the best way to form policy or force action—but they have tremendous power.

Business must be prepared to take swift—and very public—action.

Better yet, perhaps the white-haired CEOs of these organizations should know what entry-level recruiters and human resources professionals have learned fresh out of college: A cursory check of each potential employee's personal social accounts is mandatory. As discussed earlier in this chapter, there is no longer separation of "personal brand" and "professional brand." In the Social Age, anyone who says anything anywhere nearly as stupid—or brand-damaging—as Pax Dickinson is *not* a viable candidate.

Which brings us to Chapter 4, where social takes on not just a group of consumers or internal stakeholders but an industry that had not yet been born in the early years of the Industrial Age. The advent of this process was just twenty-five years ago, so it's a baby by most business era standards—and was made possible entirely by the strength of social.

In Chapter 4, we take on the evolution of social recruiting, and its immediate impact on your ability to thrive in the Social Age.

# CHAPTER 4

# The Evolution of Social Recruiting

What if one technology—a group of competing websites, really—disrupted a major component of how business is done? And not a century-old, Industrial Age process as we've discussed so far but a process that itself was in the throes of adolescence, still trying to reach its full potential.

## SOCIAL RECRUITING: DISRUPTER

We're talking, of course, about modern recruiting. More specifically, about how social recruiting has led to many recent references to the job board industry (born in the late 1990s and itself just a teenager) as a dinosaur doomed to extinction.

In the old days—or, rather, in the old-school days—employers would post an ad in the classified section of the Sunday newspaper (speaking of dinosaurs). Because an ad was sold by the space it took up on the page, words were used sparingly. Very few companies could afford a display ad; in fact, only the biggest companies could afford more than a simple ad that read like this:

*Receptionist. Exlnt computer skills reqd. Good phone voice. 2+ yrs exp strongly pref. Fax resume to 775–555–1212.*

Ad ready for publication, employers would wait for the Sunday paper to come out, then wait for the fax machine to ring; that was the indication that the ad had attracted applicants. The curly fax paper would be taken to the copy machine, copied onto flat paper, and the flat résumé thrown on the stack with all the other flat résumés on a recruiter's desk.

Don't laugh—this was high-tech in the 1990s.

When we compared it to relying on the U.S. Postal Service for several days to deliver résumés and cover letters, we felt lucky to live in an age when communication was "instant." Of course, those were also the days when a résumé was all a job seeker needed. And that résumé was the only document an employer reviewed before making a hiring decision.

Then came the Internet, Web 1.0. The pre-dawn era that teed up the Social Age.

And with it came monstrous job boards, career-building job boards, local job boards, professional association job boards, and niche job boards. Indeed, all we had to do was click the Apply Now button and good things happened. Of course, this was when unemployment was at 3.2 percent and even the worst applicants, if they were perceived by the recruiter as merely technically competent, were offered employment. No interviewing or networking skills were required; no hustle was necessary. This creative destruction didn't just create a huge new industry; it was a precipitating factor in the demise of the newspaper industry.

With that creative destruction, however, came a series of unfortunate side effects. Anyone with a pulse could apply for any job posted online. There were no filters; there were no barriers; no real work was required to submit a "for your consideration" application. A single job posting could result in hundreds and hundreds of applications. Most of the applicants were decidedly underqualified for the positions. The "don't call us, we'll call you" method of avoiding the unwanted job seeker began failing.

Human resources departments, now drowning in the volume of applications and sensing the job seekers' desperation, began hiding behind the huge CRT monitors on their desks. They stopped answering the phone. They didn't return voice mails and e-mails. What became their priority was processing the never-ending pile of applications as quickly as possible.

Regard for the candidate experience—driven from the top of the arrogance-reinforced corporate silos—became a nonissue to employers. We could hear CEOs and VPs of HR boasting, "They should feel lucky to work here—there's a million other applicants just like them!"

The hiring system was (and in many organizations, still *is*) broken. "That's just the way it is," both recruiters and job seekers would say.

And that was *before* the Great Recession hit the world economy in 2008.

## THE RÉSUMÉ BLACK HOLE

Once the recession hit, and the number of unemployed soared to well over 15 million in the United States alone, the glaring flaws in the hiring process were exposed. Reliance on applicant tracking systems (ATSs)—keyword-sniffing technology that accepts, processes, and screens incoming résumés—became a crutch for HR professionals at almost all large employers and placement agencies. The "résumé black hole" (where the résumés of hopeful applicants went in and were never heard from again) became commonplace. Although many of us didn't think it was possible, communication between the employer and candidates got even worse.

At the exact same time, the widespread ineptitude among job seekers became even more obvious. Especially during the recession, most job seekers seemingly had no clue how to search for a job effectively.

Once the recession really hit hard, many workforce veterans found themselves looking for work. Some for months or years. They learned the hard way that they had no idea how to job search in our digital world. Many of them had been at the same company since the Internet was born. To them, the Sunday paper was still a go-to resource. Stubbornly sticking with what they knew to be true in the 1990s and early 2000s, many fell into terminally unemployed status; their unemployment benefits expired before they found work.

Desperate for positive results, many workplace veterans joined the college students and recent grads, using the big job boards as their primary job search strategy. And the broken system began its own vicious cycle; poor hiring practices became self-fulfilling prophecies:

1. As more and more applications from big job boards needed to be processed, more employers needed applicant-tracking systems.

2. The more ATSs got involved, the more résumés fell into the black hole and were never seen again.

3. The more applicants expressed their frustration with being ignored, the more HR hid from human interaction.

4. The candidates who thought they *really were* qualified submitted applications over and over again—yes, via the big job boards—giving employers even more applications to process, which took the cycle back to step 1.

Of course, some job seekers learned how to win this game (at least temporarily).

They became wordsmiths. No matter how inexperienced they were and despite their lack of talent, they learned how to get past the ATS with poetic résumés full of the keywords that HR professionals told the ATS to use as a primary filter. Résumés became what recruiters wanted to hear, as opposed to what they needed to see: qualified candidates ready to do the job from day one.

The worst part? Recruiters, overwhelmed with hundreds of applications for each open position, started taking shortcuts. The volume was unmanageable. They had to utilize the tools available to filter candidates to an acceptable, workable level. And the résumés that survived weren't necessarily representative of the best candidates; they represented those job seekers who played the game best and got past the résumé black hole.

What could possibly go wrong?

Plenty. And it did. And it does. Over the past decade, more and more new hires fail to live up to employer expectations—because the wrong candidates are being hired.

Can you imagine any other aspect of your business failing this consistently—as much as 50 percent of the time—and your organization surviving? Product launches? SEC and tax filings? Investor reports?

Yet in the spirit of "that's how it's always been done" we tolerate our broken hiring system. We allow HR to fail, over and over. We fail to identify top talent. We focus on the "safe" hire rather than the best hire. We lose the opportunity to scale our team, to affect culture, to drive more revenue, to gain market share.

And we're okay with that. Because this is how it's always been done.

Is it any wonder that this broken hiring system—despite its short life span and the anticipated potential for the recruiting industry with job boards as the center of the hiring universe—was ripe for another round of destruction?

Then along came the Social Age. And with it, social recruiting. Impact. The asteroid hit, and the job board dinosaurs—though not yet extinct—were going to have to pivot to stay off the endangered species list.

## WHAT IS SOCIAL RECRUITING?

There are many definitions of social recruiting. They range from the generic (using social media sites to hire) to, as stated by Matt Alder, strategy consultant for HR and founder of MetaShift, the heady "social recruiting is a concept, not a defined technique."

While we lean toward the latter approach—that recruiting through social networks is more philosophical art than science—the bottom line for most organizations is this:

*We need good people who will succeed in their roles here; good people are increasingly online; therefore, we need to recruit online.*

A decade ago, when MySpace was still a baby and Facebook hadn't yet been born, social was "personal." Early adopters included the young and young-at-heart. Those in the Boomer age bracket were skeptical at best. Many discounted social websites as mind-numbing time sucks not worthy of their attention; social media was "for kids."

As usual, the dinosaurs were wrong.

The top five social networking sites now boast user numbers in the billions; 46 percent of the U.S. population reports having accounts on three or more social networks. Far more relevant in the Social Age, as reported by social recruiting platform Jobvite in its 2013 Social Recruiting Survey:

- ► 88 percent of all job seekers have at least one social networking profile.
- ► 75 percent of the American workforce is composed of job seekers.
- ► 69 percent of employed Americans are actively seeking, or are open to acquiring, a new job.

Today, social recruiting appears to be a juggernaut. A disrupter. An asteroid crashing into life as recruiters had understood it to be—and as they expected it to continue.

According to Boston-based recruiting software company Bullhorn:

- ► 98 percent of recruiters said they engage in some form of social media for recruiting.
- ► 97 percent reported they use LinkedIn to find or research candidates.
- ► 60 percent of recruiters said they like Facebook as a recruiting resource.
- ► 52 percent trust Twitter as a prime source for talent recruiting.

Why have all these job seekers and employers swarmed to social? Because social, despite its digital nature, puts the *human* back into human resources:

- ► Social enables us to learn about each other, even before we meet.
- ► Social allows us to make sure there is a cultural and ethical fit, even before first contact.
- ► Social organically creates referrals and mutually beneficial introductions.
- ► Social enables us to connect on a personal level, allowing us to avoid ATSs and résumé black holes.
- ► Social empowers candidates to display expertise far better than a résumé ever could.
- ► Social allows employers to demonstrate (not just to state) their culture, values, and mission.

The results are already in. Social recruiting—despite its infant state—is being given credit for fixing, at least in part, our broken hiring system. According to that 2013 Jobvite survey:

- ▶ 73 percent of employers have successfully hired a candidate through social media (up from 63 percent in 2011 and 58 percent in 2010).
- ▶ Of those social hires, 89 percent of respondents have hired from LinkedIn, 25 percent through Facebook, and 15 percent through Twitter.
- ▶ Since implementing social recruiting, 49 percent of employers reported receiving more candidates.
- ▶ More than four out of ten (43 percent) say the quality of applicants has improved.
- ▶ One-third of respondents see more employee referrals, which often lead to more valuable hires. (Other surveys have reported that employee referrals are, by far, the preferred method of sourcing candidates.)
- ▶ 20 percent of employers reported that it takes less time to hire when using social recruiting.

Dan Finegan, CEO of Jobvite, added this comment in the report: "We continue to see social recruiting gain popularity because it is more efficient than the days of sifting through a haystack of resumes. It also increases quality referral hires, which our own data on Jobvite proves are hired faster and last longer."

Unlike our friends at Jobvite, your authors (other than wishing you nothing but success in the Social Age) have no vested interest in whether you adopt social recruiting or not. However, we have a theory on why social has caused major disruption in the recruiting aspect of our business.

Employers can't control the message. In social media, it's far more difficult for companies to manipulate, to sway opinion via sound bites and slogans as they could using old-school marketing techniques. Just like your customers, potential employees now expect employers to be engaging through social media. No matter their size, legacy, or culture, on social media employers are expected to be . . . human. Caring, engaging humans.

At the same time, employers don't have to accept your résumé as fact. They review your LinkedIn profile to see how well connected you are, right now. They go to your Facebook page and run a cursory check of your character. They monitor your Twitter account to see if the "real" you matches the "résumé" you. They determine candidates' level of passion for their chosen career and industry. To determine potential for fitting in with the existing team, employers can use social to establish an applicant's likability.

And—we can't emphasize this enough—all this happens *before first face-to-face contact.*

Your authors are aware of the irony: Assumptions about a candidate are made without ever talking on the phone or meeting in person.

And that is somehow more human?

## HOW IS THIS MORE HUMAN?

Let us explain.

A social media profile, as well as the posts, tweets, shares, and updates on those accounts, is far more human than a résumé could ever be, even if that résumé was able to get through the ATS and make its way to human eyes. Photos are seen. Passions beyond work are on display, as are character, maturity, and honesty. For social recruiters, whether it's good or bad, social media has replaced the résumé as the first impression and first contact. Candidates who pass that test have essentially become prequalified. Recruiters see them as good people, a good fit, and capable of doing the work. For many job seekers, the phone and job interviews that follow are more of an opportunity to mess up than further opportunities to shine. Simply put: At that point, it's the candidate's job to lose.

More human? Yes, in many ways. More efficient? Yes! Then again, compared to the job-board-ATS-résumé-black-hole process that old school organizations are still using today with a greater than 50 percent failure rate, how can it be any *less* human? Any less efficient?

## BEWARE THE SOCIAL RECRUITING PURITANS

Like other aspects of the Social Age, some bad comes with the good. In social recruiting, the bad most often comes in the form of the Social Recruiting Puritan.

Got a picture that includes a red Solo cup full of beer and a little too much fun? To the Puritan, you're off limits. Swear a bit too much on Facebook? Not good enough for the Puritan. Talk about your passions (politics, religion, etc.), even from a confident, assured position? You won't fit in.

We said earlier that one of the flaws in our Industrial Age hiring process is the propensity to hire the "safe" candidate, the one who poses the least risk to an existing team or process. Why? Because in a typical HR department, risk is simply not worth taking. We hire the compliant. We value the quiet. Following through on what we learned from our parents and grandparents, we want people who just do their jobs without rocking the boat. Taking chances? Not on an Industrial Age HR person's tool belt.

And so it continues for Social Puritans. They look for safe, calm, and neutral.

They subjectively eliminate everyone with a passion for living life, having fun, or being anything other than vanilla.

So what's the problem with this approach?

First, a lot of highly passionate contributors are not exactly "safe," but they think creatively and deliver solutions no one else has thought of yet. They aren't calm, but they make their entire team think about how to best accomplish the collective mission, even if the course they take has nothing to do with "the way we've always done it." And many of those who refuse to stay neutral—who do the right thing even when it isn't the easiest, safest path to take—are the ones who time and again really make a difference. Think that cup full of beer, or underwear on a candidate's head in a photo from freshman year makes for an unsuitable candidate? Think someone with a less-than-attractive avatar pic can't serve the team well? We should not be so quick to judge.

Second, this line of thinking involves just a bit more hypocrisy than might be socially acceptable. Those of us in the recruiting world have witnessed firsthand the exuberant partying that goes on at conventions held by the Society of Human Resource Management (SHRM), the National Association of Colleges and Employers (NACE), and many others, including every group of two or more social recruiters anywhere near the South by Southwest (SXSW) festival each March. For one week, Austin, Texas, is full of red Solo cups, underwear where it shouldn't be, and alcohol-infused bravery that leads to harsh, less-than-safe opinions and agenda being shouted within the temporary tents.

Yes, Social Recruiting Puritans are, more than anything else, hypocrites. They judge others, yet, given the opportunity, they fail to serve as role models. They fail to acknowledge, in those all-too-rare objective moments, that everyone was young once, that we all get a little crazy, that every once in a while the Las Vegas in all of us doesn't necessarily stay in Vegas.

Beware the Social Recruiting Puritans. And should you encounter them, think about how they might do a disservice to your team, how they might limit the diversity that steers us away from crippling groupthink, and how we all need to surround ourselves with those who genuinely care about their work—and about living life.

Using a snapshot of a person's life—as we can readily see via social media—can be good. In the hands of a Puritan, the result is a team that is "safe and same." No fire. No innovation. No passion. As a social leader, do not tolerate the Social Puritan. The quality of your team depends on it.

## IS SOCIAL RECRUITING A DINOSAUR KILLER?

After many starts, stops, missteps, and miscalculations, there now are enterprises, small- to medium-size businesses (SMBs), start-ups, and nonprofits that clearly embrace all that is social recruiting. They have become kings of the new digital world—at least in regard to recruiting. They are dinosaur killers.

The best part? Those looking at social recruiting from the outside in might view some of the leaders as potential dinosaurs themselves. Legacy enterprises such as Northrup Grumman and Taco Bell—the number one and number two social recruiting companies in the United States, according to the Social Recruitment Monitor (SRM) in May 2013—are setting the pace. These two companies are the most effective in generating likes, follows, engagement, and community interaction with fans, customers, and job seekers.

Here are some additional takeaways from the 2013 SRM report indicating that other large and/or legacy organizations have come full circle, back to their human roots:

► The Verizon Wireless Careers page had the largest corporate fan base on Facebook.

► Starbucks (@StarbucksJobs) boasted the most followers on Twitter.

Many of our largest companies—including Huffington Post, Geico, Ford Motor Company, and Google—have invested heavily in social networking. And by invest, we mean deliberately engage; SRM reported that employers recruiting on social media averaged 6.2 posts per week on Facebook and 23 tweets per week on Twitter.

It is not uncommon at all to see Tim McDonald from @HuffPostLive, Shannon Smedstad from @GeicoCareers, Emilie Mecklenborg from @FordCareers, or Jeffrey Moore from @Google being part of a discussion in a Twitter chat such as #InternPro or #TChat, participating in a Google Hangout discussing best practices, or networking at an Unconference (a conference purposely without structure to allow the free flow of ideas from all participants—a Social Age creature indeed).

And they each shine in their roles. These are the "rock stars" who get it. These are the brand champions getting it done—and done right!

Four words that sum up the secret to social success:

*More social. Less media.*

The organizations really putting social to good use—and the champions who represent their brands—are not broadcasters. They don't just post their open jobs, as they would on a job board, and wait for applications to fill their in-boxes. They mentor. They advise. They blog. They build relationships. They are ever present on Twitter, Facebook, and LinkedIn. They get it.

This, in its best form, is how social recruiting works.

Does it work for everyone, for every company? No. And the reason is simple . . . Social is work. Hard work. Those of us who are practitioners of it don't get to hide behind our dual LCD monitors. Instead, our iPhones and Galaxies are always at the ready. We must answer Tweets, direct messages (DMs), instant messages (IMs), and personal messages. We must be available, approachable—and human.

*More social. Less media.*

In other words, we must be the exact opposite of what we were taught by our Industrial Age predecessors and mentors. We must forget what we think we know. To be successful, we have to be open—both personally and as a company culture. And that isn't easy for everyone, especially for the dinosaurs who work so hard to protect their vision of corporate life, those heavily defending their hierarchical status.

Thank heaven for attrition. Thank goodness for new—perhaps younger (or younger-at-heart)—blood. Because often, that is what it takes to make this crazy leap into social.

## WHY DOES SOCIAL RECRUITING REALLY WORK?

Those who are intensely passionate about recruiting through social media will tell you it works for many reasons, including that it's so much more effective than advertising, old-school employee "incentive" programs, career fairs, and, yes, job boards.

Those early adopters may also tell you that they don't consider hiring the most important aspect of social recruiting. And their reasoning is solid.

By its very nature, social recruiting means you're out there, for the entire world to see. Unlike an anonymous job posting, there is a human out front—that champion we often mention. And who better to "sell" the opportunity to work for your company than a passionate champion of your brand? Who else would you want talking to a potential team member about joining your company instead of the competition than the person who has drunk the most company Kool-Aid and shows it every day on social networking sites?

For that reason, social recruiting truly is an opportunity to do more than just get some unknown candidate to fill out an application. It's more than just hiring.

Among the first, and most important, tasks of social recruiting? Branding.

How many millions of dollars does the typical enterprise-level organization spend to increase visibility, display the company culture, and win over not just potential customers but potential employees?

As we continue to interact online with customers, the public, and active job seekers, everyone becomes a potential candidate. Through social media, we demonstrate our willingness to engage, our principles, and our unique organizational culture. Discreetly, but consistently, we increase the visibility of our company not just as an employer but as a valued member of the community.

Social allows us to connect in a way a television commercial, display ad, or job posting simply can't. Social is branding, just like traditional advertising—it's just more human.

Another aspect of social recruiting that early-twenty-first-century recruiting best practices can't touch: attracting the passive candidate.

As veteran social recruiter Steven Levy says, "Through a job board or a display ad, any recruiter can find an active job seeker. I want to find the person already employed; already demonstrating problem-solving skills—the 'purple squirrel.' I know he or she is employable!"

Getting to know passive job seekers—those not looking for work until an opportunity (or relationship) is placed in front of them—is a valuable benefit of social recruiting.

Another coveted aspect of social recruiting is employee referrals.

Why is this important? We mentioned earlier that employee referrals were considered by recruiters to be the most productive method of sourcing new candidates. In addition, according to a study conducted by the Federal Reserve Bank, referred candidates are twice as likely to land an interview as other applicants. For those who make it to the interview stage, the referred candidates have a 40 percent better chance of being hired.

Think about this in terms of the broken hiring system we discussed earlier in this chapter. Compared to the ATS-interview-popularity-contest form of hiring . . .

## EMPLOYEE REFERRALS = RECRUITING GOLD MINE

In addition to branding, finding the passive candidate, and employee referrals, many other positive aspects of social recruiting are improved candidate experience, relationship building, more committed candidates, and the building of talent communities (which we talk about in detail in Chapter 5).

A bonus advantage of social networking: It has been our experience that social recruiters—the champions and catalysts out in front of your brand-promoting opportunity at your company—are some of the most loyal, committed, and passionate team members you'll ever have. Retention among these champions is much higher than among those not nearly as emotionally attached to the brand. Drama seems to be nearly nonexistent. Work ethic is never questioned. These are the ambassadors of your company and your brand. You can't ask for more than that.

Want to move gracefully yet aggressively into the Social Age? Hire as many employees as you can with a mindset that says, "We're *all* social recruiters."

## SOCIAL RECRUITING ON STEROIDS

In early 2014, a company we'll hear more about in Chapter 12 because of its innovative work in the area of customer experience took the concept of social recruiting, and the mindset "We're *all* social recruiters," to the next level.

They went to "*Everyone* is a candidate."

Information technology giant HCL Technologies (HCLT) from India offered twelve-month consulting gigs for the roles of Ideapreneurship Evangelist, Big Data Guru, Hacker-in-Chief, Digital Voyager, and Womenspiration. The chosen consultants-to-be would be assigned a mentor in their field of choice, awarded $25,000 as prize money, and provided with $50,000 in compensation over the twelve-month period.

They offered the opportunity to win this contract exclusively on Twitter.

Over the three weeks the Twitter campaign lasted, which included a two-week question-and-answer session and a two-day Twitter chat, the campaign drew 88,000 applicants, over a quarter-million tweets, as well as worldwide press on dozens of major media outlets including *BusinessWeek* and the *Wall Street Journal*.

Obviously, this campaign was designed to involve far more than just recruiting. And it worked. There will be a time, however, when this will be the norm on social, rather than a clever marketing campaign the likes of which brought HCLT an enormous amount of positive (and nearly free!) press.

Mostly, however, this campaign shows the potential of social recruiting: the power of engaging with potential applicants in a positive manner. And it shows how far innovators can push the boundaries of social media.

## WHAT IS THE ROI OF SOCIAL RECRUITING?

So how much is all that press and employer branding street cred worth to HCLT? For that matter, how much is it worth to find just the right candidate for just the right position versus a hiring mistake who might be gone in six months? That is the basis for the one question that comes up at every social media–related event, every workshop, and every speaking engagement, every single time:

*What is the ROI of social recruiting?*

Especially for those firmly entrenched in the "social media isn't working for us!" camp, the follow-up question is: "How, exactly, do I know if social recruiting is worth the investment?" That is quickly followed with, "If it weren't for the networking, social recruiting wouldn't exist" (duh) and "Social only works because all the kids are on mobile" (duh, again). These are two good reasons to be thoroughly entrenched in social recruiting rather than in arguments against it. Here's the cold, hard truth: You may never know the ROI of social recruiting.

Here's what we do know: Not being on social media now is a big mistake. Huge. The way social is trending, five years from now any failure to embrace social recruiting—to become known to potential employees as a caring, engaging employer on social media—will be catastrophic.

As online media consultant and blogger John Zappe says: "You can't not be there, because candidates, potential candidates, and those who you hope to attract and someday hire will see your absence from the social media landscape as a negative."

Omission is obsolescence. Not playing your part, in the eyes of the social-savvy job seeker, equates to apathy. That asteroid is going to come crashing right through your floor-to-ceiling office windows. Your organization will go extinct.

That said, there are steps you can take to obtain the ROI for your social media recruiting. Social media analytics, benchmarking, and pivoting to achieve better results are all crucial factors.

Here, however, is the real issue with measuring ROI—and the reason accurate measurement is nearly impossible: Social recruiting, done well, is so much more than filling a talent pipeline with qualified candidates. Social recruiting, by definition, is also employer branding, public relations, a demonstration of expertise, an ongoing discussion of your culture and mission, long-term relationship building, and much more.

Could a restaurant, on paper, make more money if it didn't need a building for dining space? Of course, it could—on paper. However, that just isn't how business works. Soon, social recruiting will be viewed similarly. Sure, we could live without social recruiting. We could survive on tested, traditional means. Enterprise would remain intact.

As our population moves more and more toward social and mobile, do you want to be the last person standing on Monster.com?

As we stated earlier in this chapter:

*We need good people who will succeed in their roles here; good people are increasingly online; therefore, we need to recruit online.*

Social recruiting is not just a fad. It is not going to go away. Your competition is most likely already succeeding; they may even be—slowly and effectively as they display their open culture and social collaboration—poaching your best team members.

Social recruiting is, without a doubt, how business is done—in a world gone social. In Chapter 5, we'll further discuss a factor critical to success in a world gone social, including social recruiting: engagement. We refer to this subset of the Social Age where we learn to actively listen to and communicate openly with customers, employees, applicants, influencers, and community members. No more hiding behind toll-free numbers, suggestion boxes, and message-controllers—this is the Engagement Era.

# CHAPTER 5

# The Engagement Era

*Companies with unions generally deserve unions.*

*—Unknown*

W e've already used the word *engagement* a lot in this book—in every chapter, in fact. Why? Because it's the buzzword of the early twenty-first century?

No.

Because engagement is the cornerstone of the Social Age. Active listening, communicating in a deliberate manner, collecting and acting on input, providing both formal and informal feedback loops, giving recognition and expressing appreciation are all a huge part of success in a world gone social.

*Engagement* has earned its place in the buzzword hall of fame—it *is* that important.

So what's the trouble with those who throw the word around like teenagers tossing popcorn at a horror flick? They have no idea what engagement really means. To many, engagement is posting a kitten meme on Facebook. Or broadcasting the link to their newest blog post or webinar registration form. Or an inspirational picture on Pinterest. They equate the number of Twitter followers and Facebook likes with long-term successful engagement, as if 100,000 Twitter followers alone somehow made them good listeners and communicators. (One *can* have tens of thousands, even hundreds of thousands of followers and still be engaged quite actively—something some veteran Twitter users take great pride in, your authors included.)

Engagement isn't good marketing. It isn't good content. Whether speaking digitally or in person, it is our ability to communicate well with all stakeholders in any conversation—and not just employees, as the buzzword hacks seem to intimate. ("Employee" and "engagement" are too often tied together, as if there is no other kind.) In the Social Age, it is imperative that we engage with customers, candidates, vendors, influencers, advocates, and brand ambassadors—as well as employees.

And yet, there is more to it than that . . .

Engagement has purpose and is quantifiable; it is effort tied to, and perhaps motivated by, loyalty. Engagement is an emotional investment in a brand, a mission, a product, or even a leader. Perhaps most important, engagement is maximum effort in exchange for maximum results, recognition, and respect.

## IT ALL STARTS WITH THE EMPLOYEES

We give credit to the buzzword slingers for one thing: They seem to get that to succeed, engagement must start with employees. In fact, it is quite simply impossible to build an engaged customer base, inspire loyalty among vendors, and generate an attractive employer brand without engaged, passionate employees serving as a strong foundation.

In-N-Out Burger knows this. (Ever meet a grumpy employee at one of In-N-Out's drive-thrus?) Southwest Airlines knows this. (How many times have you sung along to a rousing version of "Happy Birthday" on a Southwest flight?) Conrad Hotels knows this. (Just try to make it through the lobby without receiving a warm smile and a warmer greeting from a half dozen or more staffers.) Even legacy enterprises like GE Capital and Coca-Cola get high marks for deliberately keeping their employees happy. How? Through trust and respect, and by treating them like the qualified adult decision makers they are.

We know intuitively *and* through countless studies on the topic that engaged, emotionally invested team members work harder toward achieving common goals. They feel a sense of personal commitment. They find inspiration in the company mission and often from the leaders tasked with furthering that mission. They understand and appreciate their roles in the organization; they believe in their own future and that of the company. Often, their personal brands are tied to their employer brands; when they do well, so does the company, and vice versa.

Engaged employees are far more flexible, meaning they are far more likely to adjust to changing workload commitments when necessary. Far less prone to find a grass-is-greener position with a new company, they stay longer. When workplace issues arise—and they do, even in the best companies—engaged workers show more emotional intelligence; they join the effort to find a solution.

Engaged workers have been tied to higher productivity, customer satisfaction, innovation, more effective recruiting, sales growth, market share, and profits.

Who would *not* want a team of engaged employees?

The answer, history shows, is no one. Every organization on the planet would like its employees to be actively engaged. The problem with the majority of operations born in the Industrial Age—and, apparently, those that insist on maintaining their command-and-control operations to this day—is that they don't know how to get there. They don't understand what it takes to motivate employees all the way to becoming engaged.

In the twentieth century, work was dominated by those who would show up, do their jobs, take their prescribed coffee and lunch breaks, and go home. Unadulterated effort—putting in the extra time and energy to do the job really well—came only from those exceptional employees who dared not to be mediocre, those motivated by issues outside the management style of the company.

And, in the spirit of the truism at the start of this chapter, that was exactly what most companies deserved.

They accepted substandard performance because they failed to engage well enough to motivate past mediocre. Those employees who were not self-motivated showed up to earn a paycheck, not to move the company mission forward. In most cases, the only time these employees cared about the financial health of the company was when job security was threatened. In far too many organizations an us-vs.-them, management-vs.-employee environment existed—the polar opposite of engagement.

As a result of this poor effort, and from a century-long, global failure to understand the importance of engagement, we have a lot of work to do. Even now, several years into the Social Age and with all the tools available to them, organizations are failing miserably at engagement. In fall 2013, Modern Survey polled 1,000 employees, all working for companies with 100 or more team members. The survey showed:

► Just 13 percent of workers felt "fully engaged" (maximum effort; high loyalty).

► 26 percent felt moderately engaged (moderate effort; moderate loyalty).

► 34 percent considered themselves underengaged (just adequate effort; little loyalty).

► 27 percent felt wholly disengaged (minimum effort; looking/leaving).

Overall, Modern Survey stated that six of ten employees felt little loyalty and exuded little effort; just one in eight felt valued and worked accordingly.

That is no way to live. Or work. And it is no way to run a company, especially with Millennials—who have a much different view of work than their parents and grandparents—already forming the majority of the workforce.

# WHAT USED TO BE CONSIDERED ENGAGEMENT

So we can set the stage for discussing the Engagement Era, let's step back to the Industrial Age for just a moment—because sometimes, especially when it seems we still aren't doing enough, it helps to look back at what we used to pass off as employee engagement and reflect a bit.

How many of these old-school tricks and traps do you remember? Perhaps more important, how many might you still use today?

▶ **The suggestion box** | Remember the box mounted on the wall near the time clock or break room? The one with the slot on top, the mini-lock to guarantee privacy, and the accompanying "We Value Your Suggestions!" sign? Executives proved over and over that the sign was a lie by failing to read, or react to, our suggestions. This wasn't engagement; this was false hope in a box.

▶ **The employee survey** | Every other year or so (or when a frontline manager would declare an "employee morale" emergency), we would be asked to complete the dreaded employee survey. We colored in the scantron dots. Hoping no one would recognize our handwriting, we answered the essay questions. And then . . . nothing. Zero follow-up based on the data collected. No apparent action taken. Sure, C-levels probably read the report synopsizing the results—and then the survey died a lonely death somewhere in a locked cabinet in HR.

▶ **The annual performance review** | Throughout our corporate lives, some of us saw our HR rep once per year: during our annual review. Though the performance review took many different forms, we knew before we walked into the room our direct supervisors would have already graded us on our performance. It was the HR rep's job then, with the supervisor in the room, to spin the comments in the report; everything had to be positive. This wasn't engagement, it was an annual duty that HR and supervisors crossed off the to-do list with the same *"glad that's* over!" zeal that accompanied their mother-in-law's birthday.

▶ **The "need to know" Friday happy hour** | Let's gather everyone around the common area, tap a mini-keg of beer and open some boxes of wine, dump three bags of Chex Mix into a bowl, bring out the sheet cake from Costco . . . and have an "informal" discussion among the executives, HR, and all the employees. Corporate utopia, right? No. The trouble with these "spontaneous" get-togethers? Everything was planned; every rah-rah "only tell them what they need to know—or want to hear" word was scripted; very little actual dialogue occurred, in many cases because the employees were unwilling, or afraid, to engage in real conversation ("Don't rock the boat!"). As we threw our red Solo cups away and headed home for the weekend, we often didn't feel so much engaged as we did a little buzzed from the corporate-provided alcohol—and a lot manipulated from the corporate BS.

Yes, compared to the standards set by some in our modern era, we still have a lot of work to do regarding engagement.

So let's get started, first by emphasizing that . . .

## ENGAGEMENT WAS ALWAYS A TOP-DOWN LEADERSHIP ISSUE

Even before social, engagement was always a leadership issue. It's no secret: Companies with engaging, caring CEOs who came down from their penthouse offices (or dismantled them altogether) to interact with team members, customers, and vendors always seemed to foster an engaging culture.

And still, a disconnect remains. Too many old-school CEOs, board members, and directors seem to believe that engagement is a bottom-up process driven by HR, middle managers, and veteran employees. Still others may think that employees are already engaged, that their efforts to improve engagement are working. They may think employees are responsible for their own engagement, for bringing it with them as part of their uniforms, that conditions on the ground don't matter one bit. Or they think they can engage employees with hollow incentives that in fact fail to inspire.

The reality is that engagement is a top-down matter—and the best among us lead by example in this area known to affect morale, productivity, culture, and profits.

Recently, Mark witnessed polar-opposite attitudes to top-down engagement.

Two CEOs were asked by a consultant to show a willingness to be more approachable and less aloof. Specifically, they were asked to walk their sales floor every morning for thirty minutes. The only other instruction was that the sales manager was not to act as liaison; this had to be one-on-one, human-to-human contact.

In other words: sincere engagement.

From the start, CEO No. 1—let's call him Dave—was worried. He wasn't sure how well-liked he was on the floor. After all, some tough decisions had been made recently and about 15 percent of the sales team had been laid off. But down he went, the elevator carrying him four floors lower than he had been in months.

Dave opened the door. All he could see were cubicles, stretching into the distant grayness. No faces, only voices coming from behind the Steelcase enclosures. He went straight ahead, past the floor manager's office—exactly as instructed.

Eyes down for the most part, Dave walked the aisles slowly. Five minutes into his thirty-minute mandate, he hadn't made eye contact or spoken to a single person. He did come close: A young sales rep leapt from his chair to get a deal signed off, nearly running into Dave as he left his cubicle. Surprised by the presence of his CEO on the floor, the sales rep's eyes got big, he stood up straighter and threw his chin up in the air as guys do, and he said, "Hey." Dave, not remembering the employee's name, looked back at him, threw his chin up, and said, "Hey."

And so Dave's torturous walk continued throughout the week. The occasional "Hey." Awkward eye contact. Many "what's he doing down here?" looks. Only once did Dave actively engage a team member—and that was when he thought a sales rep was not following company guidelines closely enough and decided corrective action was necessary.

Six months later, the company's next CEO—we'll call him Bud—walked the exact same floor. Same company. For the most part, the same team members. Same Steelcase cube farm. Yes, Bud was Dave's replacement.

Given the same challenge, Bud owned the floor.

Working with HR, Bud had learned the names and backgrounds of many of the reps long before ever getting in the elevator. Working with sales management, he knew who were perceived as superstars and who underperformed. He looked at each of the employee's social media profiles to understand their passions and motivators. To build rapport even before meeting them face-to-face, he sent a personalized connect request on LinkedIn. That morning, he tweeted about being excited to spend some time on the sales floor later and mentioned many of the managers and reps by their Twitter handles.

As Bud entered the Steelcase jungle, he listened. He then did something that surprised even himself. Without thinking, he decided not to "walk the floor." Instead, he went into the break room and sat with his coffee and BlackBerry.

Soon, a member of the sales team entered the smallish room furnished with just two tables surrounded by plastic chairs. Surprised, the sales rep stopped in his tracks.

"Oh, hi," he said, not knowing what else to say once he recognized Bud from his picture on LinkedIn.

"Hello!" Bud said back. "Time for a refill?"

"Yeah," said the sales guy, not so eloquently—understandable, since, unexpectedly, the new CEO was sitting in what had been, until that moment, the sanctuary of the sales team.

"Let me buy this one," Bud offered. He got up, grabbed the coffeepot, and, pointing to the chair next to the one he'd just vacated, said, "Have a seat; how do you take it?"

A casual conversation ensued, first about the traffic, then about family, and eventually about work.

Over the next few minutes, Bud repeated this process with everyone who entered the break area. Underperformers and superstars alike joined him for coffee and conversation. Before he knew it, he had gone well past his mandated thirty minutes.

The next day, Bud did the same thing. And the next. On Friday, not only did he get morning coffee for everyone, he had a local shop bring in pizza for lunch. He sat, quietly enjoying his pizza, as those two tables in that tiny break room filled with conversation. Real conversation. About stupid stuff—life stuff. Work was barely discussed.

And so this process went on for about three weeks. By then, Bud knew just about all the 110 salespeople pretty well. He'd pass them in the halls, join them in the elevator. He communicated with them on Twitter; he shared their updates on LinkedIn. He recognized their individual achievements and team milestones on both his personal and the company's Facebook pages. No longer perceived as a threat, he'd sit in on meetings without saying much. And, of course, Bud would pour the coffee. Occasionally, he would tweet:

*Hearing some great ideas on relationship building and critical listening from the @<confidential> team today. #alwayslearning*

Within about thirty days, a miraculous thing happened. Members of the sales team started doing something they had hardly ever done.

They pushed the "up" button on the elevator.

They deliberately went up four floors . . . to talk to Bud. No middle managers. No HR representative. No liaisons or filters—just engagement. Employee engagement. From the top down. Soon, everyone could sense a different attitude. Trust developed. Best practices were shared. Personal agendas were quashed.

No, it wasn't some Pollyanna version of perfect. Bud was still a results-driven boss—even an autocrat at times, who frequently got frustrated enough to drop an out-loud, red-faced F-bomb.

There was no doubt, however, that a new culture had developed. Demanding, yes, but authentic. Sales went up, dramatically. So did customer retention, unsolicited testimonials, employee referrals—and the bottom line.

The moral of this story?

A single person, especially in a top-level position, can change an entire culture. It takes just a matter of weeks—one conversation, digital or in-person, at a time.

Another important note: What Bud did was different for another reason. Rather than dictating some corporate policy change announced in a memo that parenthetically said, "Our culture has changed: We will focus on engagement, and we will communicate internally on social media. Starting now!" Bud set out to become a role model. He deliberately set the nonhierarchical, transparent example.

He was engaging. And he enabled engagement to happen.

And that, in your role as a social leader, is key. It's a point we'll discuss in some detail in Chapter 15. For now, this is your takeaway: Be that leader. Even if you aren't (yet) the CEO—maybe you are an informal leader or a mentor, or perhaps you are leading only a small team—regardless, be a leader by example. Change the existing culture—one conversation at a time.

## SOCIAL AS EARS, EYES, AND MOUTH

As Bud demonstrated so well in our story, engagement can't be mandated. We must create an open, collaborative environment where most everyone feels free to think creatively, where they know their contributions will be valued in every conversation.

In our global economy, this has never been more important. Even when we can't engage in a meeting, across the lunchroom, in the hallway, or even in the same state or country, we must be emotionally available, nearly 24/7. We must communicate effectively. We must ask the tough questions—and listen to the answers.

This is where social is a change catalyst. In the Social Age:

► Suggestion boxes have been replaced with real-time digital communication. *Two-way* communication.

► Annual surveys need to die the death they deserve; always-available feedback loops are accessories in the justifiable homicide.

► Performance reviews (dinosaurs that they are) are finding it hard to remain relevant; deliberate, real-time recognition of achievement has taken their place.

► The happy hours (your authors would like to think, anyway) still exist, but the scripted portion (and those nasty sheet cakes) are gone, never to be seen again (and when the C-levels join the party, they should need no introduction to the staff, because they've been communicating across all channels throughout the week).

In the Social Age, social networks have become our ears, eyes, and mouth—in that order.

We monitor Twitter for tweets about our brand, products, team members, and customers. We watch LinkedIn Groups for the thoughts of industry influencers (those subject matter experts, bloggers, journalists, and speakers who are both well connected and respected) and brand ambassadors (of both our products and those of our competition). We browse Pinterest to measure interest in a particular topic or trend. We blog—and comment on other blogs, even our competition's—to display expertise and for continuous self-learning.

We observe Facebook groups and Google+ communities to measure the pulse of every stakeholder involved with our organization's effort to reach our potential. And we diligently observe Yelp, Glassdoor, and other niche review sites for real-time observations from our customers, employees, candidates, and shareholders. We set up Google Alerts or install Mention (a terrific tool for filtering, organizing, and prioritizing mentions by keywords) so anytime our brand, our product, or major team members are discussed by name, we know.

Using social media monitoring tools such as Radarly, Engagor, or industry stalwart Radian6, or free tools such as HootSuite and Twitter-owned TweetDeck, we listen in a way that has never before been possible. We watch for input from myriad sources—the volume of input available is now so high that an Industrial Age CEO could never have imagined it possible. And we respond, in an authentic, accountable manner faster and more effectively, in less time than it used to take us to assemble our legal and PR teams, let alone to formulate a message-controlled response.

## CAN SOCIAL HELP YOU OUT-ZAPPOS ZAPPOS?

Let us introduce you to an eight-person company that beat the pants off Nike, New Balance, Adidas/Reebok, and even online retailer Zappos—some of the largest, most iconic companies out there.

It all started simply enough. Ted, impulse buyer par excellence that he is, woke up and decided he needed new running shoes, *stat!* So he called one of his most revered companies, the online retailer Zappos, to get some advice and place an order.

We have admired Zappos for years. The CEO, Tony Hsieh (pronounced "shay"), intentionally created a quirky, customer-obsessed culture after selling his first company, where he had come to feel like a stranger. Hsieh sold the entire operation and set out to start fresh. He wanted to build a company he'd actually like to work for even *after* it had become big. His solution: an intentionally relentless focus on culture.

As you read, please try to keep in mind that Zappos is a remarkable company, which we'll explain in more detail later in this book. (We're certain the company was having an off day when this story took place. We're also absolutely certain that, in the Social Age, too many bad days can ruin your company—yes, even Zappos.)

As we were saying, Ted woke up with running on his mind. So he called Zappos—at five o'clock in the morning Las Vegas time, which is where Zappos is headquartered. His only expectation, given the reputation of Zappos and despite the early hour, was quick counsel from a human knowledgeable in all things footwear.

Within just a few moments, it was clear that Ted's expectation would not be met. The clerk at the other end of the line was not exactly well informed on product and was far less trained and much less focused on finding Ted a solution to his unfortunate shoe issues. Frustrated, Ted said a polite good-bye—and ended the call without placing an order.

But Ted Coiné, the author of *Spoil 'em Rotten!: Five-Star Customer Delight in Action,* didn't let it go.

Knowing Zappos is famous not just for its extraordinary service but also for the active presence its employees maintain on Twitter, he decided to throw them a meatball—a pitch so slow and right down the middle of the plate that even the newest Zapponian could easily hit a home run.

He sent a tweet to @Zappos, asking for someone to call him.

No answer. Nothing.

Disappointing—but also intriguing!

Had Ted found a chink in the armor of the mighty Zappos? Ted decided to turn this should-be-easy sale into a mini-research project—one that went on for a couple of hours that morning. Ted tweeted again, asking the Zappos social media team to have a sales associate call him, informing them that he wanted to buy a pair of shoes. No one called.

Meanwhile, Ted expanded his reach. He first tweeted to Nike, the brand he already owned, and Reebok, a brand he also admired, then went directly to the running Twitter account for New Balance, another brand he liked, and the customer service handle for Zappos:

*Let's see who calls me first to sell me some running shoes (if anyone). The race is on! @newbalance @NBRunning @Zappos_Service cc @zappos*

Again, nothing.

Eventually, Zappos did reach out to Ted on Twitter. For some reason, however, the company refused to call him, even after he sent a private tweet (known as a DM, or "direct message") with his phone number. Instead, the Twitter-empowered Zapponian provided Ted with the same customer service and product order phone number he had already dialed several hours earlier, when he spoke to that less-than-helpful clerk. Ted wasn't even offered the direct extension of a knowledgeable veteran employee who would be happy to assist.

Meanwhile, in the Social Age . . .

In what has become standard practice on social media, another company—a smaller, hungrier company than the one from the land of Zapponia, a company that generates sales by closely monitoring social media channels—was hard at work. It knew that many of its potential customers buy shoes online. It knew that many of them loved Zappos. And it knew that many who loved running would order Nikes online from Zappos.

> *@tedcoine We'd love to sell you some shoes! Check out our Men's at*
> *topoathletic.com . . . and give us a call (617) 431–3800*

It turns out this socially enabled, shoe-selling start-up—specifically, an intern at the start-up—was using a low-cost monitoring tool called Sprout Social. On the Sprout dashboard (which can be closely watched from any desktop, laptop, iPad/tablet, or smartphone), that intern was most likely monitoring a combination of keywords. In this case, perhaps those keywords included "shoes," "running," and "purchase." The intern might have even been monitoring "sell me some running shoes" or maybe even "Hey, @Zappos . . . call me!"

This intern was Alex Stoyle, who followed the basic rules of social media monitoring and selling:

▶ Rule No. 1: Actively listen.

▶ Rule No. 2: Respond quickly.

▶ Rule No. 3: Meet customers where they are now.

Alex saw Ted's tweets (he listened). He reached out to Ted (he responded quickly). He asked Ted, via DM, for his phone number (he met the customer where he was then).

Alex called Ted. Alex made the sale.

Alex's employer, Topo Athletics, had just opened a few months before. Its founder, Tony Post, had been CEO at Vibram, makers of those weird-looking five-toed shoes you see everywhere. Topos are only slightly less weird, with the big toe separated from all the others. Ted was reluctant to try something weird, so Alex walked him through the technology and the benefits. When the well of Alex's product knowledge ran dry, he put a coworker, whose specialty was product design, on the line with Ted to answer more questions. Satisfied with the science behind the shoes, and now really rooting for the little guy, Ted placed his order.

And Ted told 300,000 of his closest friends:

> *I'm placing my order now with Alex at @topoathletic. This #intern grabbed my business from 4 multinational corps!! #bravo !!!!*

But that's only the start of the story. While Ted was kicking the social media tires that morning, one of his friends was listening in, too. This friend, Becky Robinson, is CEO of a company called Weaving Influence, which helps authors launch their books. Despite her own social media prominence, Becky had not had much luck with this type of social experiment either. So, she checked with Ted and asked him how it was going. Ted told her the whole, Social Age story.

A few days later, Becky developed a piece on the effective use of social for marketing and sales, where she mentioned Topo in a big way. We'll let Becky tell the story from the time she joined the Twitter dialogue between Ted and Alex:

> *I eavesdropped on the conversation. I joined in. I talked to @topoathletic about my plan for a half marathon in a few days. The day of my race, I got this tweet from Topo Athletic:*

> > *Good luck to new friend @beckyrbnsn running the Churchill's Half Marathon Ohio today #MakeItHappen*

> *Impressive! This exchange showed me the excellence with which Topo Athletic is listening and responding to customers (and potential customers) on Twitter.*

> *So, while writing a news release about effective social media use during the holidays, I referenced the exchange with Topo Athletic. When the piece got picked up by Fox Small Business Center, I sent more tweets to the company. Their response?*

> > *DM us your size and address, Becky—we'd be proud to have you in some Topos!*

> *Just six days later, an awe-inspiring package arrived at my door. Suffice it to say that I can't imagine buying any other running shoes, ever. I'm going to go lace on my Topos and go for a run.*

And the story not only continues, it comes full circle. Becky's original piece was picked up by Fox Small Business Center. Alex picked up the mention via Sprout Social. Alex reached out to Ted to say thank you. Ted and Becky both love the shoes, the company—and their engagement on social media.

It should also be noted that, as of this writing, Ted has never heard from New Balance, Reebok, or Nike. He never heard from Zappos again. And while all these well-established, well-respected companies—which most likely have entire social media command centers backed by the best enterprise-level software available—were ignoring a potential sale, an intern at a tiny eight-person company showed them all how it's done in the Social Age.

The Engagement Era is full of similar stories, from just about every aspect of business:

▶ Tim McDonald, whose story we'll feature in Chapter 11, being hired by Huffington Post Live because his future boss was paying attention on Facebook

▶ High-risk hires avoided through monitoring of a potential employee's social media account

▶ Strategic partnerships and profitable business relationships formed after a single tweet

▶ Major contracts won, simply by responding to a comment on a blog post

▶ Tens of thousands of jobs offered via LinkedIn, some well before the two parties ever met in person

▶ Millions of mutually beneficial introductions made between those who share common interests and passions

No doubt: We have to be impressed with how far the Engagement Era has enabled us to come in just the past few years. We're more authentic and communicative than we've ever been. Silos are being torn down all around us. Small companies can easily compete with legacy corporations. Start-ups can launch without a single penny being spent on traditional advertising. We build relationships. We communicate. We are accountable. We are far more able to motivate our teams toward accomplishment of a common goal.

We do, however, still have a tremendous amount of work to do. In fact, we are just scratching the surface of this aspect of the Social Age. When all companies—even those most firmly entrenched in their command-and-control processes—have transformed themselves into transparent, engaging, nimble organizations fully capable of active listening, how much progress will we make? What difference, on a global level, can we make?

This is uncharted territory for business, nonprofits, and even government agencies. The impact of engagement will not be known for quite some time. For now, think of it this way. Look how much progress was made—the quality and democratization of higher education, improvement in our overall standard of living, advances in technology and innovation, the growing trend toward volunteerism and caring for each other in general—all while nearly no one actually enjoyed their work, when we worked only for a paycheck as opposed to accomplishing a common mission, when personal agenda mattered more than sharing knowledge and aspirations.

Now ask yourself this: In a world gone social, how much further can we go? How much good can we do?

This is a transition that must take place. *Is* taking place, with or without us. And those without the expectation of engagement across all channels will not survive.

Are you ready to lead your organization into the Engagement Era?

In Chapter 6, we'll discuss the magic that happens when engagement reaches a tipping point—where advocates, ambassadors, and champions combine with customers, employees, and influencers to form a community. In the Social Age, this is the pinnacle of an established brand, for which stakeholders share your passion and mission.

For that to happen, it takes a community.

# CHAPTER 6

# It Takes a Community

*Social is not a campaign. Social is a commitment.*

*—Stan Phelps*

Your organization has gained an enviable level of traction and notoriety. Early adopters love your product; evangelists believe in the mission. Inspired, your employees are all in. Thanks to influencers and bloggers, your brand is showing up on your industry's "Top 100" and "Best of" lists. The media—perhaps both traditional and digital—respect your work, or at least your potential. You are genuinely making a difference.

For an organization in this enviable position, what comes next in the Social Age?

A *community*.

Specifically, an *online community*.

More clearly defined, an online community is a group of Internet users with a passion for a brand or a cause, or who, at the very least, are bonded by a common purpose and bolstered by companionship. The best online communities leverage existing success, develop further trust, build exponentially more human relationships with existing and potential customers, and then exceed expectations.

No pressure, right?

In the Social Age, it really isn't as difficult as it sounds. In fact, online communities span every conceivable industry and personal interest, including:

► Kiva, Kickstarter, and Indiegogo in crowdfunding

► SK Gaming and Gaming Voice for gaming enthusiasts

► TOMS and Warby Parker, with business models built on the premise of "doing good," in social commerce

► Lady Gaga and Nicki Minaj as the central figures in worship-worthy celebrity-based communities

► Presidents Barack Obama and Bill Clinton in politics

The list goes on and on. Nearly every industry has fine examples where the sense of community is so strong that the industry founders give the community—not the business model, the founding team, or the marketing department—full credit for the success they've achieved so far.

## THE POWER OF COMMUNITY

Such is the case with YouTern, an online community for young careerists founded by coauthor Mark and his team.

In late 2009, YouTern was envisioned as a value-added service bureau for career centers. The company had one mission: help college students and recent graduates become highly employable in a really tough job market.

There was only one problem: On-campus career centers had zero budget to spend on outside vendors. The recession had decimated their ranks and their operations budgets. Mark's team, just six weeks from launch in September, was at a pivot point.

How could they—as a self-funded, lean start-up—generate the required passion for the company's mission and enough traction for the brand to survive with virtually no advertising dollars allocated in the budget?

The YouTern team created a plan—a plan they believed in very much, a plan only a few organizations at the time had fully bought into: a content-rich site that would provide immediate value to millions of potential users, supported exclusively through social media.

Mark was reluctant—well, way more than reluctant. He thought they were nuts. The only thing he knew about social media at the time was that his teenage children were always on Facebook instead of doing their homework. He had a LinkedIn account but had found no value from that site yet. He had no Twitter account. He didn't even have a Facebook page.

Yet Joe and Dave and Christina—and Deb and Tony and Ellen *all* pushed Mark toward social. They predicted that, moving forward, this was the way start-ups would launch. They said that by providing valuable content, users hungry for contemporary career advice would not only find the site but help promote the mission. The students, recent grads, career experts, résumé writers, career services professionals, authors, and bloggers would all flock to a community where peer-to-peer networking, mentorship, coaching, and learning would happen organically. They would become "brand ambassadors"—and YouTern would thrive through "doing good."

Mark called "B.S."

He didn't buy it. He couldn't lead this way. He lacked experience in social media; he wasn't used to being out in front of the customer. He loved sitting back in a B2B (business-to-business) model helping those who actually helped others. And social media? Well, sticking his avatar up and articulating his thoughts for all to see frightened him, to say the least.

Three months later, with zero progress for the business model thus far, Mark was finally convinced by Christina—who had set up a Twitter account for him ninety days before—to at least try a Twitter chat, to give it one shot. If he didn't like it, fine, they'd seek investors and buy their launch using traditional advertising. So Mark agreed: "Fine, *one* Twitter chat, and then we drop this."

The next Monday, Mark joined #jobhuntchat, a career-focused Twitter chat. Much to his stubborn surprise, he met 200—*two hundred!*—job seekers, career experts, and recruiters he would never have met otherwise. He was thrilled by the selfless exchange of knowledge. He loved the balance of mentors to young careerists. He loved the leadership from Rich DeMatteo and Jessica Miller-Merrell. Mostly, he loved the "give before you take" camaraderie that pervaded the sixty-minute chat.

Mark was hooked. Mark went social. And he never looked back.

Blogging and value-added content became YouTern's operation model. Sharing knowledge in the career space—the kind of advice that enabled young careerists to get jobs in the toughest of economies—became the charter. Still, something was missing. The team, for all their passion, hadn't reached that tipping point where social took over, where good happened organically.

All members of the team worked without salaries for some time while YouTern gained traction. But they grew frustrated. "What do we have to do," they thought, "to push this over the edge?"

The answer: the press.

But not through methods commonly used in the Industrial Age. No PR consultants. No campaigns. No campus tours. Nothing that would resemble advertising whatsoever.

What happened?

About a year after all the hard work started, YouTern began to appear on those "Top 100" and "Best of" lists. Mark himself was cited as a "Gen Y expert," a champion for Millennials, and he even made a high-profile list of the "100 Most Desirable Mentors." He and the rest of the team began to guest-blog for other career and Gen Y–related publications, gaining further exposure. Mark was asked to speak on college campuses (another anxiety-producing stress point for Mark: public speaking!). YouTern's blog, The Savvy Intern, was included on many lists of top career blogs.

And then it happened: a tipping point called Mashable.

In a major spread (at least for the career world), Mashable, a news website and technology and social media blog for the "Connected Generation" (think CNN for Millennials), listed YouTern as a "Top 5 Online Community for Starting Your Career." YouTern's world changed.

Soon after, the site was mentioned in the *Wall Street Journal,* Read Write Web, *USA Today,* and many more traditional media outlets. Mark found himself on Huffington Post and Bloomberg News, talking about the plight of highly educated but unemployable college graduates and what it would take in our new economy to make them employable.

With the team putting in 100-hour workweeks for well over a year, YouTern reached that tipping point: It became an overnight sensation. In a success story that could happen only in the Social Age, *and without spending one penny on traditional advertising,* YouTern had become a *community.*

Of course, for the ambitious start-up team at YouTern, this wasn't enough. With help in the form of blood, sweat, and a few tears from Dave Ellis, YouTern's content and community manager, YouTern grew from seven posts per week to eighteen, then twenty. Dave curated the best available content from the best available authors. He and the social media team publicized the content on Twitter, Facebook, LinkedIn Groups, StumbleUpon, Reddit, and many other outlets. And he did so without spamming, without ever crossing the line into self-promotion.

The YouTern team then did the next logical thing—at least according to "best practice" wisdom available in 2011. They started their own Twitter chat: #InternPro. With the help of Eric Woodard, they began a weekly show on BlogTalkRadio. They launched a LinkedIn Group. In order to continue to create advocates, champions, and brand ambassadors, they dove even deeper into diversified content—and provided even more value for their community.

Today, YouTern remains a self-funded start-up with a huge community following. Each Monday, 100 to 200 people join the chat on Twitter. The site will see 1 million unique visitors in 2014. @YouTernMark and @YouTern are two of the top 20 Twitter accounts shared by recruiters and careerists. As a publishing brand, self-funded @YouTern, with a staff of fewer than ten, is retweeted more than huge organizations like @USATODAY and @USNews and even mega job boards @Monster and @Careerbuilder.

All this is accomplished on a shoestring budget, with no advertising dollars—but built on the goodwill of the members of the career community who found YouTern to be a mentor-driven, safe environment in which to ask tough questions, listen to the answers, and self-learn.

That is what a community does.

It bonds its members to a common cause, a subculture, or an interest such as a music genre, a particular sport, or a television show. A community can also carry a brand that just a few short years—or even months—ago, no one had ever heard of. And it can throw social support to established brands like Coca-Cola, Ben & Jerry's, the National Hockey League, or Bill Clinton, all of whom have embraced social with open arms and are reaping the benefits.

A community, in what remains a sometimes cynical, what's-in-it-for-me world, brings people together.

Welcome to the Social Age.

For many organizations, building a community is more deliberate. (As we'll see later, there are many companies that have tried desperately—some successfully, some not—to build online communities.) In YouTern's case, however, the word *community* was never in the business plan or the executive summary. It was never discussed at board of adviser meetings or internally.

It just happened. Organically. Without intention, but wonderfully welcome.

By the way, as a virtual company with no brick-and-mortar office, YouTern's break-even point each month, not including salaries: less than $1,000.

*All of this impact for one thousand dollars, total, per month.*

(We'll discuss why this is so important in Chapter 7.)

## LEADING IN THE ENGAGEMENT ERA: THROUGH COMMUNITY

Imagine leading your organization into the Engagement Era with a strong social community as a cornerstone of your brand.

What could you accomplish? How would that effort benefit your brand? Could an online community launch your organization to a level you couldn't possibly have imagined? Could it allow you to compete with your well-funded and/or well-established competitors? Could it enable you to grow your brand, without ever purchasing traditional advertising? Without ever defending your brand when things went wrong, because your evangelists and brand ambassadors would do it for you?

What would that look like? How would that be done?

For this book, we looked at many brands that have built a strong online presence, that have built a community around their brands, solidifying their position among consumers, influencers, and, in some cases, even voters. Here's how they did that—and here's how you can lead your brand to community status, too:

▶ **They are social from the top down** | It must be said that the brands that have done amazingly well in the Social Age benefit, first and foremost, from a common denominator. They believe in what author Stan Phelps says best: "Social is not a campaign. Social is a commitment." And that commitment—like every other critical aspect of success in the Social Age—is a top-down issue. Richard Branson (Virgin Group), Ariana Huffington (AOL), Elon Musk (Tesla), Jeff Weiner (LinkedIn), and many others have embraced social as a competitive differentiator and a relationship builder. Without a doubt, building an effective community starts with the trust in, and the respect of, your organization's leadership. Not the CEO yet? Not a problem. Lead your team, no matter how small now, with social as a commitment. Quantify effort, track results, and gather success stories—and then pitch your company based on the impact to your team. (More on this in Chapter 12, when we talk about Comcast's Frank Eliason and what one person can do without permission, process, or policy.)

▶ **They build on a common purpose** | The number one rule of community: Build around a common need, purpose, or agenda. Brands that build community to sell product fail. Those that think a specific platform—a Twitter chat or a LinkedIn Group, for example—forms a community fail. Those that start a community to push a message or rebuild their reputation fail. Those that attempt an online community just to broadcast *at* the members fail. Every time. Your community must be built on a common purpose and fostered through mutually beneficial communication. Not sure where to get started? Answer these two questions for your brand: (1) What difference are you making? (2) What problem are you solving? Once you have the objective answers to these questions, that forms the basis of a mission worthy of emotional investment. Don't know the answers to these questions? Struggling to articulate your mission? It is entirely possible your organization isn't quite ready for a community.

▶ **They put the community first** | Effective communities that grow organically put the goals of the community first. On all channels, they promote engaging conversation and provide value by answering questions directly, without promoting their new product line or their latest blog post on the subject. At the same time, they don't allow community members, no matter how powerful or influential, to self-promote, solicit, or filibuster. In other words, your online community must be a spam-free zone. In one example, a major Twitter chat (which at one time had a sterling reputation) began answering questions from the community by pointing the group to its latest blog post on that subject instead of answering the question. Each tweet by the host was nothing more than an insincere advertisement for the site. As they say in the Twittersphere: #epicfail. Within three months, the lack of caring—the lack of mutually beneficial communication—drove even the most passionate members of the community away. What could have been an engagement gold mine instead caused the demise of the chat—and the brand.

► **They go where the community members live** | Remember the three basic rules of social media selling discussed in Chapter 5? Specifically, Rule No. 3 states: Meet the customers where they are now. Nowhere does this rule apply more than when building an online community. You simply must learn where the majority of your potential members and ambassadors thrive online. That could be a LinkedIn Group. Perhaps a Facebook page or group would work. Pinterest is another (static, but compelling) way to grow a community through quality content. To enable larger groups to talk in real time, a Twitter chat might make the most sense. For smaller groups, or for subgroups within your community, a Google Hangout might be the best answer. Experiment. Test each channel. Then focus on the channel that best fits the demographics of your brand—even if that means "all of the above" is the best long-term answer.

► **They are consistent facilitators** | When it comes to maintaining an engaging community, consistency is king. Without a constant effort from the facilitators, and without a diverse set of deliverable content, the community will undoubtedly die a slow death. LinkedIn and Facebook groups require constant posts, interaction, and moderation. Twitter chats and Google Hangouts must be on a set schedule and thoroughly promoted so they become "calendar worthy." When topics become harder to develop, the best communities invite guest hosts and subject matter experts to join—even lead—the conversation. The commitment your organization makes to your online community carries the same weight as opening the doors of your office each morning, the same impact as your primary website. Neglecting the community, even for a week or two, destroys momentum and erodes enthusiasm for your brand. Be consistent. Be available. Be aware of the impact your community has on those who come to you for knowledge, networking, and relationship building.

► **They enable the community to self-moderate and self-protect** | When trolls attack (and at some point, they will), well-established communities do not need the organizers/moderators/facilitators to protect their members, or even their brand. The community does it for them. A troll is a social antagonist who has taken on the role of contrarian, no matter the subject, and is intent on disrupting the conversation with negative input. Consider the value of your social media team, your customer service department, or your executives—they do not need to confront a troll. Think about how your organization might put up a "Do *not* engage" sign when that negativity surfaces. A healthy community's members rush to its defense. They become the sergeants-at-arms. In all but the most extreme cases, your organization gets to remain neutral, even quiet, allowing you to avoid a potentially brand-hurting dialogue. (More on this later in this chapter.)

▶ **They encourage sharing and self-learning** | Some of the greatest online communities promote the best aspects of what your authors believe the Internet was meant to be: a place to share and learn. By sharing knowledge and best practices, the community grows, collectively. As the community grows, its members become mentors, teachers, and accountability partners. Ultimately, as the members share perspectives, questions, and expertise, this becomes a primary reason for maintaining contact with the community. In the process, your organization becomes known as a value-added brand that provides an appreciated service well beyond the products or services you sell. Like model organizations such as Warby Parker and TOMS, your organization becomes mission-driven; you become known for doing good—and for having a purpose that goes well beyond profits and executive bonuses.

▶ **They promote individual thinking** | Solid communities that survive in the long term avoid one of the largest community-killing traps: groupthink. Yes, human nature dictates that we want to be surrounded by those with common interests. However, right up until the moment the trolls take over the conversations, exceptional online communities welcome thoughtful debate. They enable emotionally intelligent disagreement. And—knowing that the members are there ultimately because they believe in the purpose and health of the community—both the facilitators and the community members allow opposing views to flourish.

▶ **They cultivate a "red velvet rope" mindset: They make community members feel special** | In *Book Yourself Solid,* Michael Port coined the phrase "red velvet rope" to describe the art of making someone feel special by working with you. As they build content, invite guest contributors, build relationships, and welcome new community members, the best communities keep this art form front and center. They never take for granted the energy each new member brings to the group; they never cross over into elitist territory by discounting one member's potential. In a thriving online community, all its members must feel special enough to not only believe the community is worth their time but to refer others from their personal spheres of influence to the community. Ultimately, communities rarely grow from the effort of your team; after all, there are only so many available staffers, resources, and hours in the day. Communities grow through enthusiastic referrals from existing members you've already made feel special because of your red velvet rope mindset.

## ADVOCATES, CHAMPIONS, AND AMBASSADORS

As your community grows, a phenomenon grows with it: Those community members who most closely relate to the product, mission, or culture of the organization self-ascend to the next level of involvement. These members, constituting perhaps the top 1 percent of all your organization's users, become advocates, champions, and ambassadors. They can make all the difference in your community—and to you as a leader of the community.

As we've discussed, social is work—*hard* work. There are only so many staffers who can be assigned to your social commitment. Imagine the power, then, in building a stable of the most passionate community members—perhaps those who are hungry to build their personal brand and gain valuable experience—to assist with repeatable tasks.

These enthusiastic members often become not just vocal proponents of the community but direct contributors to the mission, leveraging their personal networks to promote and grow the community. The best of the best become organizers of your community outreach, often filling a volunteer role such as moderator of your LinkedIn group, manager of your Facebook page, monitor of your Pinterest account, or official greeter at your Twitter chats. They actively recruit new members and entice influencers to join the community. In the best interests of the community, they take on side projects such as coordinating local meet-ups or staffing the booth at a conference. (This model doesn't work for every community, of course. In fact, it makes the legal teams of old-school corporations cringe. The key: Adopt this element of community slowly, and document all successes while mitigating risk. Maybe you want to ask for forgiveness rather than fight for permission.)

Your role, as the leader of your online community, is to identify the most passionate members—the organic evangelists of your tribe—and then build healthy, mutually beneficial relationships with each. How can they help the community? How can the community help their personal brand? Can they dedicate a few hours a week to form Twitter chat questions? To moderate discussions on LinkedIn? To promote today's top posts on Google+? To produce a radio show on BlogTalkRadio?

Take a lesson from the best nonprofits in the world: Your community is only as strong as the volunteers who support the community. Don't wait for a budget. Don't ask for permission. Build your stable of evangelists. Find a need within your community that can be filled by a current member and ask for the person's help (all the while remembering your red velvet rope mindset).

Actively seek out advocates, champions, and brand ambassadors. Your community will benefit tremendously from their effort, their critical thinking skills, and their contributions.

## DRAMA QUEENS, DIVAS, AND THOSE PESKY TROLLS

At some point, every community needs to deal with an adversarial bunch—the opposite of advocates, champions, and ambassadors—the drama queens, divas, and those trolls we mentioned earlier.

Drama queens and divas are usually the much easier groups to deal with out of this trio. Typically, a combination of those who are negative at the moment and those who can also be more than a bit self-absorbed, these distracters are generally easily managed in a community setting.

They are readily identified by statements ranging from the fairly innocent "Oh, my back hurts. I hope I can contribute to #Twitterchat today" to the far more intrusive "I know today's topic is on SEO, but my problem is titles . . . I suck at titles . . . Anyone have any advice for me on titles?" Even worse are the blatant self-promoters and spammers. For those who meet any of these descriptions, the self-importance usually doesn't go away. In fact, it typically escalates to the point that they continuously steer the conversation back to themselves or their agenda.

Your community advocates and champions must work together to bring the conversation back to the greater good. If that fails, a DM, or private message, to the diva is more than called for. If that doesn't do the trick, mention in the Twitter stream, with that person's handle clearly in the message, that the goal of this community is to serve all members, and that a one-on-one conversation with a mentor may be the more appropriate forum for those questions.

This strategy works every time. Your community is given credit for maintaining focus on the topic at hand. The drama queens and divas usually just go away when they learn that your community is not all about them.

Trolls are a different story. They don't just go away. Ever. For those who insist on being trolls, for those who consistently take their contrarian stance to the next level and insult, offend, belittle, or bully other members of the community, your authors believe very much in this community ground rule:

*Starve the trolls. Feed the tribe.*

We've talked before about how social media makes us feel more human—because we are, basically, social animals.

In that humanness, the negatives come along with the positives. The simple fact is—and you'll see this over and over again as you build your community—if someone is unhappy, bitter, or angry in person, that trait is going to cross over into social media. Perhaps even more so, as many social antagonists feel powerful in their anonymity. They hide behind their keyboards and generic Twitter handles, knowing they can be more boisterous, argumentative, and destructive than they could ever be in face-to-face communication. So they let loose—with no account-ability in place and no consequences to suffer.

This anonymous communication, without accountability, is exactly why many communities, such as AOL–Huffington Post, insist on user sign-in, using a verified Twitter account or Facebook page, before allowing comments. Anonymous contri-butions are a license to disengage filters; they enable us to say what we think before really thinking. They are, at the very least, unproductive tangents. This practice doesn't stop contributors from saying something stupid, of course. It does, how-ever, allow a brand to blacklist that commenter; it simply refuses to allow that per-son to contribute to the community. While not perfect, this is a much better option than shutting down your entire commenting system, as General Mills chose to do on its YouTube page after some particularly harsh entries in the comments section.

We strongly encourage you to take this matter seriously as you build your com-munity. Set a precedent for meaningful—if highly spirited—debate in which the community members are 100 percent responsible for their actions. When you've identified trolls, unless they are too monstrous to "feed" at all, work toward bring-ing them back from the dark side. Perhaps even ask them to fill roles within the community. If all efforts fail, however, be prepared to terminate the no longer mu-tually beneficial relationship.

After all, trolls are contagious. If your brand advocates and champions are unsuccessful in their attempts to quash the self-serving, momentum-sucking monologues—and if you don't actively push trolls back under the bridge they came from—your organization will be judged by the other members of the community. Sides will be taken; divisiveness will occur. Previously passionate members of the tribe will bail for more productive pastures; communities will falter. The compan-ionship you seek will be replaced by confrontation—and your community members will find a more productive, less stressful way to invest their time and emotional capital.

Be a good listener. Be empathetic. But be strong. When it comes to community, you can't let the drama queens, divas, and trolls win.

## IF ONLY TROLLS WERE THE ONLY PROBLEM

As aggravating and demotivating as the long-term presence of trolls can be, they aren't the worst things that can happen to an online community. That distinction is equally split between two self-inflicted community killers: apathy and arrogance.

The fix for apathy is usually quite simple: new blood. New facilitators, contributors, managers, guest hosts, topics, and advocates almost always do the trick. Typically, only those chats that lose focus or rely too much on the same old topics fall victim to the apathy bug. Of course, apathy can also take hold when the community becomes an echo chamber of thought, a victim of groupthink. When all else fails, and you are sure your online community still serves a valuable purpose, think of your community this way: "Our job is to entertain, mix fun with knowledge, and provide companionship. Are we doing that *right now?* If not, bring in the new blood!"

The second community killer, arrogance, is much harder to ward off.

Arrogance is the exact opposite of the traits we think of when discussing community. Yet, since the proverbial dawn of the Social Age, so many companies and even grassroots, organic (un)organizations have fallen victim to the arrogance trap:

▶ **Sony** | In anticipation that its personal computing products would compete well, Sony made an effort to create one of the first product-based online communities. Vaio Nation was launched in 2007. Within a year, the lead-generation and self-promotion site, which featured far too many "Ooh, look how good we are!" moments, was gone. Lesson learned: If you say how good you are, no matter how you say it or to whom, it's still old-school marketing.

▶ **Facebook** | In 2009, Facebook was already under fire for having a privacy policy longer than the typical Dickens novel. Amid all the furor of botched site redesigns, changes, and complications, Facebook made the decision to turn previously private information into public information. Facebook was ravaged by even its most passionate advocates. Gawker went so far as to call it "Facebook's Great Betrayal." Has Facebook continued to grow since then? It has: One-seventh of the world's population now has an account on Facebook. But many industry experts are convinced, as are we, that it wasn't until this misstep that niche social sites such as Pinterest and Instagram found an opportunity to step into Facebook's trust gap—and fill it. (As we go to press, Facebook is facing a similar situation with the pay-for-play model it has forced on business and the ever-increasing number of ads on the site. Watch this one closely as the Social Age matures!)

▶ **#UsGuys** | In 2011, Mark and Ted met each other as well as many of their current friends, colleagues, and strategic partners, in a Twitter community that named itself #usguys—an informal, continuous Twitter chat that literally goes on 24/7. In 2012, however, the group began to feed on each other in a manner that grew beyond toxic (think *Walking Dead* on steroids).

#UsGuys did regroup, and it thrives today. But at the time, the painful and divisive communication was like watching your suddenly divorcing parents turn into bitter versions of their previously loving selves.

▶ **JPMorgan Chase** | In 2013, JPMorgan Chase thought it had a pretty good idea, a way to catapult the brand into the Social Age: It set up a Twitter Q&A with Vice Chairman James "Jimmy" Lee. Sounds great, right? Let's talk investing, financial security, and mortgages with "Jimmy." The trouble? JPMorgan was the darling of the banking community, the exception that proved the rule, for having avoided potential destruction in the five-year global financial meltdown known as the Great Recession—until, in what can only be considered unfortunate timing, during that same week, the misdeeds of its leaders finally caught up with them (somewhat) and made the news. Oops. In all their arrogance, the organizers of the chat failed to take into account the fact that JPMorgan was now, finally, being blamed for its hand in a horrific recession (or was it a depression?) that led to many bankruptcies and foreclosures. Instead of being a town hall meeting, the Q&A quickly turned into a public lynching with tweets such as:

> *Did you always want to be part of a vast, corrupt criminal enterprise or did you "break bad"?*

And . . .

> *Is it true that, while you don't always spit on poor people, when you do, you have perfect aim?*

After realizing the direction the campaign was going, the social team at JPMorgan Chase finally gave up; they sent their own tweet:

> *Tomorrow's Q&A is canceled. Bad idea. Back to the drawing board.*

Schadenfreude? Yes, we're guilty.

## WHAT IS THE ROI ON "COMMUNITY"?

Especially when we think about the very public failures—as few as there may be and no matter how easily they could have been avoided—any talk about an online community, like social recruiting, comes back to return on investment. And like social recruiting, the ROI from community is not always easy to calculate.

Of course, this drives command-and-control CEOs and CFOs crazy. They want to track every dollar spent against a specific campaign, promo code, or discount coupon. They insist on knowing how this effort, right now, is going to help them make their goals so the quarterly report looks all shiny to investors.

Sorry, Dinosaurs. The Social Age just doesn't work that way.

You can track most expenses incurred by the community-building teams. Sure, you can use traceable promo codes and coupons to sell directly to your community. You could even tell them this is a red velvet rope offer for them and for their closest friends only. And from that effort you would create a very high-level (but perhaps overly simplistic) ROI. However, by doing so, you run the risk of creating the perception that the reason the community exists is to upsell existing customers and advocates.

This is why social, regardless of our desire to quantify everything in old-school terms, is more of a commitment than a campaign. Building a community is, perhaps in the simplest terms, a productive long-term investment, like advertising. Or maybe even static overhead, like rent and utilities. Without it, however, you have no place to do business; you have nowhere to generate customers for life, brand ambassadors, and mutually beneficial relationships. As we discuss in Chapter 14, perhaps no matter how hard we try to put a macro perspective on community building—on all of social media, for that matter—ROI is an Industrial Age business principle that might not apply to a world gone social.

Today, ROI is determined by many business issues other than just dollars. Passion. Advocacy. The "do good" company mission. The feeling of being on the right side of that red velvet rope. Listening. Anticipating. Communicating.

In the Social Age, creating a sense of community around our brands is how business is done. Those organizations that fail to realize this as fact, and continue to measure success using old-school standards and Industrial Age business practices, will die a slow death.

In Chapter 7, we'll talk much more about the impact of the Social Age on those legacy corporations that refuse to change and choose to run their organizations using twentieth-century best practices despite all the advances available to them, including the building of community. We boldly discuss how social collaboration will end the way we currently lead and the way business is done, ushering in a new definition of success.

# CHAPTER 7

# The Death of Large

$W$e've already seen that social collaboration will change—*is changing*—life as we know it.

Fueled by changes in our global economy, the way we now view work and the widespread distrust we have of large enterprises, the time for a global change came sooner than most people expected. Despite our collective surprise, however, we now know social media as the catalyst that will bring an end to the way legacy enterprises act, lead, operate, and profit.

## THOSE UNWILLING TO CHANGE
## WILL CEASE TO EXIST

For many, the Social Age will lead to their demise; those unwilling to change will cease to exist.

Sound far-fetched? Even ridiculous? Stick with us while we build this statement out.

We'll start with a quick overview:

- ► **Be nimble or be dead** | Few large companies are capable of the agility needed to remain relevant in a constantly evolving marketplace.

- ► **Go nano or go home** | Nano corps, or fluid, self-forming groups that move from one organization to another, will get most projects done.

- ► **Management is unnecessary** | Engaged knowledge workers armed with collaboration technology mean there is now no need for hierarchical management.

► **Managers cost too much** | Companies can no longer afford to pay the low-ROI "management tax."

► **How far can you scale flat?** | In our social economy, scale is the only barrier to a company's growth.

► **Small is here to stay** | The strongest companies—those with enormous annual revenue and market caps—will have few employees; they will be in no danger of collapsing under their own weight.

► **Social will be the bane of large** | What makes today so different from 2008? Or from 1908, for that matter? What used to be cute and interesting (the small, flat organization) is now compelling; social and collaboration technology turn the nimble, flat organization into an irresistible force of nature.

We expect a lot of pushback on most of what we share with you in this section. In particular, it's only natural for those with personal and professional interests deeply entrenched in the status quo to rail against what we discuss with you in the pages that follow. We accept this, and understand the onus of proof lies firmly on us. So before we go any further, we ask you to keep the Law of Change clearly in mind:

*Change happens only in reaction to irresistible market pressure.*

In other words, while you may see a company here or there do something unusual and even inspiring—perhaps in the way it chooses to operate—most companies will not change just because they want to, and certainly not just because they can.

*Most companies will change only because they* must *change. They have no choice. Adapt to current market trends, or die.*

The impact of social, as an irresistible market pressure, is already compelling that change. We, too, resisted this change at first. We resisted coming to these conclusions. They sounded too . . . *out there,* even to us.

Observing converging trends over five years and collecting the data for this book, however, gave us a unique perspective on an evolution of business unfolding before our eyes. Studying companies that are nailing most or all of these aspects of twenty-first century business right now, today—well, we couldn't tone down this presentation and still stand behind our work.

The way we'll all do business in the Social Century is every bit as different from the methods of the Industrial Century as that period was from the Agrarian Millennia before it.

Here, we'll show you.

## AGRARIAN TO INDUSTRIAL

For perspective, let's look at history. We know how many of you feel about history lessons, so we promise to keep this short.

There was a time, not many generations ago, when all companies were small. If you made finely woven damask cloth, as Andrew Carnegie's father, William, did, you probably did it on a one-man loom in a corner of your modest home. You might sell that cloth to your neighbors in the village market or, like William, sell it to a merchant who also bought from many other weavers. That merchant then exported the products.

If your business was prosperous, you might take on an apprentice or two, and maybe even hire a few laborers; you might move from the living room into the barn or a backyard shed for more space. This was cottage industry, and at the time young Andrew Carnegie was born, nearly all industry was still run this way.

But the Industrial Revolution changed a lot of plans.

Advances in technology made large factories possible. One eager capitalist could employ hundreds, even thousands, of laborers to work huge mechanical looms. William Carnegie and all of his craftsmen peers fell victim to progress.

In just ten years, the senior Carnegie went from being comfortably upper middle class to being completely out of work. He could not produce enough damask at home to feed his family. Destitute, William had to borrow the money he needed to buy passage to America for himself and his family. Once in America, they joined family members already among the ranks of the desperate working poor.

They continued this way until Andrew, learning well the lessons regarding the efficiency of technology and scale, became an industrialist himself.

The year William Carnegie finally threw in the handcrafted damask towel and abandoned his cottage weaving business was 1847. Textiles, among the first industries to industrialize, flourished in factory form throughout the balance of the 1800s. Of course, other industries saw the same shift and transformed their operations from cottage-level production to massive factories owned by a wealthy few and managed by large, efficient, bureaucratic hierarchies—like the military, which many thought was the best model to follow at the time.

By the time Henry Ford brought the assembly line to automobile manufacturing in 1913, cottage production was dead in just about every field imaginable. The *enterprise,* or "very large company," ruled.

Large still rules business today, a full century later.

# IS THE INDUSTRIAL CENTURY BEHIND US?

Is the massive enterprise—the now century-old world order—meant to hold court forever? Is it still efficient? Is it still the superior way to do business? Or did scale serve its purpose when our economy was based on manufacturing? And now, in our knowledge-and-creativity economy, perhaps that purpose is no longer being served?

If the enterprise is no longer the most efficient way to do business, that can mean only one thing: Something superior, something more modern, has replaced that model.

The last time such a shift occurred was this elongated period of industrialization: Electricity came from hydroelectric or coal power, machines automated work that had once been labor intensive, and bureaucracies commanded conformity and controlled labor—because that labor required massive numbers of people, and because it was very simple, assembly-line work.

Could social really change all that?

Could we already be entrenched in a nimble, creative economy both enabled by and driven by social media and social collaboration? Are we leaving the Industrial Age behind? Is the Social Age ready to take the throne?

As we write, a quick scan of our desks shows us why some enterprises are unlikely to disappear anytime soon. Ted writes on a MacBook, made by Apple, a large enterprise; Mark writes on an Acer laptop running Windows 8 software by Microsoft—three very big, enterprise-sized companies. Desks are much cheaper to make in a factory than by a solo craftsperson or a small company of ten or so people. Large companies supply electricity, Internet access, and natural gas. Printer paper, paint for the walls, windows to look out of (when we finally look up)—all these are made by large enterprises.

And it's hard to imagine that changing in the short term.

Or is it?

Ted's MacBook says it was "Designed by Apple in Cupertino, California. Manufactured in China." Interesting. The manufacturing arms of companies—specifically, American companies—used to be much bigger. At the peak of U.S. economic dominance over the rest of the world, all of the manufacturing and assembly work was done in-house.

Now, it's standard to innovate products in one company, then wholly outsource manufacturing to a different company. Whole IT departments are outsourced, or (more often) every job in IT but those of the top executives, who guide the service provider, is outsourced. Design is often outsourced, creating opportunities for firms like Silicon Valley's Ideo, the design and innovation consultancy, which has grown to 550 employees, as well as many similar (and smaller) companies.

Marketing is often outsourced; consultancies large and small abound to provide services such as legal, accounting/audit, janitorial, food service, postal—and, yes, even social media. Often, this amounts to one enterprise buying services from dozens of other, often smaller, companies.

Where once there was Ford Motor Company, which seemed to manufacture everything in-house but the tires, now there are many smaller companies, consultants, contractors, service bureaus, creatives, solopreneurs, and even cottage industries coming together to act as a network of companies motivated toward a common goal and all working toward the mutual (sometimes incestuous) good: revenue, profits, and sustainability.

And this trend is just getting started. Even manufacturing may not require permanent enterprises in the future, as we'll show you next.

## WE'RE ALREADY SURROUNDED BY "NANO"

A few years ago, we heard a fascinating NPR feature about a former pharmaceutical executive, Dennis Goldberg, whose one-man company explored new-drug invention. He attracted a few million dollars of venture capital (a token investment in the pharma development world). He contracted Charles River Laboratories, a Boston-area enterprise, to run experiments on batches of his potential drugs right beside their own. Charles River was happy for the additional revenue. If any of the results looked promising, Goldberg would then sell his patents to Charles River or another interested pharmaceutical company.

With this model, and without the need to build and staff manufacturing plants or fill them with several levels of management, Goldberg was able to develop drugs for a mere $6 million—one-tenth what it might have cost just a decade earlier. Profit margins were enormous. Risk was reduced. And, rather than the $60 million to $80 million a traditional pharma company would spend on infrastructure, Goldberg was free, and certainly nimble enough, to create new patents.

This fascinating story inspired Ted to write on the "nano corporation," a name inspired by nanotechnology, a field in which, for instance, microscopic robots will one day soon be injected into humans to clear stroke- and heart-disease-inducing plaque out of arteries. These *nanobots* can come together and form themselves into a larger (but still tiny) robot for a task, then break apart again into individual component parts, each going on to its next challenge when that initial task has been completed.

About a year later (and independently), our friend Dave Aron, a genius IT analyst whose specialty is advising enterprise CIOs, took another shot at this concept that seems to sum up the theory quite well. Rather than *nano corp,* he called the self-forming team that comes together for a project and then disbands or moves on to the next project, often with a different enterprise as its client, a *cluster.*

If nanobots can assemble to complete a larger task then disband until another, bigger project comes along, it seems organizations—or *nano corps,* groups of people with a common mission, regardless of the product or client—can as well.

Just ask Bronson Taylor.

## CAN YOUR COMPANY INNOVATE THIS FAST?

Here is the genesis of this chapter, the "Aha!" moment that brought years of observation and rumination together to help us realize where the Social Age—really, a social *revolution*—is likely to take us, perhaps sooner than we think.

As you read this, keep in mind this is what finally did it for us. It's the straw that broke the virtual camel's back, but in a good way: Think of the camel as the large, slow, grouchy beast unable to move quickly enough to keep up with the technological changes all around it—and incapable of change.

Ted has been a fan of technology start-ups for well over a decade now—his immersion in the field started not long after the dot-com bubble burst in 2000 (Ted is famous for his timing). While he advises mostly midsize companies and enterprises, he considers his start-up friends to be "his people." Ted is a huge *fan* of technology (from afar) and of the intrepid entrepreneurs who create our digital world from the pure air of their imaginations.

Ted was talking to one such company founder, Bronson Taylor of Growth Hacker TV (GHTV). Bronson and his brother, an engineer, have worked on multiple projects together, just as good nano entrepreneurs do. Most recently, Bronson met with a business development (a.k.a. "sales") entrepreneur who wanted to hire Bronson for his techie and marketing skills.

When asked about his availability and interest in the opportunity to work for Mr. BizDev, Bronson countered, "I was just thinking we should hire *you.* Why don't we become partners instead?"

And they did. Just like that, they became partners.

When Ted met Bronson in Naples, Florida, seven weeks after that partnership decision, GrowthHacker.tv was live and earning money. The three founders did most of the work, collaborating long distance between Kentucky and Florida.

For those to-do items not in its collective wheelhouse, however, this nano corp goes the nano route—that is, it doesn't hire and employ; it outsources.

▶ When it needed a weird video to use as background for an announcement on the site, it bought a video from an online service.

► It used another service bureau to outsource the voice-over for that announcement (a delightful female Australian voice, excellent branding it could not have done in-house).

► It hosts its website with a service provider found on (you guessed it) the Internet.

► It uses an outsourced service to process credit cards.

► It uses a free e-mail service to stay in touch with visitors to the site and with customers.

► It uses Skype as a video recording tool, for which it also pays a small monthly fee.

Executives with access to a healthy expense account likely spend more on one client dinner than this company's entire monthly operating budget. No exaggeration: The company's monthly break-even point when Ted first met Bronson was less than $1,000. *Yes, one thousand dollars.*

What does all this amount to?

On one hand, you could say, "Big deal! Those are just three guys removing themselves from the hiring pool by starting their own little company. The large companies of the world are not exactly going to notice three missing would-be employees out of seven *billion* potential workers."

And that's a good point. But being immersed in the tech start-up realm, we see this instead: Anyone with a good idea and similar drive can start and run a company just as GHTV (and YouTern, as we discussed in Chapter 6) has done. There is no need to go hat-in-hand to a bank, look for investors, or save for decades to finance a new operation. All the technology this team needed to start an educational TV show is right there, nearly free. Their camera is already on their laptop, or on their phone (which is now perfectly acceptable to viewers; many even prefer that grassroots approach for its "authenticity").

Where a major television network, production company, or established digital media site might spend millions of dollars and employ thousands of people to launch a new series, these guys just did it, on their own, with close to no money, in less than seven weeks.

Bronson is dedicated to giving a great interview (and he does), so the guests have something they'll be proud to share with their networks. And they do.

*A community is born!*

GHTV reaches hundreds of thousands of potential customers per show, as the guests interviewed by Bronson share their episodes via Twitter, Facebook, LinkedIn, and Google+, as well as on their blogs and company websites, in their e-newsletters—you get the idea. All of which costs GHTV, and the guests, nothing or close to it.

Is this an example of the end of the enterprise? Does this indicate the "death of large"?

Let's pose this question a different way: Long term, how can a large, bureaucratic, "stay in line and do your time"–style company *afford* to compete against nano?

*Perhaps more important, does social media make nano unavoidable?*

*Does it make change inevitable?*

## THE PERFECT KILLER APP

Done right, and by bringing together a small team of inspired professionals to knock out a top-notch product, the nano corporation is the perfect "killer app."

When the project is over and the product goes live, the teams disperse to the four winds, ready to take on their next projects. Different teams, partners, and collaborators then market and sell the products. These teams themselves can be composed of nano corps, such as independent, small distributors or *channels*. (Nothing futuristic there—tech firms have been selling via channels for decades already.)

Nano teams self-assemble, disassemble, and reassemble at will. They can't afford to support a large bureaucracy, and the members certainly wouldn't want to anyway. They don't have time to stagnate, to be unproductive—they're making something. They are driven by passion, and then they're done.

Does this describe how your company operates? If not, are you at least a *little* nervous right now?

Keep reading.

## GO NANO OR GO HOME

Ever stick around at a movie to watch the closing credits?

Hundreds of team members come together for several months, or even years, to make the movies we watch. Then the film is "in the can"—and the people who made the film are done, too. While the director, cinematographer, and members of the cast may go on to work together several more times, the crew for this particular film disassembles just as fast as it formed; individuals and small teams go off to their next project. Hollywood has operated like this for a century now.

The Hollywood model—even when making blockbusters with budgets of $300 million—is all about nano.

How about our legacy enterprises? Can they do the same? Can they assemble large project teams from individuals and small groups, create something for the enterprise to sell, and then disassemble just as fast? Can each team member move nimbly to the next project, with a new creative force driven by different passions; different motivations?

Actually, we're already well on our way there.

If you look at the history of the corporation, what you saw for much of the early years was the drive to employ every possible job function in-house. But as early as the 1970s, this acquisitive urge began to diminish, and the fringe role of consultants became more commonplace.

Look at how most companies operate today. Walk the halls of most workplaces, and it's often hard to tell who is a full-time employee and who's a contractor, a consultant, an intern, or an outsourced service provider. Where once the megacorporation existed, today numerous companies come together to get work done. Is it so hard to extrapolate, to follow this trend to one possible conclusion, which is the existence of thousands of small companies where once there was one?

Think about what that means—what needs to happen, to make that happen.

This workplace revolution would require a culture-wide entrepreneurial mindset. A way of thinking we haven't seen since William Carnegie was forced to walk away from the loom. A way of doing business not witnessed since the farmer walked off his land to find factory work in the city.

Can we do it? That is a question only our most forward-thinking educational reformers can answer.

But we are optimistic!

## WE REPEAT: NOT ALL ROSES AND RAINBOWS

The process we're describing here isn't for everyone. It won't work for every company. And some companies will maintain their own version of a competitive edge.

After all, large organizations really aren't trying to compete in the "entrepreneurial spirit" category. They aren't trying to keep up with the power unleashed by social. Not exclusively, anyway.

Let's face it, big companies have two things that give them a leg up in the war for talent.

One is their deep pockets. If you are not the entrepreneurial type but you've got talent and you want a steady paycheck, a large company stands a good chance of crushing the most innovative nano corp when it comes to hiring you. It's typical for employees at start-ups to be paid wages that are much lower than market rates, with an upside sell that includes stock options (potentially worth millions *if* the company is one of those rare huge successes), a passionate work environment, and making a big contribution to a little team.

A lot of workers, especially once they have kids and a mortgage, would rather take higher pay with a seemingly more stable employer. Health benefits remain highly attractive to many. Throw in a 401(k) with matching funds plus vision and dental benefits, and, for many, a start-up doesn't stand a chance.

The second consideration is pride of association. We humans are ruled by our own mental shortcuts, and one of those shortcuts our brain relies on *a lot* is status by association, also called *social proof*. In the eyes of many who are not cut out for the entrepreneurial life—who don't want to carve out their own future—it's better to be a janitor at a famous enterprise than a vice president of a company no one's ever heard of. Many enterprises benefit from what Seth Godin calls the "Bat Boy Syndrome," whereby even being a bat boy for a pennant-winning team makes you a winner, too. In the war for talent, that is how Disney, Facebook, and many others win their fair share of battles.

After all, when we go to a party and get asked the "What do you do?" question, many of us would rather answer, "I work at Google" than "Bob's Innovative Solutions, LLC."

So if deep pockets and social proof continue to play in the enterprise's favor, what's going to spell its doom? What will cause the "death of large"?

It could just be that the way large companies are managed—in particular, the human side of that management—is the source of the trouble.

## THE DEATH OF LARGE IS MORE THAN SPECULATION

Remember Bronson Taylor, from GHTV?

He is one of three partners. They're in business together; no one's the commander. That is working just fine for them, but their company is minuscule. How about in an enterprise, when a company has 20,000 . . . 80,000 . . . 150,000 employees spanning a large country or even the entire globe?

In that case, how many commanders do entry-level employees have between themselves and the CEO?

And what about bureaucracy? When Bronson and his partners decide to make a move, they do it—often literally in the moment. If one of them is working on his own project that day, or is traveling, the amount of time that decision might wait for him is overnight. That's it. Not even twenty-four hours.

In our largest companies, by contrast, how many committees and task forces does a suggestion for change have to endure, how many months or even years have to pass before a good idea is implemented—if it ever is? One aspect of life in a bureaucracy that seemingly never changes: Killing a project during its long gestation period is a lot easier than keeping it alive to reach fruition. If a company feels pressure to report strong quarterly earnings, the second thing to go (after employees) is any risky project with no "right now" ROI. Creative ideas outside the norm are often the first to go—sometimes right before they reach maturity.

Finally, when it comes to deep pockets and layers of bureaucracy, is "scale" still cheaper and more efficient than a cottage business, as it was in the twentieth century?

In mining iron and refining steel, yes, scale still wins. But how many organizations in our advanced economy still make simple raw materials? In the century of the creative knowledge worker, scale just doesn't apply. And when creative knowledge work is the product, can the company stay competitive with a large bureaucracy to support? With all those executives' salaries to maintain?

It seems that management visionary author Gary Hamel might have been on to something when he dubbed our large companies' current predicament "*diseconomies*" of scale. When nearly every worker is an educated adult fully capable of making sound decisions, and implementing and improving processes, the necessity of paying a huge staff of professional managers six or seven figures to keep workers in line is a sucker's bet.

In our social economy, the long-term odds favor the house—the small, nimble, nano house.

## HENCE, THE DEATH OF LARGE

Over the long haul, legacy enterprises that do not embrace social are in big trouble. They're marching blithely off a cliff, completely unaware that they're doing it. If nothing else, they will no longer be able to compete with other, similar organizations that leverage their deep pockets and prestige—and at the same time, *do* unleash the power available to them in the Social Age while working through small, focused teams rather than a top-heavy bureaucracy stuck in the 1950s.

Want evidence?

► Think Montgomery Ward, JCPenney, and Sears vs. Amazon and its 17 million likes on Facebook.

► Consider the fine community work that Ford, and to a certain extent new kid Tesla, are doing compared to competitors General Motors and Chrysler.

► Ponder all the old-school beverage companies slowly going away, while Red Bull rocks social media with 36 million likes on Facebook and 1.5 million followers on Twitter.

► Look at the work *The New Yorker* and *Rolling Stone* are doing on Twitter, and compare it to that of just about any dying magazine brand (and there are plenty to choose from).

► Spend a few moments looking at the engaging social media accounts of Virgin America, and compare them to the broadcasting and defensive stance of United or Delta.

► Compare the long-term value of coffee brands like Starbucks and Dunkin' Donuts to Folgers.

► Think about how Huffington Post's 200,000 tweets have driven the younger demographic to a site operated by AOL, perhaps the Internet's first original legacy corporation.

If we're going to make a difference and save a few of these companies from self-imposed extinction—and in the process make the world of work a better experience for employees of all levels—now's the time.

That list of enterprises getting social—and going small—the right way is absolutely a list of exceptions. For the other legacy firms, the hourglass is just about out of sand.

Meanwhile, the little, nimble guys, the nano corps, are popping up everywhere—and thriving! We've given you only a few examples. Moreover, GHTV and YouTern are only niche organizations. Dennis Goldberg renting space and selling patents to Charles River Labs is merely one other, and the movie industry? Well, there's nothing normal about Hollywood! Maybe these are all flukes. Maybe an entire economy could never function this way.

Maybe.

But do you want to be the guy who stubbornly stands at the loom while the world around you progresses? Do you want to be the leader who hangs on to the assembly line and mass production mentality long after that model was proven ineffective?

Didn't William Carnegie and his peers see their way of life as secure; they were happy craftsmen proud of their work; they believed their continued success was inevitable. Today, the exact same thing can be said about the leaders of legacy enterprises who believe so strongly in their Industrial Age model—and perhaps too strongly in the "too big to fail" mindset—and make the choice not to adapt . . .

Until an irresistible market pressure changes everything in a given market in a virtual heartbeat.

In business and in economics, nothing is inevitable. Absolutely nothing is unchanging.

Social is every bit as powerful and unstoppable a disruptive force today as the assembly line was 100 years ago.

At the start of this chapter, we laid before you seven factors that, together, spell certain doom for our largest companies as they exist today. So far, we've discussed the need for agility and the advantage of being nimble and nano. Now it's time to really dive into the exciting, frothy waters of disruption. In the next chapter we introduce you to several remarkable companies that have turned their backs on bosses and haven't looked back since.

It's time to discuss how "flat" works. Prepare for a whole new world—and a whole new way to lead your team and company—in the Social Age.

# CHAPTER 8

# Flat: The New Black?

What if you start a company and don't have any "managers" at all? You hire only mature, responsible adults and you treat them accordingly.

## WHAT IF EVERY EMPLOYEE MADE BIG DECISIONS?

Within the company's customer-centric culture, employees make their own choices, including all manner of decisions about the company itself: strategy, spending, customer interaction, product design—*everything*.

Communication, even among virtual and separated employees, is organic. No more useless meetings that serve only the grandstanders and bureaucrats. Conversations flow both at the office watercooler and at its digital counterparts via Twitter, Facebook, IM, and Yammer (or whatever other internal messaging tool you might use).

Each team member is fully accountable for decisions; your company thrives or languishes depending entirely on them. As founder, you have no title or, if you do, it's only for outsiders, not your coworkers; you refuse to be treated as "the boss." Even the best parking spaces go to the earliest risers, not those who have risen through the ranks.

Sound hard to wrap your head around? A little too "out there" for you?

We hear where you're coming from. Both of your authors were mentored by those who cut their teeth in the Industrial Age, and this type of model—well, to those mentors this probably sounds great for an Israeli kibbutz or a 1960s-era California commune. But it's certainly not what we were taught, or you, in B-school, is it? Frankly, this would make our fathers' and grandfathers' heads explode. There needs to be one "the buck stops here" boss, someone to take the credit—and the blame. Right?

Now let's put a twist on this question.

What if a *competitor's* company was founded this way, and you soon discovered they were kicking your butt? More innovative products. More efficient operations. More market share. More profits. And the best young talent flocked to this innovative company . . . while you consistently struggled to find good people.

What then?

Good business leaders don't change on a whim; they don't change their org charts because of a fad, and they certainly don't force change upon their organizations because they figure the experience will be fun. They inflict change upon their organizations (yes, we said "inflict") for one reason only: to obey the Law of Change:

*Change happens only as the result of insurmountable market pressure.*

Guess what? That pressure is upon us all. Right now. Change in how we operate our organizations is afoot, and we don't get to vote based on how we feel about it. We either adapt, or we sit back and watch the competitor—the one embracing the "flat imperative"—grow, while we fail.

Say you're a producer of video games—not the Pac-Man and Space Invaders that your authors grew up with at the arcade, but the incredibly elaborate, graphically vibrant alternative universes that today's gamers spend an average of 1,000 hours per year playing—games like Grand Theft Auto VI, Bioshock, and Assassin's Creed V. (Don't know those names? Establish a game room somewhere in your office, and see how many twenty- and thirty-somethings flock to work for you—you'll learn.)

This is big business—$70 billion in annual revenue, with one of the highest profit margins of any industry.

Among the thousands of entries in the gaming marketplace, there is one company that outshines them all. Per employee, this company is more profitable than Microsoft, Apple, or even Google (where, last we checked, each employee generated $1 million in annual revenue). This firm is privately owned. At the time of this writing, its cofounder, Gabe Newell, was worth $1.5 billion himself.

And he refuses to let anyone call him "boss" (though he reluctantly allows the press to call him the company's president).

Welcome to VALVᴱ, a $2.5 billion company that produces the überpopular games Half-Life, Left 4 Dead, and Counter-Strike, among others. It's also creator of the Steam portal (think the iTunes store, but for games), which sells not only VALVᴱ games and products, but its competitors' products as well. (That's gotta be galling, huh? Knowing every time you sell your games, your rival is taking a piece of your action? Gamers love Steam, though, so if you want their business, you've got to go where the gamers are.)

Most important to the discussion around the flat imperative: VALV$^E$ employs more than 400 passionate team members. And not one manager. Not a single one.

In fact, employees so dislike taking on project leadership roles that VALV$^E$ veterans laugh about how they often dupe a new hire into taking the lead when the time comes to collaborate; staff members rarely choose to lead a second time.

"Wait a minute!" we said when we heard this. "So they *do* have leaders, after all. Not so 'flat,' are we?"

Wrong! Yes, the game designers need to work together, of course. These are incredibly complex endeavors, involving graphic artists, story crafters, and coders (VALV$^E$ even has a position for on-staff economist, if you can believe it). So they choose one person to coordinate work on a given project as they create a new game or improve an existing one.

But unlike the autocratic, General Patton–like "Leaders-with-a-capital-L" we're used to from our Industrial Age upbringing, VALV$^E$'s temporary leaders have no command-and-control authority. As with the other flat organizations we've studied, following is at all times an opt-in choice made—and continually made again—by the other workers on the project. The project "leader" is nothing more than a central knowledge repository, with no authority to compel obedience or dispense rewards.

This truly is servant leadership, not in the "humble boss" spirit of the phrase, but quite literally leadership based on serving the team. Though no one at VALV$^E$ used this term with us, a project leader seems in many ways no more than a communication point—"home base," if you will.

As for Newell, the billionaire founder? He works in an office with three other employees, who all chose to work there with him. His desk is the same standard issue as everyone else's—which is great for him. If sharing the office with any one of his peers on a particular morning isn't working out, he can wheel his desk anywhere else in VALV$^E$'s headquarters and park himself there. For a day. A month. Or forever.

Yes, every new hire at VALV$^E$ is given a desk—with wheels. And irrevocable permission to use those wheels.

It is explained in the (really fun to read) employee handbook that workers choose whom they work with simply by moving their desks and are enabled to move again whenever they like. They don't need to ask anyone before initiating such a move, which is good because . . . well, who would they ask? VALV$^E$ has no bosses.

Here are just a few other fascinating aspects of this remarkable company:

▶ **Each employee is bound to profit** | VALV$^E$ team members are *much* more cognizant of their own ties to the profits than in a typical company—

something we've seen again and again in flat organizations. Financial transparency and employee accountability are absolutely essential components of self-leadership. No matter your role at VALVᴱ, if what you're doing doesn't positively impact the bottom line, you'd be wise to find ways to improve performance—or find something else to do.

▶ **Make a decision, any decision** | All employees at VALVᴱ can make any decision they feel is necessary—at any time. Regardless of the magnitude of the decision, they have no higher authority to convince, pitch, or ask permission of—no boss, no task force, no product development department. The focus and only decision-making point: the gamer experience and profit margins. This is true even on the company's biggest projects and products: Employees can change the code on even the bestselling game in real time. If the change doesn't work, they are solely responsible for changing it back, quickly.

▶ **Ignore industry norms** | Finally—and this is something else we've seen in one example after another of highly successful, employee-driven companies— VALVᴱ performs the exact opposite of industry norms (often referred to as *best practices*, a term we loathe and equate with "never better than anyone else"):

▷ The company pays its employees much more than it must. VALVᴱ is profitable, and Newell knows this pay rate is fair; perhaps more than fair. If employees feel their employer is paying an unfair wage, they disengage—and you've lost them.

▷ Most of VALVᴱ's employees understand their work is valued and meaningful; many, we dare say, would take less pay rather than abandon that motivating aspect of VALVᴱ's culture.

▷ VALVᴱ refuses to outsource labor to a cheaper locale. Newell asserts that's actually stupid. He claims the quality of their products and the heart of their innovation comes from not being cheap and shortsighted.

▷ VALVᴱ views the idea of employees working long hours as inefficient. Except at the crunch time of a new release, if you don't leave work at a reasonable hour and have a life, you're probably not good at your job—or your workmates aren't pulling their weight. Both are considered unacceptable.

▷ Because VALVᴱ recognizes that work-life integration is critical to the sanity and health of its employees, this provides the opportunity to develop friends, interests, and passions outside of work, which then fuels creativity and innovation at work.

▷ Our favorite? VALVᴱ hires a lot of misfits (or if you'd prefer, "unusual suspects"). Instead of filling the ranks with nothing but Phi Beta Kappa engineers who write code fast (and do nothing else to contribute to the culture, innovation, and success of the company), VALV$^E$ hires people with all sorts of interesting backgrounds, including many creative types from Hollywood. This culture makes groupthink nearly impossible, and it makes their games, and their unexpected innovations, much more dynamic.

Is VALV$^E$ perfect? Hardly.

While the company strives to hire only responsible adults with high emotional intelligence who fit well within the culture, the occasional mistake happens. And Newell readily admits they need to get faster at replacing people who don't fit their culture or don't meet the expectations of other team members.

Despite its quasi-utopian business model, there has been at least one disgruntled employee to leave. One gray area: In a podcast that features interviews with influencers from the gaming industry, former employee Jeri Ellsworth publically denounced VALV$^E$ when she compared the company's culture to a cliquey high school.

With some studies showing that just 4 percent of gaming employees are female, some might argue that the entire gaming industry is far too male dominated; certainly, VALV$^E$ is not immune to this criticism.

So not even the most amazing company gets everything right every time. Still, if you're going to be mortal like the rest of us, isn't it better to operate a company that's incredibly profitable? One where the workers manage themselves? One where decisions are made for the right reasons, rather than to please a boss?

## FROM ZOMBIE SLAYING TO TOMATO PROCESSING

Maybe you're thinking, as one executive remarked to us, "This is great for an industry like gaming, but we don't build products that kill zombies. We're in a grown-up business. A legacy business, with hundreds of blue-collar employees and certain expectations from the communities in which we operate."

Taking this into consideration, the assumption may be that a high-tech start-up staffed primarily by well-educated team members is the perfect place to start and maintain a flat management structure. No senior employees. No unions. No baggage. Perfect contemporary breeding ground for a flat culture, right?

Perhaps it would be far more difficult for a more traditional business—one that has been around for four or more decades and produces a tangible product that we might find on store shelves, an organization that didn't grow up with technology or using social media as an engagement tool—to implement a flat management style?

Maybe not.

Canned foods is about as old-school as we can get, right? Can a food processing plant, with a major operation in a small California farming town less than 100 miles from Silicon Valley—yet worlds away—operate flat?

Ask Morning Star, the nation's largest processor of tomatoes.

Based in the California cities of Williams and Los Banos, Morning Star doesn't have managers—and it hasn't since the company's founding in 1972. How does it pull that off, when many employees (or "colleagues") are lifelong manual laborers without formal education? And when nearly 90 percent of them are considered seasonal employees?

For a bit of insight, let's start with Morning Star's website, on the Self-Management page:

> *The Morning Star Company was built on a foundational philosophy of Self-Management. We envision an organization of self-managing professionals who initiate communication and coordination of their activities with fellow colleagues, customers, suppliers and fellow industry participants, absent directives from others. For colleagues to find joy and excitement utilizing their unique talents and to weave those talents into activities which complement and strengthen fellow colleagues' activities. And for colleagues to take personal responsibility and hold themselves accountable for achieving our Mission.*

Right now, you're likely experiencing one of two emotions: elation because this sounds like such a great way to do work, or discomfort because it's a bit touchy-feely for you. Either way, this copy is likely not what is displayed on your firm's website, is it? "absent directives from others"? "joy and excitement"? "weave those talents"? "complement and strengthen"?

"Oh, come *on!*" we hear many of you saying.

Here's the thing, though: Whether you love it or hate it, this works—exceedingly well. Morning Star started in 1970 as a guy (founder Chris Rufer) with a truck, hauling tomatoes from fields to processors. Four decades later, it's the biggest tomato processor in the United States. Even the most bellicose skeptic must respect that level of success—and the fact that Morning Star is world-renowned for its management style.

The keys to pulling off this flat structure?

► The focus on mature, responsible adult team members.

► The specificity of expectations and performance.

How many employees at *any* firm unmistakably understand what their role is *and* how it tracks directly back to the company's success?

Far too few.

Indeed, lack of meaning at work—lack of understanding the company strategy and how the employee personally affects the execution of that strategy—is a huge factor in the malaise of low morale dragging company profits down, not only in the United States but worldwide.

All too often, employees come to work to do *exactly* what their boss expects of them, and no more, so they can get paid. The boss changes the directions from time to time—"moving employee cheese" as Spencer Johnson put it in his bestselling book *Who Moved My Cheese?*—and the employees do exactly what they are told, again.

Eventually, employees are forced to shrug off what they perceive as a negative work environment, poor communication, and autocratic management. Not able to find any passion from their current job or from the leaders assigned to make sure the job gets done, they continue to work toward "following their passion" as they've been told to since college. The result, as we've discussed before: minimum effort expended to do the seemingly random tasks assigned them—all the while, they look elsewhere for more meaningful work and a genuine sense of contribution.

That is not the case at Morning Star, where workers are truly self-directed. So self-directed, in fact, that they write their own expectations—and then commit to doing what they've written.

That document is called the Colleague Letter of Understanding (or CLOU; pronounced "clue"). The often handwritten letter states the worker's role, specific duties, and how the worker's performance will be measured. The CLOU is negotiated with, and ultimately approved by, other nonmanagers with whom the employee will work.

The entire purpose of the CLOU is to ensure that part A fits smoothly into slot B—and that the entire operation runs as a single, integrated unit.

As workers gain more skills, they tweak their CLOUs to reflect their skills, impact, and additional responsibilities. Pay is decided upon by committees of peers, and it is based on performance against the expectations stated in the CLOU. Issues such as inequitable pay are handled up front with peers; no issue is left unresolved. Which begs the question, does this work? In their more than forty-year history, has anyone ever filed a legitimate complaint against Morning Star for inequality? We couldn't find one. Nor any complaints regarding civil rights issues, sexual harassment, or any of the other issues most "normal" companies deal with at one time or another.

So, it appears self-management isn't *non*management; it isn't chaos.

Even in an industry as markedly unsexy as tomato processing, self-management works. It *really* works. It works in both an incredibly profitable, innovative industry like gaming as well as in a low-margin, low-tech commodity field like tomato processing.

Still, we had to ask ourselves another question, one that harkens back to Chapter 7, "The Death of Large."

## CAN FLAT SCALE?

VALVE's 400 employees, Morning Star's 3,000—as we looked at flat companies, we asked ourselves: Is there a limit to the size of a company when it has no, or very little, traditional management?

We suspect there may be, but there is another large, thriving, pancake-flat company: W. L. Gore & Associates.

Founded in 1958 by Bill Gore (a former DuPont researcher who loved the science he was doing but didn't like the bureaucracy his employer had saddled him with) and best-known for its Gore-Tex line of waterproof clothing, W. L. Gore is unquestionably the most-studied flat company in the world. And for very good reasons, with which you might already be familiar. We don't want to tread over territory you may already know, but to continue this important conversation, let's settle for a summary of the important points around Gore's success:

► Gore is privately held, incredibly profitable, and remarkably innovative.

► Outsiders hired into the firm find it takes about a year to figure out their own role at Gore. (That is an awfully long time—what would Wall Street say?)

► With no official title, no administrative support, no reserved parking spot, no executive washroom, many outsiders find it tough to *ever* fit in. (Flat can be stressful, as Rick Wartzman of the Drucker Institute pointed out in a compelling *Forbes* article titled "If Self-Management Is Such a Great Idea, Why Aren't More Companies Doing It?".)

► Just about the only person at the company with a title is the CEO, Terri Kelly (a primary reason her role comes with a title: because it's easier for the outside world to think of someone as "in charge").

► Kelly was elected to that position by her peers and then confirmed by the board. (Would your company's CEO survive an election? A confirmation?)

Gore, with 9,000 worldwide employees, seems to answer the question "Can you scale flat?" in the affirmative.

How the company does that is interesting.

As Malcolm Gladwell observes in his must-read bestseller *The Tipping Point:*

*How Little Things Can Make a Big Difference,* Gore is one big company that operates as a whole slew of small companies. It has a hard-and-fast rule that no business unit may grow to over 150 employees—the size at which, Gore feels, cohesive human groups seem to splinter into cliques and colleagues become strangers. So at Gore, when a unit approaches that magical number, it is split into two units, each focused on a smaller portion of the business the single unit once served. Gore purposely avoids bureaucratic, autocratic cliques by breaking up even their most successful units.

So can your organization, no matter how large, scale flat? The answer is yes, it's quite possible—but perhaps only if you behave like a small firm, if you deliberately avoid the "death of large."

## FLAT: MORE THAN JUST AN INTRIGUING CONCEPT?

You could ask: Is flat simply the latest fad? Or will it drive success in the Social Age?

Consider for your approval:

Management is expensive—prohibitively expensive, actually. For proof of this statement, take your own firm, or any other nonflat company you wish, and perform this exercise:

1. Total the salaries of all the managers; include benefits, bonuses, and any other form of contribution.

2. Follow the same process for all administrative staff members dedicated to supporting those managers.

3. Account for travel expenditures for all these individuals and those who travel to support them.

4. Factor in the proportioned rent for their office space and the expense of their technology, office equipment, and services such as Internet and phone access; also include their various software as a service (SaaS) expenses.

5. Calculate the total investment in training, motivating, and retaining the managers.

6. Total these expenses, and add about 5 percent for contingency expenses (recruiting, relocation, etc.) not already noted.

The total represents the "management tax" your company pays to support the established hierarchy—and, quite possibly, to enable bureaucracy. If you truly want to calculate how much money your company spends for *not* being flat, consider also factoring in the work-hours lost in meetings, as managers pull each other and/or workers out of productivity-driven tasks (making or selling) to talk to them—or to talk *at* them.

You might also account for the hours workers spent interacting with the software that modern corporations use to oversee their workforces—the customer relationship management (CRM) that executives foist upon the sales and customer service teams to monitor them, the legion of HR processes, and the modern-day paperwork that must be filled out to justify decisions and cover our collective asses. Without management, all those hours would likely be spent on mission-critical tasks.

When you have a number—or even a range of numbers—that accurately depicts your organization's management tax, consider this: Your firm would move that entire number from the expense column to the profit column . . . if your organization were flat.

This is a good reason for any business owner or board of directors to at least pause to think about how their business might look—and operate—with little or no management.

Yes, it seems different—so "out there." But if "out there" means avoiding what amounts to billions of dollars wasted on management tax, well, that's a *lot* of money.

Still, we've just begun. There are two even more compelling reasons to consider a flat org structure to be more than just an interesting idea, even a compelling one.

## EMPLOYEES PERFORM BETTER IN FLAT ORGANIZATIONS

Much better, in fact.

Treehouse, a self-learning platform that teaches users to build a website, write a mobile app, and even start a technology business, went flat in 2013. Employees there report feeling empowered. They say communication has greatly improved, while turnaround times on project issues, decision making, and budget allocation have been significantly reduced. Ultimately, the employees feel a sense of ownership of their projects and their contribution to the bottom line.

Jason Fried, founder of Basecamp (formerly called 37Signals), the web-application company where "flatness" is said to be a core value, told Inc.com that those who thrive in a flat company aren't those who necessarily crave old-school recognition like dedicated management responsibilities and promotions that come with prestigious titles, but are those who thrive on accomplishing the mission in front of them. He also says that the company's foray into more traditional management structure (assigning a dedicated manager to improve a department and watch over the team) was wholly unsuccessful. Fried commented, "Groups that manage themselves are often better off than groups that are managed by a single person. So when groups do require structure, we get them to manage themselves."

Granted, the sample size of flat companies is still much smaller than the control size of their competitors. We are also happy to concede the fact that no one ever hears about flat organizations that fail. Surely there have been a few flat companies that didn't survive, whether or not it was because of their flat operation or other business issues.

Further, it's difficult to find a publicly traded company that is flat—perhaps because this is a strategy for long-term success, not necessarily current-quarter profits, or perhaps because companies founded as flat are so profitable that owners see no reason to sell stock.

Difficult, but they're out there. Sun Hydraulics (NASDAQ: SNHY) of Sarasota, Florida, went public in 1997 as an answer to succession planning: Two of the founder's three heirs did not want to participate in the business; the third is active on the board. Bob Koski, CEO from the company's founding in 1970 until his death in the mid-2000s, brought this manufacturing firm public. Sun continues to grow enviably year after year, with sales of over $200 million in 2013.

How flat is Sun? Aside from the corporate officers (legally obligated to have titles), the only job title is Plant Manager—for the employee who waters the plants.

This remarkable 900-employee multinational organization is innovative not just in technology, management style, and environmental and community leadership; it is a net exporter to the rest of the world, including to China. And as is the case with all the flat organizations we studied, employee engagement is through the ceiling.

Engaged workers exhibit much less absenteeism (and presenteeism, where they are physically at work but operate in a far-less-than-optimum manner) than workers at their hierarchical rivals. That alone is worth its weight in gold—and it is where many aspects of social come alive in a flat organization.

Engaged workers aren't merely at work doing what they're paid to do. They also perform better at the tasks a command-and-control structure cannot incentivize or scare them into doing—all the noncompulsory stuff that is so essential in this knowledge economy. They share—on Twitter, IM, Jabber, Yammer, and Facebook—their successes, failures, lessons learned, and the shortcuts found. Via text and e-mail, they celebrate wins and communicate innovative solutions. Where once these team members were intentionally divided and conquered (and even forbidden to carry and use "personal" devices while "on the job"), in a world gone social they communicate freely.

And that isn't all:

► Engaged workers innovate more, because they care and because they are free to fail.

► They are far more willing to go that elusive extra mile when times are tough or when it's crunch time for a deadline.

► Engaged workplaces find it much easier to hire top talent—after all, who doesn't want to work for a company they can love?

► As discussed in Chapter 4, engaged workers are much more likely to recommend their friends to work at their company, even without referral bonuses/bribes as incentives.

In short, engaged workers give more of themselves. They share. They grow. They make better decisions. They prosper.

Add the benefits of everything from improved engagement to removal of the management tax, and we hope you've already entered the realm of the imperative, of "must-do" rather than "oh, that's interesting."

But we aren't even close to finished yet . . .

The main reason a company must go flat harkens back to the Law of Change:

## CHANGE IS THE RESULT OF INSURMOUNTABLE MARKET PRESSURE

In the Social Age, when your competitor goes flat and you don't, you're up the creek.

How on Earth can you compete with a company with drastically lower overhead and workers who are so much more engaged, productive, and innovative than yours?

As many companies discover (including stalwarts like those in the American auto industry), there is plenty of room for inefficiency when a market is vibrant and incredibly lucrative (like video gaming is right now). It is entirely possible that VALV$^E$'s biggest competitor, Electronic Arts (EA; worth $4.8 billion as of this writing), will get away with maintaining the hierarchical nature of its existence. It will still thrive, albeit with a monstrous management tax to pay, like an anchor dragging along the ocean floor as the ship of commerce sails on, oblivious.

But look at Morning Star. It sells an absolute commodity, a "me too" product if ever there was one. You don't go to the store saying, "I need my Morning Star!" and happily pay 20 percent more for the company's sauce; you likely have no idea which products even *contain* Morning Star tomatoes and which contain a rival's paste. So Morning Star can't possibly charge more for its product.

It simply must run in the most efficient, engaging way possible.

If you want to compete with Morning Star for market share, you'll have to do it under the weight of your hefty management tax and through the less-than-inspired work of your less-than-engaged employees.

How long can you keep that up?

The same scenario plays out with Gore & Associates. With its amazingly diverse product line, this company operates in a vast number of markets and industries—and thrives in each! Would you deliberately compete against Gore? Maybe *you* would, but we are really glad we don't have to. At least not through a management-heavy, slow-to-adapt, traditional business model that might bleed billions trying.

Times have changed. Today, as you read this book, we're deep in the midst of a cataclysmic (and wonderful) change in the way business is done. What used to be considered impossible is now happening. Fueled by collaboration—and built on the foundation of organic communication with a click of a button or a share sent via the touch of a screen—the Social Age is upon us.

Companies that used to be outliers—like VALV$^E$, Morning Star, Sun, and Gore—will become the norm. It's already happening at organizations like Basecamp and Treehouse. Same with Semco, a Brazilian firm we've been tracking for years now, and Menlo Innovations, a disruptively innovative software firm based in Michigan.

Again and again, flat companies with open communication, authentic leadership, and engaging cultures are crushing it—and they're coming to a market, and an industry, near you.

## HOW DO YOU FLATTEN HIERARCHIES?

In late 2013, Zappos announced that, in order to prevent bureaucracy from infiltrating the company as it continued its growth, it was going flat—a change the billion-dollar online retailer owned by Amazon will have implemented by the end of 2014.

The only thing is, Zappos isn't going flat. It's going flat-*ter.* The company's move toward a Holacracy (from the Greek word *holon,* meaning a whole that is part of a greater whole) is arguably a step in the flat direction.

Perhaps like you, we had a lot of questions about Zappos, the move to flatter, and the model. Let's take a look at some of the answers to those questions:

▶ No, Amazon does not control how Zappos is run; although Amazon bought Zappos in 2009, CEO Tony Hsieh is given free rein in running the company; the parent and child firms are completely distinct.

▶ Yes, a lot about Zappos is "a little weird"—a trait it encourages in employees. Engagement is very high. Customer service is legendary. Hsieh is a healthy-culture zealot. Zappos doesn't do things like everybody else, so the idea that the company is changing its management structure shouldn't surprise anyone.

► It's true that many aspects of Zappos have always leaned toward inclusive. For instance, Zappos.com's home page used to sport a video of Hsieh in his CEO's "office," which was a cubicle in the center of the cube farm at headquarters. Yes, at the center—the top dog didn't even sit near a window.

Ultimately, Zappos is a company where the CEO is accessible to the rest of the staff on a daily basis, an aspect of the company that is well within the spirit of a more open, democratic—and flat—workplace. By this virtue alone, Zappos is way ahead of most companies out there.

Still, until the press release stating that Zappos was going flat was read by millions, the CEO sat at the top of a familiar-looking organizational pyramid. There were managers and managers of managers, as at most companies with 1,500 employees.

But soon there won't be. Or, at least, they won't have the title "manager."

Still, to think of a Holacracy as flat, without bosses and subordinates, is inaccurate. A Holacracy is perhaps best compared to a Venn diagram, where workers may belong to several different "circles," each with different responsibilities. At Zappos, some of the circles have command authority over other circles, and while they don't use the word "manager," their leaders manage.

Clear as mud yet?

The bottom line: Zappos is taking an important step away from hierarchy. It is deliberately distancing operations from hierarchy's handmaiden, bureaucracy.

That's an important point. Hsieh has no interest in running a lumbering, regimented, calcified company. With this step, he's backing his firm away from Industrial Age management and toward something that is more *in the direction of* flat, and certainly (despite naysayers) more in the *spirit* of flat.

Zappos isn't the first Holacracy; it's just the largest to date. Medium, a publishing platform and the third company founded by Evan Williams of Twitter fame, is a Holacracy where employees "focus on the work that needs to be done rather than the people who are in charge." So, too, was Ternary Software, which lives on today as HolacracyOne, a consulting firm with Brian Robertson, one of Ternary's founders (and the person credited with inventing the term *Holacracy*) as CEO. Its mission: spread the Holacracy gospel to all who will listen—including Zappos, which HolacracyOne is helping to make the shift (and therefore turning Holacracy into the new black among bloggers, management consultants, and self-anointed thought leaders).

A Holacracy is a move toward the flatter end of the spectrum for leaders who just aren't ready to jump in with both feet. Does that sound like you? If so, we have some advice.

## GOING FLAT CAN HURT

By this point, we hope your question is "How do we get some of that flat for ourselves?"

Our best answer: Start that way. Be flat from day one, when your company is still just you and your best friend in a bar, drawing on a napkin.

But it's possible you're already past that stage, as Semco was when Ricardo Semler took over the company from his father in the early 1980s. As Zappos is in 2014.

Can you go flat if you didn't start that way? Yes, absolutely. Is the shift likely to be ugly? It sure was for Semler. His must-read book, *Maverick!*, chronicles the experimenting, missteps, and, yes, the firings that took place as he wrestled his father's foundering old-school business from its executives and set out in a new direction—one that not only saved the company but made it many times more successful than it had ever been before.

Firings. Let's not gloss over that. Sociopathic CEOs aside (and they aren't unheard of), nobody wants to fire anyone if they can avoid it.

Does going flat mean the company must dismiss its management entirely?

This is something we struggled with as we discussed this section of *A World Gone Social*. We are dedicated to the human side of business, after all, and managers (most of them, anyway) are human. Advising our readers to lop off the top and middle levels of their corporate pyramid doesn't sit well with us.

And we have precedent as to why it shouldn't sit well with you, either.

In the 1970s and '80s, corporate America realized it had one, two, even three levels of management more than it needed. When they began clearing that dead wood from their headquarters, the first white-collar recession in our history occurred; in the restructured economy, a mass of mostly middle-aged white guys found themselves undervalued, overpriced, and unemployed.

For all who have struggled with our most recent recession/depression and who may be saying, "Big deal—join the club," it was also the largest mass exodus of collective institutional wisdom these companies had ever faced. Losing knowledge and wisdom—and, in a world gone social, the relationships nurtured by those managers—is bad for any organization's competitive posture.

No, we do not advise wanton layoffs. We do *not* suggest tossing aside the knowledge holders and relationship owners and *teachers,* which is what the best managers tend to be.

For flat to work, however, managers have some hard adjustments to make, just as the organizations themselves do. Those accustomed to position-power (and the perks that go with it in an Industrial Age bureaucracy) may very well decide not to stay. Then there's the issue of pay. A vice president earning a quarter million dollars or more in the old management hierarchy may not welcome compensation decisions being made by those who are now peers, as in many flat orgs.

There is nothing easy about any of this, and no one-size-fits-all recipe for success. That's why a slow, methodical approach may serve your organization better than ripping off the Band-Aid.

## FIRST, GO FLATTER . . . THEN A LITTLE FLATTER

This is why we're optimistic about Zappos' move from traditional hierarchy to Holacracy. There are still bosses in a Holacracy, even if the role is couched in gentler terms; specific team members retain responsibility for specific decisions.

*Maverick!* is full of examples of Ricardo Semler returning from a vacation or a business trip to find his workers had redesigned the factory or moved him into an ever smaller office, or even launched a new business unit. He enjoyed that type of thing, so it worked for him on an emotional level (as well as a financial level). He was dedicated early on to complete workplace democracy and saw his role more as defender of institutional chaos (and innovation, and engagement) than as the boss with all the answers—and all the power.

Tony Hsieh hasn't signaled that is where he's going with the Zappos Holacracy. He's still CEO—and not just in name. The worker bees won't be opening Zappos Airlines without his consent.

So if you're still a bit old-school, yet you understand the need to reinvent in order to survive, a Holacracy may be the right next step for you. But you may not know how to pull the trigger. And if you're not sure you can pull it off—in your department, division, or the entire organization—you need more information and more expertise.

The good news: In the Social Age, we can learn about any subject in a matter of days. We can absorb every blog on the subject of flat organizations and Holacracies. We can learn from the mistakes of others. We can build relationships with leaders in similar positions on Twitter, LinkedIn, and Facebook.

We don't need a master's degree in flat leadership. We don't need to be experts in going from the top of a silo to a Holacracy, and then to a flat organization. We simply need to know the experts. We need to learn from them as mentors. We must gain from their experience—and their willingness to share.

Hsieh would probably tell you that his strengths are culture, customer experience, and motivating others to care deeply about a common mission. He would likely *not* say that he is an evangelist or an expert on the subject of Holacracies. But he knew who was, or he asked his community and those within his mighty (and well-deserved) personal network to find out who was.

He came across HolacracyOne—and enlisted its help. He built an army of ambassadors from within Zappos to champion the idea. He gained top-down support from his current "managers"—even those who will be impacted most by this shift in leadership style.

He pulled the trigger, and as a result there is no doubt that Zappos will remain on the leading edge of innovation.

In the Social Age, this is how business is done.

Let us make our case . . .

## FLAT *WILL* BE THE NEW BLACK

Since the first chapter of *A World Gone Social,* we've talked about how customers must be listened to—and companies must react quickly to what they hear. We've discussed how employees are doing the listening; through social, they are your company's ears. And we've shown that it's now mission-critical to engage with all stakeholders and build communities to amplify the voice of the advocates, champions, and brand ambassadors found on social media. In Chapter 7, we talked about the imminent "death of large"—and the need for companies to get small, to go nano, so they can compete for customers, innovation, new team members, and market share.

So, with all that in mind, let us ask you . . .

In the Social Age, how can any organization do *all of that* in a management-heavy bureaucracy that operates in "the way we've always done it" (TWWADI) fashion with thirteen layers of decision makers functioning as service and innovation roadblocks?

Here's our ten-step thought process: how we see a company, over time, reacting to the imminent crisis caused by a long-standing bureaucracy failing to adapt to the Social Age. This is why we think—why we *know*—that in the Social Age flat is the new black:

1. Social is changing the way we work, hire, learn, listen, and communicate.

2. A business that chooses not to engage and collaborate with employees through social will find the majority of its employees "actively disengaged."

3. Companies that do not engage and collaborate with employees, it is easy to deduce, also do not listen actively to customers (which economy of scale dic-

tates would need to happen through those very employees who have grown accustomed to being disengaged).

4. Those customers, tired of being talked *at* and not listened *to*, will defect to a competitor that places the social strategy of the company—and the power to serve the customer well—directly in the hands of frontline employees who do the communicating, decision making, and reporting of brand perception up the chain of command.

5. The CEO of the company—thirteen layers of management away from those communicators and decision makers—will not understand the failings of the brand that are so obvious to everyone else and will be slow to react; brand erosion will occur, slowly at first and then like the deafening roar of a herd of dinosaurs.

6. The company will begin to be overrun by an existing competitor or a start-up that sees an opening and offers a service-oriented, marketable solution.

7. That company finally will realize that the loss of employees, customers, and market share is acute, that the enforcers of the TWWADI policy are barriers to communication and blockers of action and innovation.

8. To remove TWWADI from the equation and to begin the process of becoming competitive again by making the organization one giant listening device—to finally become socially active—the company simply must go flat, or at least flat-ter.

9. Once flat-ter, those in the C-suite (who, through change ignited by insurmountable market pressure, now understand that listening and engaging must be at the core of the company's culture and service model) will be much closer to their feet on the street: the empowered frontline employees.

10. Finally, the organization will be nimble enough to effect real change—as a direct result of listening—almost exclusively through social.

We know that the flat management style has its detractors. We know that this, more than any other section in this book, might raise eyebrows. And we know that social hasn't yet served as the impetus for a major organization choosing to go flat-ter. Not even Tony Hsieh—truly a social CEO—mentioned this as part of his reasoning for moving Zappos to become a Holocracy.

But it will happen.

Of this, we are certain: Companies must systemically change to take full advantage of social. In the Social Age, a CEO cannot be a dozen or more layers of bureaucrats away from the organic, unfiltered perception of the brand. Quick-enough change cannot be effected that far removed from the reality that the flat-ter competition thrives on when making critical decisions.

Some legacy company, much larger than Zappos, VALV$^E$, Morning Star, or W. L. Gore, is going to make this leap. It will be the trendsetter.

And you can say you heard about it here first, in *A World Gone Social*.

In Chapter 9, read how your flat (or flat-ter) organization will learn, live, even thrive, without all those managers—specifically, without their industry knowledge, personal contacts, and influence—by utilizing intellectual crowdsourcing we call OPEN.

# CHAPTER 9

# The OPEN Challenge (Ordinary People, Extraordinary Network)

*We live in a humbler age.*

—*Adam Grant*

To help you answer any question or solve any problem you might face, which would you rather have at your disposal?

► The top expert in that field

► One thousand completely ordinary, everyday people, chosen at random

What if we changed the parameters and allowed you to tap the collective wisdom of a dozen Nobel laureates, professors from the most prestigious schools, best-selling authors, and advisers to heads of state and put that dream team against a random assortment of people replying to a query posted on the Internet? Surely you'd think these top experts and authors would beat the pants off a randomly selected sample from the general population, right?

If you've read James Surowiecki's *The Wisdom of Crowds*, you already know the answer. Written all the way back in 2004 (when most of us were, let's face it, still mired in the Stone Age of Web 1.0), Surowiecki's fascinating book explores the magic of crowdsourcing—a magic that many current leaders and organizations still wrestle with or outright ignore today.

A worthy example comes from 1968, when the U.S. Navy lost a submarine, the *Scorpion*, in the North Atlantic as it headed back to port. The officer in charge of locating the missing sub, John Craven, had a seemingly hopeless task—including beginning the search with nothing better than a twenty-mile radius of the *Scorpion*'s last known position. Craven faced a challenge much worse than finding a needle in a haystack, because his haystack was an ocean.

In those old days—or old-school days—Craven would have been expected to form a panel of naval and oceanic experts; he would rely exclusively on this small team of specialists to narrow the search for the sub. They, it was assumed, knew what Craven needed to know.

Instead, he asked for the thoughts of a diverse group of experts in several different disciplines. So groupthink didn't occur and so no opinion would be diluted, Craven did not allow these experts to contact each other; they worked independently. He then collected their best thoughts and amalgamated the answers.

In the end, not one of the experts' individual best guesses was even close to the actual site. However, the composite location—the combination of the group's thinking—was remarkably within just 220 yards of where the sub was ultimately found.

Through crowdsourcing, the Navy found its sub.

The wisdom of crowds is so profound, so unimpeachable, and your authors have been using it so frequently for years now, that we've given it its own acronym.

## OPEN: ORDINARY PEOPLE | EXTRAORDINARY NETWORK

In the way that most really promising ideas are born, this concept came to us by accident.

First, our wonderful friend Suzanne Daigle, the renowned Open Space meeting facilitator, planted the seed the day she called Ted "ordinary." There's a great story behind this, but we'll spare you. Just know that, in her defense, she insists it was meant as a compliment.

Second, Ted stumbled across the Wikipedia entry for "Open Space Technology." On that page, under "Ideal Initial Conditions" are these unintentionally prophetic words regarding the problems that Open Space is best at solving. They involve:

> *... a high level of complexity, such that no single person or small group fully understands or can solve the issue.*

Without question, this defines the benefits of living and working in the Social Age:

▶ On any given day, in many areas of endeavor, any one of us can be completely ordinary—no matter how expert we are in another area.

▶ Together, however, we make for an extraordinarily powerful network able to solve any challenge, no matter how complex.

▶ Any of us—and potentially *all* of us—can tap into such a network at will, obliterating the chasm between the knowledgeable few and the rest of us.

Hence, Adam Grant's epigraph at the start of this chapter. Or, as your authors like to ask:

*When we're all experts through our networks, then what does "expert" even mean anymore?*

We're absolutely convinced that this question is worth pursuing further. Of all the trends and changes we identify in this book, OPEN is the most actionable and the most urgent—a vital combination that can transform any individual's career and any organization's prospects for the future.

Let's be honest, there will always be subject matter experts in any field. They may have years of academic study behind them and work as Ph.D.s in our most august research universities, or they may hold prestigious titles at the R&D departments of the largest companies. Or they could be autodidacts, the hobbyists all around us who just really care about, say, nineteenth-century model trains but hold down a day job selling life insurance. Regardless of the context, some will always know more about a given topic than others.

That truth does not obviate OPEN at all. What subject matter expertise means in the Social Age is that these experts are available to *all* of us, and they make our networks that much more extraordinary.

In this exciting new time we live in, the Social Age, knowledge is no longer power because so many people are only too willing to:

▶ Share their own knowledge

▶ Connect their friends and acquaintances with one another

Obviously, some of us are not as willing to do this as others. Some of us—especially those born and raised in the "hold your knowledge close and enemies closer" generations like your authors—come to this beneficial realism more slowly than others.

In Adam Grant's phenomenal bestseller, *Give and Take*, he breaks down the population into one of three different giving styles. Most of us are what he refers to as "matchers," which is to say, we keep a running tally in our heads: I did this favor for Bob, so he owes me now. Or Jamie helped me out here, so that means I'm on the hook to help Jamie in the future. Matchers will do favors for you—introduce you to a knowledgeable friend, for instance—as long as they're relatively confident you'll do the same for them. This alone makes the social web flow.

The second group is what Grant calls the "takers." We don't have to spend a lot of time on them. Some among us take without giving, including most trolls, drama queens, and divas, who are cynical or bitter and self-serving to a fault.

The most interesting group, and also by far the most successful, is what Grant calls "givers." Unlike matchers, givers don't keep score; they just give. And by being so relentlessly helpful to their friends and even acquaintances, givers inspire those around them to either turn from matchers into givers or at least be on the lookout for ways to help the givers, who so clearly deserve that help. How to be a massively successful giver? That's what Adam's must-read book is all about.

## SIX DEGREES OF SEPARATION IS DOWN TO TWO

Just a few years ago we had "Six Degrees of Kevin Bacon," whereby everyone in Hollywood was connected to that actor through a string of mutual relationships. Now, in the Social Age—and through a series of relentless givers—we, as our buddy (and relentless giver) Tim McDonald says, have maybe two or at most three degrees of separation. Meaning: Nearly everyone active on social is connected to everyone else on social by no more than a friend of a friend or two.

And each one of those connections is a resource—perhaps an expert ready to help find a solution to a challenge you are facing. And each is a potential member of your extraordinary network.

Have a problem and don't know who to ask for help with a solution?

After you've established yourself on Twitter—and have helped others by serving as a member of their personal network—Twitter is your go-to resource.

Have a question and Google search isn't working for you? Just tweet out the question to your followers: "Who can tell me . . . ?" The bigger your network, the more likely you'll receive the answer you're looking for—maybe even just a link, but often *exactly* the link you need—at any time of the day or night. Ted has been using this to beat Google, since his Twitter follower base was about 20,000 (it's now well north of 350,000). But you can implement this strategy with just a few Twitter followers. Why? Because all of those followers have their own connections; they are already OPEN.

This all sounds great for your personal brand, yes? To find out if that new Wendy's sandwich is as good as it looks on TV, if you need a quick answer to a question, or if you really do want an introduction to Kevin Bacon.

But what if you're running a business, and your own researchers have hit an impasse? Say you're a start-up out to create an artificial ankle on a budget, and your internal all-star team of engineers, computer scientists, and anatomy experts has come up blank on a specific issue? In the Social Age, is there a better way?

There is.

Remember the submarine search described in *The Wisdom of Crowds*? Crowdsourced know-how is always available—if you're OPEN.

That is exactly what Jay Martin of Martin Bionics (now part of Orthocare Innovations, an independent orthotics and prosthetic research and development group) did. Author David Burkus writes about Martin's conundrum, and how he freed himself from it, in *The Myths of Creativity.*

The Expert Myth has us believing that the most experienced and pedigreed expert will naturally outperform someone less experienced or less knowledgeable. But Martin found just the opposite. Frustrated by the lack of results from his experienced researchers and burning through his seed capital, with a major deadline fast approaching, Martin fired his staff and started over, bringing on a team of inexperienced—yet OPEN minded—interns instead.

The interns didn't know what couldn't be done, so they did it. The end result, despite many thinking Martin was crazy for firing all his well-educated and experienced experts, was that Martin Bionics developed an innovative new prosthetic that became an industry standard.

As with the *Scorpion,* the lesson of Martin Bionics, is that ordinary people can solve problems with a high level of complexity, by coming together and working toward a common goal.

In the Social Age, there are companies whose entire business models are built on the foundation of OPEN.

One such company is Innocentive, the "open innovation firm."

Innocentive runs contests, open to the general public, designed to solve the innovation needs of its clients. A typical project for Innocentive: "the future of clothes washing technology challenge." The winner of the challenge—the person or group who revolutionizes the laundry process that uses no liquid, creates no wrinkles, and does not damage clothes—would be given a $40,000 prize. For this challenge alone, Innocentive received nearly 600 submissions. As we go to press, the winner has not yet been determined. However, imagine the savings for Innocentive's client: greatly reduced R&D costs, salaries, recruiting, benefits—all expenses that might cost an Industrial Age firm several million dollars.

Yet, through an OPEN-based process, Innocentive's client pays only $40,000 (plus Innocentive's fees, of course).

Could OPEN be a business model that allows earners to work independently or in nano mode? Can companies work around their most vexing challenges using OPEN? Can the Social Age enable everyone involved to be more agile, more nimble—and small? If ordinary people like John Craven and companies like Martin Bionics and Innocentive can do it, can't we all?

## SO, ARE EXPERTS OBSOLETE?

Your authors, along with our partner, Shawn Murphy, run SwitchandShift.com. The site proudly features a "League of Extraordinary Thinkers"—a core group of thought leaders from our own OPEN circles.

So how can we say experts—or "thought leaders," as they are also known in the Social Age—are not valued? How can we discount those who have proven themselves genuinely worthy of a term thrown around way too often on the Internet: *expert*?

That's entirely fair. Do we believe in expertise, or don't we?

Short answer: Of course we do. As mentioned earlier, some people just plain know more about any given topic than do most of us. Our league is composed of bestselling authors and high-profile speakers, CEOs, and educators; psychologists and neuroscientists; top-tier consultants, professors, mentors, and futurists; even a military general. They're way smart, yet consistently demonstrate humble confidence. There's nothing ordinary about these people.

And that's no contradiction to OPEN; Martin Bionics aside, it's actually the best part.

Yes, you can put your extraordinary network against someone else's expert any day. But the best part of the Social Age: *You don't have to choose!*

Let's face it, we're all profoundly nonexpert at some subjects. You might go the Dalai Lama for spiritual advice, but to do your taxes?

But what if you grew your personal network so you had not only the Dalai Lama but dozens of rabbis, scores of priests and ministers, countless more imams and swamis, and some noted atheists thrown in for good measure? And what if your network included thousands of partners from Deloitte, Ernst & Young, and PwC? And NPR's Click and Clack, master car mechanics the Tappit Brothers (Tom and Ray Magliozzi)? *And* Kevin Bacon?

Your network can. And for many ordinary people on social media, it already does. Even if those high-powered niche experts are not in your direct OPEN, they are to some degree available to you through the extraordinary networkers within your sphere of influence.

Chances are outstanding that, even if your own social networks are still tiny, you have links to people with vast, robust networks at their disposal—and chances are also great that many of those people are givers who take delight in connecting one acquaintance to another or to their entire network.

OPEN does not mean ordinary people are the only people who will remain. What OPEN really means is that, first off, experts can't get by as high-and-mighty oracles. If they try to do so they'll be left out of the conversation, and their personal expertise will suffer as a result. In this humbler age, it isn't cool to be haughty. As we learned in Chapter 6 while talking about community: Arrogance is out, even for the elite few who could have any preexisting claim on feelings of superiority.

OPEN also means that our personal networks are extraordinary, in part, because there are subject matter experts in each, and they're all connected into one global network. With the right approach, people who set a profile on any social media site are able to tap into that one global network as soon as they make their first few connections.

In short, experts remain valued—and through the power of OPEN, we can all have experts in our network, no matter how ordinary we are in a given area of expertise.

Maybe the question isn't "Now that we're all experts, what does expert even mean?" Instead, we might be wise to ask, "Now that we're all experts, what about *any* of us is just 'ordinary' anymore?"

That is why the Social Age is so exhilarating: Through the power of OPEN, there isn't one thing ordinary about any of us.

## TAPPING THE POWER OF OPEN

Ordinary people who together form an extraordinary network may sound very cool and all, but . . .

How do you make it work for your business? That is what the rest of this chapter is about. Within the discussion, we'll take you full circle to wrap up the "death of large." Because with OPEN, "large" is—well, it's not only a disadvantage in the Social Age; we're convinced it's a terminal condition.

Let's start with what the dinosaurs would consider a bold statement:

*No matter who we are, the more OPEN we are, the more global our impact.*

When we form social relationships (and then leverage those relationships to become friendships via the phone, Skype, Google+ Hangout, in person when possible, and so on), our personal networks become infinitely better, deeper, and richer than whatever we can knit together exclusively through local face-to-face relationships, as we did in the Industrial Age. No matter where we live, no matter how spectacular those local networks are—and no matter how much good those local personal networks can do—a global OPEN sphere of influence is far more powerful.

Are we right? While the dinosaurs roll their eyes, we submit for your approval:

► There is no "either/or" at work here. Your local, in-person friends and colleagues don't disappear because you've gone social. Rather, social connections allow you to augment your existing and growing local networks with even more brilliance.

► Think of all the talent right where you live—people who would be excellent to know, but who you never bump into. You are in close proximity, but never seem to find a reason—or a way—to connect. With social, regardless of where you live, the sharing of common interests drives connections. Because you're both involved in a Twitter chat about your shared interest, you may meet each other when you never would have otherwise. Distance becomes a non-issue.

► Think of that Twitter chat (or LinkedIn group, or Facebook fan page, or Pinterest board, or, well, you get the idea). Through those channels, you are quite likely to meet absolutely fascinating people who share common interests—but who bring unique and diverse backgrounds, attitudes, and ideas. Via social, you can begin a friendship.

► Instead of being limited to the brilliance in your own backyard, through social you have the best minds in the world at your disposal, some of whom are likely to be helpful to you in your career, or challenge your way of thinking, or introduce you to their friends.

Your authors met this way. In a group called #UsGuys, on Twitter. We worked together for almost a year before *ever* meeting in person.

Ted met Shawn Murphy, cofounder of Switch and Shift, this way as well. Over time, they realized they shared a very closely aligned worldview. Shawn asked Ted to write a guest post on his blog, and it was such a positive experience for all concerned that they communicated by e-mail, then phone, all the while making a faint connection stronger. Eventually, they launched a blog together—a blog that will reach 1 million visitors in 2014. Yes, they set out to create just a two-guy blog, nothing more ambitious. Who would've known where that would take them?

In the Industrial Age—with Ted in Florida, Shawn in Sacramento, and Mark now in Seattle—the three of us would most likely *never* have met. Yet there are millions of "Ted Meets Mark" and "Shawn Meets Ted" stories out there. And in nearly every case, it is our commonalities that bring us together.

Welcome to the Social Age. And to OPEN.

Yes, there are billions of people out there on social media. The great thing about social, though, is that we find common interests and narrow down those billions to hundreds, or sometimes dozens. Mark, Ted, and Shawn were drawn together by a passion for reintroducing the human side of business into our working cultures.

It isn't just Ted, Mark, and Shawn who believe this, of course; there are probably about 300 very active, and OPEN, thought leaders on Twitter who lead an ongoing discussion around business leadership.

And all 300 of them, in just a relatively short amount of time, have come to know and respect each other. The trolls have been pushed back under the bridge. The drama queens and divas self-filter. All that's left are those relentless givers who know each other and our respective niche in the leadership space. When new givers organically join this informal OPEN circle, they get to know every other member of the tribe. Their ordinary appearance—sometimes stemming from a single tweet, comment, or blog post—exposes those very ordinary people, perhaps even social newbies, to an extraordinary network.

This scenario happens every day—and with every niche. It happens for artisan bakers, gamers, and graffiti artists; parents with small children and caregivers of parents with ALS; auto and travel enthusiasts; and, as you might imagine, social media evangelists, too. You name the topic of interest, there's an informal online community where the members all know each other—and thrive from the experience.

## OPEN EXPERIENCE, NANO OPERATIONS

In Chapter 7, we shared the way Bronson Taylor and his partners run Growth Hacker TV, as an incredibly agile nano corp. Switch and Shift is a nano corp as well. So is YouTern. Yes, the partners are tied by legal paperwork, so it's a real business in that respect. But that's pretty much where any resemblance to a normal organization ends. Beth Nicoletto, Switch and Shift's Heroic Senior Editor, lives near Fresno, California. Our social media intern attends Ohio State. We have never come together as a group. As of this writing, Shawn and Ted have met only once in person, Ted and Mark just once, and Mark and Shawn just a few times. None of us have ever met our editor or intern face-to-face. So we can see each other—so we can be human—meetings are run via Google+ hangouts.

The Leaguers and our many guest writers? We've met very few of them in person. In the Social Age, it just isn't necessary to shake hands before working together.

Can you run an entire company via the tools of social and collaboration media? If you can't, you should be able to. We're doing it. And it's working quite well. Many of Basecamp's customers are as well: Basecamp, and the myriad other collaboration tools available today, enable just such virtual teams to thrive.

Switch and Shift is fueled by OPEN—it's a business that is all about the network. YouTern has been built on the strong shoulders of OPEN. Granted, there is very little ordinary about the Leaguers and guest writers who contribute to those sites. Or the guests on Shawn's *Work That Matters* podcast or Ted's *The Human Side* TV show. Or the contributors to YouTern's weekly #InternPro Twitter chat.

But please don't forget our earlier statement: When we say "ordinary," we do so convinced that *everyone* is ordinary in most respects—even the most remarkably accomplished professionals. Regardless of how extraordinary these people may be in their respective area of expertise, though, in the long-term these networks—and the combined strength of communities like Switch and Shift and YouTern—will nearly always be more powerful in the collective than *any* one individual.

## CRAFTING YOUR OWN CONSTELLATION
## THROUGH OPEN

In our travels we uncovered a company right under our noses that has turned OPEN into a remarkably fluid and, we're certain, remarkably profitable business.

Meet Ray Wang.

The first thing to know about Ray is that we were loosely connected to him for years without having any idea what he was really up to. (Remember those 300 thought leaders who all knew each other in the leadership space?) Ray's bio has said for a while now that he's founder of Constellation Research, whatever that is.

Then Mark was speaking to one of Switch and Shift's Leaguers, Dr. Janice Presser, about his notion of turning a subset of our social network into a mutually beneficial "constellation," where trusted members would refer each other for projects they couldn't fill or couldn't fill alone. Yes, Mark actually used the word *constellation* with the good doctor. And she said, basically: "Oh, like Constellation Research. Know Ray Wang?"

So Mark did speak with Ray. The gist of his business is beyond fascinating to us—it's not going too far to say that we see what he has already been doing for several years now as the future of business, combining the need to be nimble with the architecture of the nano organization, working with members of his constellation as peers rather than employees—pretty much everything we discussed in Chapters 7 and 8 of *A World Gone Social*.

Ray's firm advises companies on thorny issues like technology vendor choices and consults with these companies to bring the choices to fruition (that's the very macro-level view of an obviously much more complex way that he and a whole bunch of other people pay the bills). Interesting to us is that Ray calls himself a researcher, not a swaggering CEO. (Remember Adam Grant's "humbler age" quote that began this chapter?) And he does employ a number of other researchers, whom he considers his inner orbit; they constitute the core group of his business. Sometimes that's all he needs, so his business is on the relatively small side.

But there are two more concentric rings to Constellation Research as well, and with these rings Constellation can grow overnight to be a little bigger or even a lot bigger, complete a project, and then shrink again or reconfigure with different members as needed to take on the next project.

The basic idea in all of this, be it Constellation Research or another more informal group entirely, is this: In the Social Age, when our orbit overlaps with someone else's, it's almost impossible for us *not* to find each other online. And when our orbits intersect, teaming up on work in our own little nano corp is—well, it's almost unavoidable.

We all have our own constellations. Joining together to form larger, closer affiliations enables us to enjoy our individual autonomy, without the need to sell ourselves into servitude to an old-school corporate master that tells us where to go and when to go there, and keeps most of the money from our work for itself.

This isn't for everyone, of course!

But here's the thing: Remember the Law of Change? That "insurmountable market pressure" that builds up until change occurs?

Companies are beholden to it, so the trend toward smaller parent firms employing only workers skilled in the company's core competency, contracting with outsourced providers (of any size) will happen. It's already happening, and has been trending this way for about a decade already.

More than half of the 70-million-member workforce in the United States will be considered "independent workers" (contractors, temps, independent consultants, and those small companies with fewer than five employees) by 2020, according to a prediction that was part of MBO Partners' 2012 independent work preview. In 2013, MBO estimated there were already 17 million workers meeting this description.

Insurmountable market pressure is already bearing down on more and more of these independent workers. No matter what some might think about how this negatively affects society—and though some companies are doing this not in the interest of going nano but to avoid paying for benefits reserved for employees, such as healthcare—this is already a reality.

Employment visionary Carleen McKay calls these nontraditional members of the working community the "Contingent Workforce." Many of these independents like to call themselves freelancers or solopreneurs.

The same individual may at times work as a solopreneur or as part of a nano corp by joining forces with trusted colleagues in his or her constellation. Some of those constellations will be like Ray Wang's core staff, employed permanently, while others will come and go. But if they're good at what they do, there is no reason (in a healthy economy) that these individuals will consider themselves anything other than fully employed.

Why has the recovery from the Great Recession still not seen a resurgence in employment? Why haven't jobs tagged along with any perceived resurrection in the post-recession economy?

Perhaps because the very notion of full-time, long-term employment is a relic of the bygone age—an aberrant and short age in the history of the world. Yes, there was a time when loyalty worked both ways—when employers and employees worked to their mutual benefit. Employees looked forward to the proverbial gold watch; most employers awarded that gold watch (and a pension) in exchange for a lifetime of service.

For the most part, though, workers did not feel they were entitled to mass, full-time employment until the 1940s. By the 1970s, however, companies were already dismantling their mammoth operations. That thirty-year stretch was not normal, nor was it sustainable. Look at Pittsburgh in the 1980s. Or Detroit as this book goes to press in 2014. That is what is left of the full-blown Industrial Age in the United States.

This is the insurmountable market pressure that leads to change.

This is the Social Age.

And this is why OPEN is so critical to your personal success—and to that of the organization you strive to lead well.

## THE SOCIAL AGE HOLY GRAIL: OPEN WITHIN OPEN

Remember Innocentive, the "open innovation firm" that taps the power of OPEN to crowdsource R&D for its clients?

There's another OPEN company that takes this a step further.

Olapic is a visual commerce platform that tells its clients' branding stories with curated customer photos and videos, helping those brands improve the shopping experience and increase sales. It was also the company smart enough to seek out Ian Greenleigh, the model practitioner of OPEN thinking, as the director of marketing.

That's right: an OPEN individual working for an OPEN company that uses OPEN methodology to generate its core product.

This is the Holy Grail of the Social Age—and we have it today.

We met Ian Greenleigh a while back when Mark and Ted interviewed him on Human Side TV to discuss his new book, *The Social Media Side Door: How to Bypass the Gatekeepers to Gain Greater Access and Influence.*

Ian is sharp as a tack, ambitious, and at times outrageously funny—sometimes, it seems, without meaning to be. In his deadpan style, he just says what he really thinks (and some of what he really thinks will have you snorting coffee out of your nose).

A self-professed—and perhaps devoted—introvert (not exactly what most people think when they think "networking god"), Ian leveraged OPEN to a truly astonishing degree. Graduating in the depths of the Great Recession, the only job this prelaw student could land was in sales, which he hated—so he blogged on behalf of his company, and then contacted the people who commented on his posts to sell to them. He wasn't good at sales, he decided, but he had a knack for marketing, so he decided to land a marketing job with a firm he admired in Austin, Texas.

He did this through some very creative social media "side doors," which led him to write his book, for which he interviewed some of the top minds in marketing and beyond, which led to articles and interviews in dozens of the top marketing and business venues, including Mashable, *AdAge, BusinessWeek,* and *Harvard Business Review.*

This in turn took Ian to New York, where he became director of marketing for Olapic, the OPEN e-commerce site with the OPEN product line.

In many respects Ian is a quintessentially ordinary person.

But from nothing, in the midst of the Great Recession, a career change, and a side hustle, and through extraordinary use of social media, he has crafted for himself a truly extraordinary network.

Meanwhile, Olapic is an incredibly ordinary company that had the smarts to seek out and hire ordinary Ian. Together, they—and their concentric OPEN circles—make for an extraordinary network and a team capable of crowdsourcing innovative brainpower and creative thinking from OPEN focused contributors.

What could be more Social Age than that?

In no time, what seems like serendipity—a perfect alignment of all the planets to form a cascade of mutually beneficial relationships—will be considered ho-hum, business-as-usual.

In a world gone social, this is your company's and your industry's future.

And, no matter how social your organization is now, this is your opportunity.

## READY TO THRIVE?

Have you set up accounts on Twitter, Facebook, and LinkedIn?

Your OPEN community is already developing.

Not on social yet, but ready to thrive?

Jump in. Headfirst. Set up your accounts. Have a great head shot taken that shows how likable you are. Work with someone you trust to build a solid profile bio. If you're not sure where to start, emulate the profile of someone already nailing it on social.

Most important, regardless of your experience level on social: Ask good—no, *very* good—questions.

And then share the answers—because that is what relentless givers do.

By asking good questions, you've already become a self-learner and an active listener. By sharing what you've learned, you're establishing your reputation as a giver. By building relationships with those already entrenched in social with their own OPEN communities, you build credibility for your personal brand—and the brand of your organization.

And here's the thing: Social is so new, so novel, that you aren't that far behind. It's not like it's 1848 and you're still creating products on a loom while your competitors have a huge factory that takes up a city block in London or Chicago. We—all of us—have only started to realize what social can be, and what it can do.

But you need to be OPEN minded. And you must get started.

There is nothing harder to it than this. It's how we all begin with social. And let us tell you something: It works.

OPEN works.

Yet it's just the beginning. The Social Age is a new world. Your world.

And that is good, because you won't like the obsolete alternative. You don't want to be that person mired in Industrial Age wisdom but without the foresight to embrace what is coming next.

Resistance is futile.

As our buddy Jim Claussen, from IBM, says:

*If you can't embrace social, get used to obsolescence.*

In the next section of *A World Gone Social,* we'll tackle issues that deeply impact your success in the Social Age: customer service, marketing, and leadership. We'll begin by enabling you to position yourself as a social leader—what we, thanks to Jim Claussen, call the "Blue Unicorn."

CHAPTER 10

# The Social Leader:
# A Blue Unicorn?

*My passion is the social executive—or rather, bringing the social leader*
*to organizations. Right now, they're about as common as blue unicorns.*

—*Jim Claussen*

Remember back when George H. W. Bush was president, and he made headlines because he had no idea of the price of a gallon of milk? (Stick with us—we promise this isn't a political diatribe.)

The first President Bush wasn't just off—he was off by a few dollars. The dustup wasn't over the price of milk but what it represented. One of the president's most important duties is setting economic policy. When it comes to a staple of most American households—well, not having the slightest clue what that staple costs was taken as a fairly big indication that perhaps the president was out of touch with the typical voter. Perhaps fatally out of touch.

Did that one gaffe lose him the 1992 election? Hardly. Did it drag down his overall favorability? Absolutely. And remember what a tight three-way race that particular election was? To win, he needed every little boost he could get.

## A LEADER COULD LEARN . . . A LOT

Today's business leaders can learn a lot from President Bush's milk woes. Specifically, what if you had an easy-to-use set of tools at your disposal that allowed you to see directly, *unfiltered by your staff,* what your customers *and* competitors' customers think of your company? How your employees *and* your competitors' employees honestly perceive the company culture. And what your investors *and* your competitors' investors think of your company and its rivals in real time.

A leader could learn a lot. Probably enough to spot opportunities and challenges before most anyone else, even among all the sameness and noise that without question exists on social media. As Jim Claussen, IBMer and founder of Executive Social Academy, says:

*The leader that listens to social signals and also empowers employees to listen for signals, increases a company's ability to spot new opportunities. If employees see their leadership listening and discussing what they hear, they will do the same.*

With that kind of collective listening power, a person could rule his or her industry—especially if the leaders of rival companies snubbed those same tools as a fad, irrelevant, or for some entry-level cube farmer to deal with. In fairly short order, an insightful leader with myopic counterparts like that could dance circles around that rival.

Of course, if this were a common occurrence, we wouldn't have a snappy title for this chapter.

Jim Claussen coined the term *Blue Unicorn* to describe the rarity of truly social leaders—and listeners—in today's workforce. He says:

*Social listening gives the initiated an unfair competitive advantage in spotting opportunities, unmet needs, competitive weakness, and new rivals. Listening through social analytics provides deep insights into the customer experience. This is key—because today, customers don't choose a product; they choose a responsive brand that not only listens, but provides a personalized exceptional customer experience.*

What if *you* had some easy-to-use listening tools like that?

You do.

And there is no excuse for leaders of any size organization to be wrong about the price of milk. Ever. Again.

Social media (and the analytics that help us measure our impact, which we'll discuss in Chapter 14) is the most revolutionary tool executives have ever had to learn, interact with, and capitalize on, all while building their personal and corporate brands. Simply put: The Social Age changes everything for executives of the twenty-first century.

## HOW SOCIAL IS YOUR CEO?

*Despite this obvious trend, regardless of how incredibly easy it is for senior executive leadership to engage in social (the foundation of today's connected economy), I'm still searching for the Blue Unicorns.*

—*Jim Claussen*

So here we are, six years into the Social Age, yet data from information house Domo and the leadership-focused site CEO.com confirms that only 30 percent of Fortune 500 CEOs have any social media presence at all—that's right, *at all*.

And those who do? Their social media presence is often just another broadcast arm of the PR or marketing department—or if it isn't, it sure appears to be. For instance, is Michael Dell on Twitter and LinkedIn? Yes, officially. Does he tweet? Yes, tweets go out from his account, with links and corporate announcements, and plenty of retweets of others who praise Dell. It's media, sure. But is that *social* media? Poor Michael Dell needs a new social media account manager, or a new coach, before we'll count him as actually "active" on social.

*More social. Less media.*

Now, we doubt anyone close to Dell will tell him this, but the time is going to come when, if you are a CEO in a world gone social and you have a social presence like his—or, worse, no social presence at all—maybe you should find a new line of work.

One more thought on Mr. Dell . . .

Imagine, with all of the influence he and his organization carry now, how much impact could be generated if he were socially motivated. For a time the youngest CEO to ever break into the Fortune 500, he is already considered by many to be highly inspiring. His work in taking his company private is more than well regarded. What if, empowered by the ability we all have on social to hide behind our keyboards while we gain confidence, he could abandon his reputation for shyness and take his Texas charm for a ride on Twitter? Exhibit his wisdom and influence on LinkedIn? Or do a Google+ Hangout with our future leaders?

Again, here is Jim Claussen:

*Consumers want brand captains with an opinion. They crave visionaries. They want to know what the company stands for; the company's values; what they believe in. Connected consumers want to engage with a company that stands for something and they want to be part of a conversation around those beliefs. They want to be part of a tribe—and to be part of a tribe, you have to have a leader.*

Can you imagine the compounding influence? Or the positive impact to Dell's brand? How many Apple users, still trying to make Tim Cook look and act like Steve Jobs, would now consider a Dell product?

With so few Fortune 500 CEOs and social leaders in general engaged on social, it is absurd how easy it would be for a leader like Michael Dell to create uncontested competitive differentiation. Companies spend millions of dollars getting their CEOs in front of eyes during prime-time television or an NFL game, when there is no more effective way for a brand to influence the marketplace, and to influence buying behavior, than a single tweet.

Charisma sells.

Social sells charisma (and trust, and respect).

In a world gone social, that is how business is done.

Now, we know what some people are thinking as they read this: "You're going to throw out some excellent chief executives—not just Michael Dell—because they don't have LinkedIn accounts, or because those they have aren't active? Because they don't have their own blogs, or, if they do, they don't reply to the comments on their posts? Because they never tweet, or their tweets are just commercials for their company? What a ridiculous bunch of hooey!"

Yes, it's true: Those who still haven't noticed that the Industrial Age is over use words like *hooey*.

And a lot of them still run our largest companies.

Now, are we anti-enterprise? Absolutely not. Some of our biggest companies and best customers are incredibly well run and are beautifully positioned to sail into 2020 and beyond. Many are expected to be even healthier than they are right now as we move further into the twenty-first century:

► We deeply admire what Unilever is doing to be not just profitable but *moral* under Paul Polman's guidance.

► Berkshire Hathaway's leader and driving force for decades now, Warren Buffett, is one of the most committed bleeding-heart capitalists you're ever going to meet; there's no mistake that his company thrives because he is at the helm.

► Southwest Airlines is big and only getting bigger, and we're certain that's because of the standard set by Herb Kelleher and the current stewardship of Gary Kelly (and because of their active listening, as we outlined in Chapter 3).

These CEOs, and so many others doing honorable, profitable work, came into their leadership roles well before a CEO was expected to be social. In his defense, that includes Michael Dell.

That's changing fast, though. All you have to do is look at the impact Richard Branson, Arianna Huffington, Doug Conant, and other social CEOs have had on their industries to see the direction in which social leadership is going. By maintaining a consistent social presence, being an engaging communicator, and showing a little of their personality—their ambition, drive, and Social Age business style—these three social CEOs have had a significant impact on their brands' digital presence.

After this current crop of well-performing leaders has retired to their well-appointed homes and go on to receive their honorary degrees from a dozen universities, the social CEO will be the norm.

> *An engaging presence on social media will not just be "nice to have," it will be considered a leadership competency.*

The fact is, many Gen X CEOs are already on social. It makes sense that the percentage of Millennial CEOs and leaders on social goes even higher. This is where they already live; this is how they often choose to communicate. That likely won't change once they've become chief executive officers and board chairs.

And let's not discount the buying power of the 76 million Millennials. In whom do you think they will place their confidence: a communicative, open, authentic CEO sincerely active on social media or a person who sits in a penthouse office looking down at the little people?

Let's take it a step further: Who do you think they'll trust more—those model social CEOs or CEOs who, although on social media, fake activity through interns or entry-level staff members, relinquish their voices to proxies, and never personally lay a finger on a keyboard?

## BEWARE THE INSINCERE SOCIAL LEADER

If you head up a multi-billion-dollar company, or even if you are a Millennial leader still finding your niche, neither your personal nor the corporate brand can afford to allow someone (even a sharp intern like the one from Topo who sold those funky shoes to Ted) to set up some social accounts for you, monitor them and report back to you, and interact with your fans on your behalf without gradually increasing direct contribution and engagement—from you.

Your thoughts. Your voice. Your personality.

As Jim Claussen says:

> *If you are invited to a business dinner with a client, do you send a pimply-faced intern wearing your clothes to the dinner to go around the table and introduce himself or herself as you? No!*

Outsourcing social is *not* the desired end state for our corporate leaders. That is why we take issue with Domo's claim that 30 percent of Fortune 500 CEOs are social. Yes, someone is doing social media in their name. The leaders actually engaged with their accounts themselves? We'd venture that its closer to 3 percent than 30 percent. You can tell just by doing some social listening for a while, as we have.

So what should a leader do, if not outsource social to an intern and move on to more "important" matters?

Getting baseline help is just step one. It's meant to get you started, then keep you moving in the right direction. Not internally wired for technology? Is this concept foreign to you, personally? We get it. Mark was in the same position not too long ago. Do what Mark did: Surround yourself with people who can help with the mechanics and logistics. Mark mans his own keyboard, but that isn't a requirement for social. The words—*your voice and insights*—are what generate trust and demonstrate integrity. Let someone else do the keyboarding, but do *not* abdicate your voice.

Step two is to learn to interact as 100 percent yourself—even if you do it only from time to time, maybe three tweets per day for starters, just to add a little "real you" to the mix. Show some personality and some character!

This reverse-mentoring, wherein an intern or talented team member teaches you everything they know about social, results in many side benefits. First and foremost: Learning social from a digital native's perspective, Mark discovered firsthand, is an eye-opening experience. (To this day, Mark attributes his online persona—and the close connection to how he thinks in person—to his team. Otherwise, he is convinced, he would have been one of those "I must act a certain way—like a CEO or something" sorts on social, instead of being himself.)

Mind you, your authors—during our workday, and at night, and on weekends— probably spend a lot of time on social. We are hooked. We drank the Kool-Aid, and now we each spend about two hours every day, Monday to Monday, building relationships, participating in Twitter chats, and commenting on blogs and Facebook posts. Mostly, as you might have gathered already, we tweet . . . a lot.

But that is *not* required of a social leader. After all, we run online communities. It's our job, as well as our pleasure, to spend that much time engaged with our friends and followers.

To be considered a sincere, engaged leader on social means you need to throw in "you" *once in a while.* When you understand the social tools that are available, you can use Buffer, TweetDeck, or HootSuite (all of which offer free versions) to schedule tweets throughout the day while you are actively leading your business. Although not perfect—meaning that it's not the spontaneous version of you 100 percent of the time—this solution is *much* better than nothing.

And nothing is what 70 percent of Fortune 500 leaders are dedicating to social media at present.

Here's a bonus: Through this relatively simple, inexpensive process, you'll avoid the "why bother?" perception generated by some CEOs' social presence, such as

Warren Buffett's Twitter account—which, assuming it's actually his, was set up for all the wrong reasons and then abandoned. He's sent five tweets since the account was opened in May 2013; he follows zero other Twitter accounts; since it was opened, the account soared to over a million followers and then dropped by 25 to 30 percent, which is only to be expected, given Buffett's distinct lack of engagement.

At least on social media, regardless of how else he otherwise contributes to the world, that account positions the Oracle of Omaha as an insincere—or at least an uninterested—social leader.

Finally, here's the third step for leaders dabbling with social: understanding.

If you run a consumer brand and don't have your own first-person fluency in "new" media (quotation marks to denote irony), then it is only a matter of time before you're considered a dinosaur. You—personally—are doomed to professional extinction.

## WHAT IF THIS JUST ISN'T YOU (YET)?

You get the theory. You understand the importance, both to your career and to your organization.

But what if this just isn't you? What if you aren't the right person to jump into social? What if you, with your current confidence level in social, are the square peg and social is the round hole? Maybe you have a thorny disposition, are a bit insensitive at times, or lack patience? Maybe you think everyone on Facebook is a bunch of kids—and who has time for all those babes on Pinterest?

Okay, we get it. As we've already discussed here, surly and social are not a great combination. Let's not hurt the brand while you get over being grouchy.

Let's face it: You aren't alone at Camp Curmudgeon. Think Warren Buffett is going to wake up one day and start tweeting twice an hour? (Not likely, although we would love it if he did!) Does this make you a bad leader? No. (Not today, anyway.)

So how do you get your firm moving toward a social C-suite?

Look around that C-suite. Who there is the most social right now? Who participates for personal branding reasons, or from a digital native's perspective? Who loves speaking to a live audience, writing, and mentoring? Who is the person most likely to enjoy a Twitter chat or a Google+ Hangout?

Whoever that is—you've found your future ambassador.

That is the person who can best represent your brand on social. That is who should lead the transition from "We're not really on social" and "Social doesn't work for us" to "We realize the importance of social to our business. A member of our C-Suite engages routinely on the social networks, is ensuring that social is integrated seamlessly into our business strategy, and is serving as a mentor to the rest of the executive team, as well as the teams that directly serve our customers."

Maybe you're the wrong social ambassador, for now. So go get the right ambassador, and learn as quickly as you can. Adapt, grow and lead!

## THE VERY REAL SENSE OF URGENCY

Even if you run a B2B company rather than a consumer-facing firm, you—or another ambassador, a social leader, at your company—*must* meet your customers and potential customers where they are, which is online more and more every day. You need to see for yourself what your competitors are up to, what relationships they are building, who serves as their champions and ambassadors. You need to make friends with other leaders both in your industry and beyond. You must expand your view of the universe from the tiny orbit of advisers who gobble up a good portion of your time.

No matter what your brand stands for, regardless of your product line or the services you offer, it is absolutely crucial that you understand every last bit of this brave new world your company is operating within. It is, without the least bit of hyperbole, a completely different world out there than it was as recently as 2008. Pretty much nothing is the same. And that's just *so far, right now,* when most leaders—and therefore most companies—are still treating social like it's something new, or just a low-cost channel on which to broadcast corporate messaging.

That last part is what really has us all fired up in this book. Today, far too many leaders think of social as a frivolous distraction that's sure to go away if they ignore it a little longer. Or they see it as a disappearing technology, like the fax machine. Or, even if they believe social has some potential, they see it as little more than just another marketing channel. (As we'll learn in Chapter 13, social is a *terrific* marketing channel, and will only continue to get better.)

They fail to realize that very soon social and collaboration technologies will be integral parts of *every* aspect of the company's existence, so seamlessly interwoven that they won't even be worth remarking upon.

Social media will be the way we communicate with every stakeholder imaginable. It will be how relationships are developed. It will be how partnerships and alliances will be formed.

Social media will evolve from being specific to a "department" or "team" tasked with messaging and communicating to being fully immersed in the DNA of *every* department, every operation, *every* employee, every day. Social media will be as common as the phone sitting on every desk; in time, social will be used *more* than that phone.

"Social business" and "social networking" will just be "business" and "networking" again in the not-too-distant future. After all, we don't do "phone business" or "phone networking," do we? We don't have a "phone department." The phone is just a tool to help our businesses function effectively.

*That* is where social is going. That is what social will be.

It's your call: Get on board, or be a sobbing dinosaur when your organization gets left behind.

## THE POWER OF THE SOCIAL LEADER

In 2012, the consultancy BRANDfog conducted a study asking all levels of employees throughout a wide range of industries, in companies large and small, for their opinions on an array of aspects of social executive leadership.

*Eighty-two percent of respondents said they trust a brand more that has a CEO who is active on social.*

That's all well and good, you may be thinking, but you aren't a CEO (yet).

This issue, of leaders being social or antisocial, goes way beyond a title, however; it impacts every leader in the twenty-first century.

Why?

Because social isn't only a matter of corporate branding; it's also the best tool available for *individual* branding. And if you don't think you personally constitute a brand, well, you've been living under a rock in another century.

In the Social Age, each of us is a personal brand.

Let's face it, whether it's the employee's own idea or the employer's, the average American employee now switches companies every three years, and boards of directors switch out CEOs, on average, every two and a half years. That means we should really think more like members of Congress (well, except for that whole 10 percent approval rating thing) who know they are up for reelection—and perhaps a new job—every two years.

In today's economy, you need be in perpetual "campaign" mode.

And what better way to establish the desirability of your own brand than online—where, as we discussed at length in Chapter 4, social recruiting is a virtual 24/7 news cycle.

But where to start? As a leader, or a potential leader looking to go social, it's important for you to focus your energies in ways that work best for you and also that will have the biggest impact (with luck, as most do, you'll find the sweet spot where the two overlap).

With that in mind, here are a few ideas to help you become perceived as a bona fide social leader:

▶ **Build credibility by blogging** | Want to establish expertise in your field? Blog. Start your own, with your name as the URL. If that seems a bit too ambitious or is outside your comfort zone, contribute to your company's blog (assuming there is one and employees are allowed to participate). Another option we highly recommend is to write guest posts on established, popular blogs beyond your company's branded properties. Work toward becoming a regular contributor on as many of these blogs as possible. Build your readership, and then set your sights higher and higher. After all, it doesn't hurt to add "Contributor at *Forbes*" to your LinkedIn bio.

► **Blogging not an option? Comment!** | No time to blog yourself? Not a good writer, and a good editor isn't available? Still having trouble getting invited to guest-post on a blog you enjoy? Make a reputation for intelligent commentary in the comments section on other authors' posts. Many blogs even link comments through an integrated service like Disqus or Livefyre, where all your comments are indexed, regardless of which blogs you interact with. These popular plug-ins to WordPress, Blogger, and many other content platforms make building your commenting reputation—and thus your brand as a social leader engaged with blogging communities of relevance to your industry—much easier. Trust us, do well at articulate commenting, and you will get an invite to guest-blog.

► **Leverage LinkedIn and Google+** | Want to build a tight network of friends? Want to be OPEN? Begin by joining a LinkedIn group or Google+ community in your field and aligned with your passions. LinkedIn is a powerhouse, with over 250 million users focused on their careers. G+ gets mixed reviews, yet millions of professionals call it home. Indeed, G+ has earned a solid reputation as a networking spot for small business owners and small to medium business (SMB) executives who don't feel LinkedIn is social enough or Facebook is professional enough for their objectives.

► **Join a Twitter chat** | Another way to establish your reputation as a social leader is to take part in a weekly Twitter chat centered on your area of expertise. There is no end to the list of chats: #HBRChat (moderated by *Harvard Business Review*), #CXOTalk (focused on technology for top executives), #TChat (recruiting, talent, HR), #LeadwithGiants (leadership), #custserv (customer experience and engagement). Of course, for those just starting their careers, there's YouTern's #InternPro chat. We'll also mention #humanbiz, which in addition to being the hashtag we'll use to discuss *A World Gone Social,* is a hashtag used by many top experts in the leadership space all week long.

► **Use Twitter hashtags liberally** | Twitter hashtags (the "#" sign), which act to identify certain keywords that find and attract others with similar interests, are a great way to turn the millions of people on Twitter into a very small, focused group. In addition to the hashtags associated with the Twitter chats already mentioned, which retain their relevance throughout each week, we recommend #leadership, #CMO, and #CXO. You can also use hashtags focused on your goal to generate a credible brand as a social leader, such as #branding, #influence, and #career. To help reduce your social media learning curve, search popular social media–related hashtags such as #social, #socialmedia, #SoMe, and #socmed to see who is talking about effective approaches for social media.

► **Engage and emulate an established mentor** | The single best way to become knowledgeable on social? Mentors. And not just engaging them in conversation but emulating how they interact on social. What do they do so well that they've earned their place as superconnectors and influencers? Check out the Ted Rubins, Cheryl Burgesses, Tim McDonalds, and Angela Maiers of the social world. Look at how the Stacy Donovan-Zapars, Mark J. Carters, and Shawn Murphys represent themselves online. Connect. Engage. Learn. And by all means, until you get a handle on what is worthy of the "relentless giver" status you hope to obtain, listen intently to your social mentor.

► **Hire a reverse mentor or intern** | In Chapter 6 we talked about Mark's team bringing in a reverse mentor to help him learn social. As Mark can attest, $15 per hour can buy you a massive amount of social knowledge in a short amount of time (which we'll talk more about in Chapter 11).

These are just a few ways professionals of all descriptions are building their brands—and thus their careers as leaders—on social media. Really, the sky's the limit, and, as we'll discuss in the final chapter of this book, we don't even know what's next—only that we need to be firmly in the mix, or we'll be left behind. It's absolutely stunning to us that more executives aren't social. But then again, one way or another (by holdouts getting with the program or by being replaced with hipper, more socially savvy successors over the next couple of years), this certainly won't be the case for long.

At the 2013 IBM Connect conference, Ethan McCarty, IBM's director of social strategy and programs, shared a study his firm conducted, results of which we find hilarious. See if you can guess what our issue with it is before we tell you.

► Overall, 17 percent of companies had social executives currently.

► Fifty-seven percent planned to have executives on social within the next three to five years.

Okay, we'll give you a second. What do you see as the issue with that second statistic?

Here it is: If you *plan* to go social, what stops you from doing it *now*?

In the Social Age, as we've already learned through the monumental change that has occurred since 2008, three to five years is *forever.* And too late.

Case in point: Mark's Twitter account, at press time, shows about 27,500 followers. Mark's team opened that account about four years ago. The number of followers—and Mark's perceived influence—has grown organically and consistently since then.

If you open your social media accounts now and are even moderately active on Twitter, how many followers will you have three to five years from now?

*Why wait?*

Remember in Chapter 7 when we advised leaders to go nano or go home? To be nimble or be dead? To make decisions as quickly as Bronson Taylor at Growth Hacker TV or you're already out of business and just waiting for the memo to arrive by stagecoach?

*This is what we mean!*

As any teenager can tell you, it takes little time to establish a rudimentary presence on any of the major social media sites. Profiles are actually designed on purpose to be easy for users to set up. Because if the process is too arduous, people will quit halfway through.

If you're going to get on social, then for heaven's sake, *get on social!* How can you take three years to *plan* to do something that takes five minutes? Building a social media control center? Opening an office in Ireland? Sure, those things take a while.

Opening a LinkedIn account? Five minutes.

For goodness' sake, you can establish a mobile Twitter account while waiting in line for your triple venti, half sweet, non-fat, caramel Macchiato at Starbucks. In the Social Age, we don't think and do "slow" or "we need a formal plan to analyze the impact of blah, blah, blah" anymore.

Although, as Tom Peters and Robert Waterman so eloquently pointed out in 1982 in our favorite chapter of *In Search of Excellence* the best leaders have never been slugs about making decisions and acting on them. "A bias for action" is how the authors described the best leaders of the day.

In 1982.

Three years to get on social? Come *on!*

## WHO'S SOCIAL NOW?

Without question, the career tracks of some leaders are better represented on social than others; some roles bring built-in exposure to social while others . . . not so much. Anecdotally:

► Chief marketing officers (CMOs)—although not nearly as many as we'd like to see, head of marketing types, and almost all public relations professionals, seem to be much more socially active than chief financial officers (CFOs).

► A ton of HR leaders are hyperactive on social, where facilities and supply chain professionals are not—at least not yet.

► Sales professionals are flocking to social faster than gold miners used to climb up Alaska's Chugach Trail (albeit many for all the wrong reasons), while IT pros, with the possible exception of chief information officers (CIOs) and chief technology officers (CTOs), which we'll talk about here in a bit, haven't yet climbed on board.

► Leaders in accounting, security, legal, and administrative positions, it seems, are almost nonexistent on social.

► In addition, many industries are far more apt to be on social than others. Digital media, publishing, music, and entertainment tend to be all over social, while engineering, medical, insurance, and financial firms are far behind in their adoption of social media.

► Regardless of industry, as you might imagine, there is a significant difference in usage of social media by generation. The majority of Millennials and members of Gen Z (those born from the late mid-1990s to the present) are already entering the workforce. These *digital natives* (as they are known because they were born into a world dominated by technology) are thoroughly immersed in social. The older people are, the less likely they are to spend significant time on social networking sites.

And then there are the CIOs . . .

## 100 CIOS IN ONE HOUR

A few years ago, and way before Twitter became the juggernaut it is today, Ted was doing some work with a major IT advisory firm that wasn't (and still isn't) heeding the advice of its own experts.

Understanding the potential of social to find and build relationships with the company's core constituency (enterprise CIOs), Ted woke up one Saturday morning with an idea: "I'll take an hour this morning to see if I can find and follow 100 CIOs on Twitter. While some will surely already be our clients, many more won't. Rather than *tell* my CEO why he needs a social media strategist, I'll *show* him."

So Ted did exactly that.

First, he set up columns on Twitter management platform HootSuite: one for "CIO" and another for "IT." Each person who tweeted with either term in a tweet came up in one of the columns, and Ted checked the bio of each, putting the CIOs on a list he'd created just for them.

That was slow going, though, so in a couple of minutes he tweeted out:

*I'm making a list of CIOs. Any out there right now?*

A number of them raised their digital hands to be added to his list. That was much faster than his searches of tweets with "CIO" or "IT" in them.

But then he hit the jackpot.

What most people—especially marketing types—still don't get is how very conversational Twitter is. You don't just say stuff or broadcast your links into the ether; on Twitter, you can conduct sometimes quite-involved conversations, one sentence at a time. (That's why tweet-chats are fun: They're conversational, not declarative.)

And that's what made the remainder of Ted's hour-long project so much fun. Others on Twitter asked him what he was up to: Why was he asking for CIOs?

Ted's response: "To see how many I can get in an hour, as a way of kicking the social media tires."

"Oh, try this . . . ," someone would say, and the suggestions kept on coming. (The other observation that many nonparticipants don't get about social media is that people who use it are inclined to be very helpful. Social, even.)

That hour flew by for Ted, as his friends told him who already had lists of IT pros he could scour or even lists of nothing but CIOs. The CIOs following Ted kept identifying themselves, and his other followers who were IT leaders introduced him to their bosses if those CIOs had Twitter accounts.

At the end of that Saturday morning experiment, Ted didn't have 100 CIOs, as he had hoped. He had a little over 1,000.

One thousand.

*In an hour.*

Now, we'd like to tell you that Ted's CEO found this information useful, that leadership at this IT advisory company started taking social more seriously, that they stopped being the cobbler whose children had no shoes and began transitioning into the Social Age instead.

But we can't. Nothing happened at all.

You can lead a horse to water, but you can't make it think.

# GETTING UP TO SPEED

So you're an executive, you have no social presence as you read this, and we've convinced you.

You are now ready and rarin' to dive into social!

Or, perhaps more realistically, you aren't ready to dive in, but you now realize you're running a knowledge deficit and you understand how that can be detrimental to the company you're steering or helping to steer.

This book is a terrific way to start, but you really need something tailored more to your particular company, preferably face-to-face lessons that will give you a chance to ask all the questions you have about social and how it can affect your career and your firm's prosperity. Where do we recommend you go for such help?

To answer that question, regardless of which of the aforementioned two categories describes you, first we're going to take you to a wedding.

"A *what*?!" you're thinking. But bear with us; it'll take just a minute, and the perspective provided is priceless.

Have you ever planned a wedding? Have you ever *paid for* a wedding? We've done both. If you have, too, what is the one thing you noticed about putting on a wedding?

Was it the cost, by any chance?

Even more than the overwhelming amounts of unsolicited advice, even more than trying to figure out how to seat the in-laws so you don't have the Hatfields and the McCoys feuding at the reception, even more than weighing the desire to have an open bar versus the certainty that an open bar is the last thing Uncle Tommy really needs—more than any of that, what we noticed most glaringly is the wildly inflated price of everything.

On any other day except Valentine's Day and Mother's Day, go shopping for a nice bouquet and the florist may gouge you a bit, but nothing exorbitant. Ask that same florist to provide the exact same bouquets for each table at a wedding reception? Four times the regular price.

It's a wedding. They know they've got you.

Catering? Same deal. How is a lukewarm chicken dinner possibly worth $80? Unless you live in New York City, you probably couldn't find an $80 chicken dinner if you tried, could you?

Over and over for every line item, the expenses go through the roof when the vendor knows they're for a wedding.

What we've noticed, as bootstrap/start-up guys by calling who have spent a tremendous portion of our careers both as employees and as advisers at enterprises, is that large companies are just like weddings! When vendors know they're selling to an enterprise, prices skyrocket—prices for goods or services that, were they to be purchased by a five-person garage start-up, would just be, um, stupid.

And we know exactly why. Two reasons why, in fact:

1. It's much better for a company to pay more, even a whole lot more, for quality it can trust. We're actually on board with this. One of the core business lessons we share with leaders is never to compete on price but, instead, to stake your ground as worth *a lot* more than the competition and then to charge *a little* more. The nuances of this business lesson are ones we would explore in depth in another book.

But the second reason enterprises pay so much for many services? Well, the other reason appalls us:

2. It's not the purchasing executive's money. Let's face it, when you're away on business and the company picks up the tab, you eat at Shula's or Morton's and don't think twice about it. But, except for the most special occasions, how often do you eat there when you're picking up the tab yourself?

This second reason for crazy consultant prices plays into the "death of large" because not only are large companies too often slow, overly careful, and bureaucratic, they're also incredible wasters of money. The management tax isn't just the salaries and benefits of all those managers and staff in the hierarchy; the purchases these companies make—routinely at four times the going rate—are a factor, too.

At this point, it's possible you're rolling your eyes and saying to yourself, "Here we are on another anti-enterprise tangent!"

Well, maybe. But this whole wedding-and-enterprise-price-padding thing? It's time we come full circle.

## HAVE WE GOT A TWO-DAY COURSE FOR YOU!

So your executives are woefully behind in this whole social "fad." Finally, the CEO admits that maybe the Social Age is upon us, that this isn't a fad so much as the way things are done now. Time to get leadership up to speed, fast! The company is behind, and when you're behind the only thing that matters is catch-up speed. Not price. Not value. Not even common sense.

So where better to send the top dogs for a crash course on all things social than a company in New York, where the group will receive a private crash course in social media for only—wait for it . . .

*$60,000 per person.*

Seriously. Not six thousand. *Sixty.* Not for the group. *Per person.*

Can you say, "Here comes the bride"? We aren't saying this organization (which we deliberately choose not to name) doesn't put on a terrific two-day workshop. It has a solid reputation. And part of what the course imparts is not just what a Facebook page should look like but useful lessons on digital user experience and how to think like a start-up founder (before you're put out of business by one). That's good stuff.

But consider the price tag, and let's think of some alternative ways to invest that sum. Say you want ten leaders to catch up to speed. That's $600,000 . . . for two days.

How many highly qualified digital media experts could that employ for a year each? At $150,000 each, four highly qualified professionals with existing OPEN communities of their own, advising and coaching the top staff for a solid year? At $75,000 each, eight more junior-level, socially savvy mentors more than capable of holding the social hands of executives? At $12 to $15 per hour, twenty eager interns—for an entire year?

Chances are, even the interns could help a lot more than ten executives will learn in two days, only to go back to their day jobs where fourteen-hour days with no breaks are the norm, leaving no time to implement what they learned at the cost of $600,000.

Of course, that dinner and several drinks at Morton's in New York amounted to good team building, right?

As we might put it on Twitter: #justsayin.

## BEWARE OF CHARLATANS, GURUS, AND NINJAS

So if spending that much to cram-session your way to social knowledge isn't a feasible solution, how *do* you decide who to hire for the social coaching you need?

Do you hire the first person who spams you with offers that use the words *expert, ninja,* and *guru*? Do you sign up for their offer of a glossy webinar or free white paper that has the word *secret* in the title?

No.

Here is a short list to get you started:

▶ **Look within** | You probably already employ social media experts whose talents your company is not using. Especially if your company is large, these socially adept team members could be buried deep within the organization. Show some gumption and unearth them. Someone among your rank and file would love to help—it might even be their dream assignment.

▶ **Look for thought leaders** | Outside your organization, there is any number of social experts creating impact for companies just like yours. First priority: Check their social profiles. Hint: A thousand Twitter followers does not an expert make. We cringe every time we see that in a profile—which, in the course of one day, is often.

▶ **Ask for (and find) references** | As in hiring decisions, check references, both formally and informally (on social, a great way to do that is to lurk: just listen to your prospects for a while as they interact with others). Discover what their peers think of them. Are they listed or ranked anywhere? Where, and for what?

▶ **Read their work** | Read their blogs. A lot. Before you hire them. Blogs show not only their level of expertise but also how they approach their work. If they've written a white paper, an e-book, or a print book, read those, too.

▶ **Consume video** | Watch their videos—press interviews, keynotes, and their YouTube channels. For very well established social media consultants, check out their talks at TED, TEDx, BIF (Business Innovation Factory), or similar venues. Hint: In the Social Age, those at the top of their game have video available. If not, well, you know.

▶ **Look at how they market themselves** Specifically, what do they call themselves? Hint: If their job titles include "Guru," "Ninja" or "Whisperer," even their mothers laugh at them. And aren't our moms supposed to love us no matter what?

Life is too short to get swindled. Money doesn't come that easily (even if it isn't ours). And the ROI of social is already difficult enough to determine. Be careful. Be smart.

Most important: Use your OPEN network.

They know.

## IF THIS CEO CAN FIND THE TIME . . .

What's your excuse?

You may be skeptical about the idea of captains of industry tweeting or blogging or coming to a Google+ Hangout to mix with the little people. "Sure," you might be thinking, "some twenty-something start-up CEOs may be social (especially when their start-ups are themselves social media platforms), but no grown-ups are, right?"

How about a bank CEO? Banking is a heavily regulated industry with perhaps the stodgiest, squarest reputation in the business world. Would that convince you?

Peter Aceto, the CEO of Tangerine (formerly ING Direct Canada), has been on LinkedIn, Facebook, and especially Twitter for years now. He's also an active blogger, writing twice monthly on the Tangerine blog. Over the past couple of years, both online and by phone, Peter has become an insightful, truly generous friend. And not just because we're anyone special online. If you observe Peter's tweet stream any day, you'll find him just as interactive, generous, and real with everyone.

Peter is a relentless giver.

So we'd like to share a little insight from this quintessential social leader. Rather than chop up what was a compelling conversation among Peter, Ted, and Mark, we're going to show you the entire interview.

Stick with this, please, until the end. If there is any doubt about why you need to become a social leader, well, this might OPEN your mind.

### 1. You are the CEO of a bank. Why did you get social in the first place?

Peter: About five years ago, we had a meeting where we talked about trends, and social media came up. That night, I opened my Twitter account. I was quite taken by the process. Tools aside (be it Twitter, Facebook, or whatever), the technology that can facilitate leaders building relationships, sharing and learning—and being in direct communication with customers and employees—was compelling.

In our competitive world, banking, it can be hard to show how you are different. When I look at my business and market, there are some really big banks over 100 years old—and in that arena we're a challenger. It was clear this could be a differentiator for us. We can have open and honest conversations with our customers, where our competitors probably can't, or won't be able to for a long time. For us, social is a competitive advantage. We're quick and nimble—we can be there before any else is. And we can have open and honest conversations with customers, potential customers, and influencers.

From a personal perspective, I really enjoy social; this worked for me. I enjoyed the dialogue with colleagues about innovating, being a challenger, and building community. This allowed me as a CEO to [be] different and distinctive, to learn what our customers/the public thinks about us and build or improve upon it accordingly. And from a consumer confidence perspective, people can go back five years to see who I am and what I stand for.

### 2. So in those five years, what's the verdict? How has social helped?

Peter: Social on the outside is important, but we built social on the inside, too. Our internal collaboration tool is called "Orange Grove," where our 950 employees can connect; it is where we create a culture of communication—while also establishing social as the way we communicate, internally and with the public. Orange Grove helps me make sure our people understand our vision, strategy, how we're doing, how we can do better . . .

On the outside, we started with just one Twitter account, mine. Now, we have many Twitter accounts that help us communicate on a local, regional, and niche level. We're also using social as a customer service channel. We didn't plan on that, but customers reached out organically; we learned through experience that customers want to communicate via social about service issues.

For instance, early on I got a tweet on my personal account from a disgruntled customer—turns out we were late in delivering his paperwork, and it was the day of his closing, so we were screwing the whole thing up for him. The minute I learned that, I ran over to the staffer who could fix that and we did, in ninety minutes. That was a significant differentiator. Our competition could not do that.

In the five years since I started, our competition has gone social, too. They are learning and are trying to catch up. Their leaders still aren't social, though, so that remains a competitive advantage for us.

I have customers who've said, "I've been watching you personally online for two years now, and I want to be your customer."

What's the ROI on this? Even more to the point, how many customers have we won who haven't told us this? You can't measure that.

### 3. Tell us more about Orange Grove, your internal social media tool. How do you use it and what have you learned from the experience?

**Peter:** We're customer-client focused, but the best impact we can have is on our people: If they're inspired, if they love coming to work every day, our customers are going to feel it.

Our people want to know the why: "Why do I want to support the mission, what does it matter to me, is what we're doing important to me and in line with my values?" Our intranet really helps address those issues. Plus, our mission is to help our customers build their dreams through better finances. We can explain how we're doing that via the intranet.

How much learning do I do from the employees via the Orange Grove? A lot! One of my posts is titled *The Right to B\*@#h*, which means giving employees a safe place to say, "This little thing is such a pain in the ass, I would think my company could get rid of that." Mostly it's small stuff, like "I would imagine this process would be without paper, since our customers are paperless." I read that and said, "We use paper for that!?" and we fixed it.

Because our people feel they have the right to b\*@#h and that my staff and I are doing something about it, we're making the company run better, and making the employees feel better about working here, too.

My hidden agenda is trying to smash the stereotype of the CEO— all the bull crap like office on the corner of the top floor, my own elevator: That nauseates me. This is foolish—companies can't run like that anymore. My goal is to remake the role of CEO. Social and collaboration technology is helping me remake the role of CEO, it lets me lead by example.

**4. What's your advice to your C-suite peers who aren't social?**
Peter: In twenty years this going to be a no-brainer—leadership will need to be social. Already I've heard a couple examples of boards judging CEO candidates by their social presence, so it's already coming. This may be best practice today, but there's no doubt in time that this is going to be the expectation of consumers: The brands they want to be loyal to are bold and transparent and social. Employees feel this way too.

Sooner or later this advantage will shrink, but I'm always amazed at how slow things are to change, but right now it's an advantage when a CEO is social and does it well. On the other hand, if you don't believe in it [authentic social engagement], and if you want to share positive public relations stories only, you can actually do damage to your brand. You can't fake being real when being social.

**5. Do you throw away a personally good CEO just because he doesn't belong online?**
Peter: There's a lot more to being a leader than having a personality; today, in this transition period, I'm not sure not being social is going to kill you. Maybe other top leaders can represent the brand to the public and the employees if the No. 1 guy can't be social. Five years ago, this wasn't even on the job requirements list, but now it's on a lot of company's lists. When boards are looking for their next CEOs, this will get on the list of a lot of companies sooner or later. I think at some point in the not too distant future, social presence will be among a board's top five aptitudes when vetting CEO candidates.

At Tangerine, I've started the social C-suite. I started it by myself; now I have five more of our top twenty execs who are social. If I were really bad at it, I could have brought them on, because I wouldn't know how to guide them with what's worked for me and what hasn't.

**6. You ran a commercial for Canada's version of the 401(k), the "RSP." Tell us about the dustup over that spot and how you fixed it because you were on social.**
Peter: Yes, the RSP is Canada's version of the 401(k)—a retirement savings plan. It's much more complicated than it has to be, so we made a commercial asking if

you're irritable and moody . . . which could be symptoms of RSP. So in the commercial, we asked: "Are you suffering from RSP?" The idea was if so, Tangerine can help.

We ran this by focus groups, market tested it—the issue of mental illness never even came up. So we ran it. Millions of Canadians saw it.

At first I got one tweet, then a couple more, saying "you're making fun of mental illness" and "you guys are <expletive>s." I was obviously surprised, but I met with the team. At that moment, we decided to keep going with the ads.

But there were a bit more tweets that indicated the ad might be insensitive; it was never a lot, maybe fifty in all.

But one guy made it clear. He explained in a tweet, which he linked to a YouTube video he'd made on the topic, that one of the biggest problems with mental illness is that it carries this stigma, so nobody talks about it, even when they're in trouble.

He said that his son was away at his first year of college and he committed suicide; the father didn't even know his son was even experiencing any problem. So, this dad explained that making fun of mental illness just isn't right, because it causes more stigma and silence on the part of those who are desperate for help, like his late son.

This got to me. I understood what the father was saying. Even though the numbers of negative remarks were never high, we met again and decided to pull the TV ads.

Risking the brand, which is the one thing that is most important to us at Tangerine, is just not worth it, even though the ads were expensive to produce and we had already bought the ad slots on the TV networks. We pulled them because it was the right thing to do.

To my surprise, we got a lot of positive reactions to that move. Fixing a perceived misstep actually has its upside, where making no missteps does not.

When you screw up and fix things quickly, you'll get 100 references from someone who is just so impressed, you've locked them in for life. That's one reason I love responding at 11 at night, or on Sunday, and often within an hour. I copy key people and promise we'll fix the problem within three hours. Customers don't get that kind of responsiveness from other brands, certainly not from bank CEOs. It creates a lot of goodwill and loyalty among our customers. That's why I love being on social.

Peter gets it.

Peter is a Blue Unicorn.

As he said, he is building a team—from the C-suite to the customer-facing employees—that gets social.

The building of a team that competes well in the Social Age is a challenge every social leader will face. Because today—with the new expectations of customers and employees and with technology that enables us to find each other, make meaningful connections, and even work side-by-virtual-side across different time zones and on different continents—we must build a collaborative, socially enabled team.

And for that, we invite you to Chapter 11.

CHAPTER 11

# Building a World-Class
# Team for the Social Age

Your mind is OPEN. You are ready to lead in the Social Age.

But you can't do this alone. You need to build not just a network of advocates and ambassadors; you need a team capable of competing well in the Social Age.

(Note that we didn't say a "social" team. Remember, in just a short time we'll all drop the qualifier in front of phrases such as *social media, social marketing,* and *social teams*—it will just be *media, marketing,* and *teams,* as it should be.)

The first step, and perhaps the most difficult for any organization: understanding where you stand now. What tools and assets are currently in place? Which team members are already engaged on social—and which are not but should be? What policies will need to be instituted, changed, or (especially vital to your success) abolished? Is your company culture conducive to social, and, if not, what will need to change?

How social is your leadership? How social does your leadership need to be—right now?

First things first.

## HOW READY IS YOUR ORGANIZATION FOR OPEN?

Recently, Ted spoke at the annual conference of the National Association of Corporate Directors (NACD). At the conference were about a thousand directors from many of America's largest companies (including a director from United Airlines, who confided over lunch that he isn't a very big fan of guitar-playing, United-bashing Dave Carroll).

The meeting was interesting for a few reasons. For one, the attendees spanned the spectrum when it came to their social media savviness. More were on this end of the scale:

► "No presence at all."

► "I'm just on LinkedIn."

► "How do I send a Twitter?"

► "Social media? My kids do the Facebook. It's not for me."

Yes, "*a* Twitter" and "*the* Facebook."

Still, they were there to learn, and they were certainly a smart bunch. So, to help them understand the current social health of their organizations, Ted sent these stakeholders home with ten questions they had to get answered before deciding their best course of action:

1. What is our social media strategy, and how integrated is it with the rest of our corporate strategy?

2. What is our policy regarding social media use at work? Why? Who set it?

3. What social media training do we provide to our employees? Or do we?

4. What collaboration technology do we use? Who chose it? How is that going for us?

5. How do we utilize social to engage with our customers and vendors?

6. How do we best leverage social to engage with our employees and candidates?

7. How do we use social to engage with outside organizations such as industry associations and university research teams?

8. What is our CEO's social media presence?

9. What are our top executives' social media presences?

10. Within our core team, who are our thought leaders—and what is their social media presence?

While you answer these questions, we'll get a cup of coffee. Go ahead. Take your time . . .

[Insert refrain from *Jeopardy* here.]
    Okay, ready?

We bet you can see a couple of themes in this line of inquiry. To help your stakeholders—and you—see the value of OPEN, let's look at each question, one at a time:

▶ **Question 1: Social media strategy** | If your company has a "social media strategy," *that* is a problem. Certainly, your marketing department should be working with PR, advertising, sales, and customer service to represent the brand best in the public eye. However, your organization should have a clear *business* strategy—and your social media should wholly support that strategy. Having a separate strategy for social—one not fully integrated into your overall mission—is a huge red flag. (Sorry for the trick question.)

▶ **Question 2: Social media policy** | Your employees are going to use social media at work. It's social, and they're human—it's what we humans do. Social used to be standing around the watercooler or taking a cigarette break. Now it's Twitter and Facebook. If your folks are huddling outside with the smokers to take a Twitter break because they aren't allowed access at work, there's a bigger problem than just their inconvenience. Or if the dinosaur at the front of the leadership pack is worried about staff goofing off on social during work hours, then you have a trust issue, not a social media issue.

▶ **Question 3: Social media training** | Meet Ted Rubin, author, social media A-lister and accomplished CMO. Ted is passionate about helping companies provide social media training to employees as a benefit. His argument is as compelling as it is simple: Who isn't going to love their company when it teaches them a skill that helps them build their career? Certainly it's more useful to them than a paid day off or a plaque. Although social media training is a savvy strategy for long-term growth and prosperity, Rubin points to American Express as one of the few large companies that has caught on to this notion and is doing it to *very* good effect. (More on this in Chapter 12, where we talk about the compelling traits of a social leader.)

▶ **Question 4: Collaboration tools** | Depending on the size of your operation, collaboration technology for use inside the organization is big bucks—upward of $15 to $45 per user per month for enterprise solutions like Sharepoint, IBM Open Connections, and Saleforce's Chatter. Theoretically, there's a good reason: These tools have made it a snap for people throughout the organization's many departments to work together. Once contained within purpose-dedicated silos and connected only through middle managers, individuals, regardless of their primary mission, can now communicate directly—and far more effectively. This is just one more reason we insist that *flat* is an imperative, rather than just an option. Employees and other relevant participants are able, through collaboration tools, to get work done without going through channels, without waiting for permission, without being blocked by the bureaucracy—none of that need get in the way any longer. By the way, if a collaboration tool isn't in the budget, a 2013 study by Avanade UK showed that most collaborators would rather use at work what they already use at home to collaborate. Facebook, specifically, was the collaboration tool of choice 2-to-1 over Sharepoint, 4-to-1 over Open Connections, and 6-to-1 over Chatter.

► **Questions 5 to 7: Engagement** | Remember Rule No. 3 of the basic rules of engaging, monitoring, and selling through social media from Chapter 5? That rule simply states: "Meet customers where they are now." For most organizations, that means Facebook, Twitter, and LinkedIn. It could also mean Google+, Pinterest, Instagram, and Reddit. Find out where you're engaging with customers, vendors, employees, job seekers, and outside organizations, and see if there are any holes in your engagement process. Where do you need more ears?

► **Questions 8 to 10: Social media presence** | The last three questions relate to the social media presence of the company's most visible representatives—or, at least, those who in the Social Age *should* be most visible. Let's face it, you know it, we know it, everybody knows it: There is something sexy about the three letters C-E-O. Ever since Lee Iaccoca arguably became America's first modern celebrity CEO when he took the helm at Chrysler in the 1980s, the top-dog spot has been a public persona, not just an unheralded functionary who steers the corporate ship. We're not saying all CEOs would make very appealing public figures or those with the most charisma are going to be the best at actually leading. But right or wrong, in a world gone social people do look to the big cheese as the number one representative of a brand. And for that rep to have no presence on social media, well, that could be merely a wasted opportunity. Or it could be a dangerous opening through which some very unwanted attention can come your way. Same for the top executives, and same for the internal experts and thought leaders.

For instance, say one of the managers within your supply chain goes to a conference and is part of a roundtable discussion. You know some people in the audience are going to be tweeting the best (and worst) nuggets real-time out to the Twittersphere. Anonymous as the supply chain function is within your company, your brand will be tied to its people's words and social profiles. The best way to capitalize on good press? If your team has Twitter accounts and LinkedIn profiles, they can retweet some of those nuggets later and copy-paste them to LinkedIn, where (you hope) they belong to a supply chain leader's group. If there's something less than savory being said about them? Maybe they, the social media team, or PR will catch it and minimize the damage, as discussed in Chapter 5. Voila! Crisis averted and/or opportunity gained.

By asking, and answering, the ten questions listed here, you can objectively assess the fitness of your own organization's current social presence—a realistic snapshot of where you stand now and what must be done next so you can successfully transition from a twentieth-century model to being a twenty-first-century organization driven by an OPEN mindset.

Here's the key: Don't ask these questions of just those in leadership roles.

Ask everyone.

## LOOK INSIDE: THE POWER OF INTERNAL CHAMPIONS

Remember: Being social is a human instinct.

The Industrial Age beat the human out of us. All the while, however, the best leaders, salespeople, customer service reps, help desk staff, recruiters and many more, were the best humans. They could solve customer problems in such a way as to sell and serve *far* better than their peers. They could assuage the angriest customer or solve the biggest technical problem with poise. They could hire those who could not be gotten and lead teams toward accomplishing what on the surface looked like impossible goals. Throughout the Industrial Age, no matter how process-oriented we became, those humans were always our superstars.

Today, social enables these humans. Despite its digital nature, they flock to social as if it were an irresistible force. This process is organic—it doesn't wait for permission, a policy, or a promise.

Social just happens.

With all this in mind, we'll make you a bet.

We'll bet you that the early adopters of social within your organization right now are not in formal leadership roles. We'll bet you that right now they are working—and perhaps even building an OPEN community—from within your marketing and public relations teams and most certainly from inside your customer-facing sales and customer service departments.

We'll make you another bet.

We'll bet you that those at your company who know more than anyone else about how social works have never been asked how social works. Or why it works. Or what works well for them and what does not. How your customers, vendors, and applicants perceive your company. And where you, as a leader, can leverage existing communities—and launch your version of OPEN.

How do you find these social superstars?

Remember "Bud" from Chapter 5? The CEO who walked the floor, poured coffee, bought pizza, and connected on LinkedIn?

Bud was OPEN. In fact, Bud was the epitome of OPEN. He led, engaged, and communicated by example.

To lead your team into the Social Age—and to build a world-class, socially enabled team—you must be Bud. You must go into the trenches to identify who is excelling now, regardless of what the fourth manager down the line thinks. You must find your internal advocates—the champions of your products and services, the ones who are most passionate about their roles now.

Those are your brand ambassadors, your social superstars. Motivated effectively, they are the core of your internal OPEN community. Sit down with them. Learn. Pour coffee. Engage. Buy pizza.

Build a plan.

Who among these superstars can reverse mentor even the most recalcitrant social dinosaur? Who has the ears—meaning, the respect—of other team members but maybe doesn't have "manager" in the title line on his or her business card? Who has the best product knowledge, even if neglecting to use the customer service scripts provided by management to solve a problem?

Now, we know what this sounds like: rebellion.

Quite the contrary.

This isn't a mutiny. We aren't deliberately seeking out the rebels and outcasts.

We are simply asking you to consider that the most likely source for knowledge, inspiration, and organic leadership may just come from the most unlikely places, far from your existing management team.

Does that mean you should replace your current managers? Initiate the flat imperative, immediately?

No. But remember: Your goal is to lead your team, department, or organization confidently and successfully into the Social Age. To do that, you may have to mix in some revolutionaries with the regulars. The end result may be the most diverse—and the most challenging—team you've ever led. Done right, this may also be the most rewarding professional experience you'll ever have.

Find your internal champions. Ask Ted's ten questions. Then ask a lot more. Actively listen to the answers. Then build your team of internal champions.

This is the core of your OPEN constellation.

Now it is time to add to your team, perhaps from the outside. First, though, as we always do, we must take a look at where we stand now. What is our employer brand? Why would socially minded superstars want to come work for us? Or if they're socially savvy and working for us now, why would they want to leverage (and perhaps risk) the personal brand they've built away from work to represent our company in an official capacity?

Hey, we didn't say this would be easy!

## WHAT IS YOUR CURRENT EMPLOYER BRAND?

It's time. Time to bring in the new blood. Time to take your organization deep into the Social Age.

Human resources, chances are, already has many requisitions open. Each one of those has a job description, as well as promotional copy for the job boards. Each of those postings contains copy at the top that talks about what a dynamic, fast-paced, quickly growing company you are and that you care about your people. You might even include the company mission statement, so carefully written in 1992, which tells everyone what your company is supposed to be.

But is it?

What is your employer brand, really? What makes your organization different? For example, think of The Container Store's focus on the customer. Virgin Group's passion for the user experience, shared by all 400+ companies in the Virgin empire. Or In-N-Out Burger's focus on consistently high-quality food delivered with a smile by valued employees.

Now, how closely is reality tied to the way you want the world to see you as an employer? What do past employees, those within your industry, your customers, and those talking about you on social *really* think? What do current employees actually think of your company?

Not sure where to start getting the answers to all these questions?

In Chapter 5, we talked about the two independent studies showing that in the United States, 70 percent of workers are either disengaged or *actively* disengaged (yes, they're actively out of love with the firm or possibly even working *against* the best interests of the company). So let's start there. How does your company fare in this area? How engaged are your employees now?

We emphasize: Don't ask leadership this question. Do not ask the VP of human resources. Go into the trenches!

Why?

We believe that deep down in the bowels of an Industrial Age management system, a blindness to the truth exists—an insidious form of bias psychologists call "false consensus," where those in charge think everyone shares their opinion, and where that opinion is formed by what they want to think rather than by current reality.

What CEOs don't like their companies just fine? Who in human resources (considered perhaps the department most responsible for employee engagement and company culture) is going to think (or admit) that they suck at engagement and that the culture is less than healthy? This is not where objective answers come from. This is not where we find authenticity.

Your employees know. Your customers know.

You need to know.

Therefore, you must provide a safe environment, so the people who *do* know can tell you what they know.

Tangerine, a bank with over 1,000 employees, does this very well. The company CEO, Peter Aceto, bluntly calls these no-holds-barred meetings "B*@#h Sessions"— seriously, that is the name on the employee meet-up invites! Given that name, and the top-down interaction that occurs, we know these are spirited, yet deeply authentic, discussions around how Tangerine can improve its products as well as how it serves its customers.

The alternative to this open talk—to listening to those who know the real problems and most likely know how to fix them—is to go on believing what you *think* you know or spouting what is written on the company About Us and Career website pages, no matter how distanced that is from reality.

And when that happens, you are stuck in the worst possible position as you build your Social Age team: hypocrisy.

## THE WORST KIND OF HYPOCRISY

*"Busted!"*

As you begin to add to your internal OPEN community, that is how socially aware candidates—the exact people you must hire to build your Social Age team—are likely to perceive a company that talks a good game but whose reality seems much different.

Take a real-world organization that, on its beautifully written About Us and Careers pages, talks about how much it cares about team members, what an innovative, open company culture its employees enjoy, and how its founders are considered collaborative innovators who have been recognized by their industry for . . . blah, blah, blah.

And then, on Twitter, Facebook, LinkedIn Groups, Glassdoor, and dedicated forums for job seekers, quite the opposite seems true. The founders, though Steve Jobs–brilliant, come across as ill-tempered autocrats who expect every employee to work well into the evenings and on weekends without compensation or choice. The direction of the company seems to change every time the venture capitalists visit or a quarterly report is due. Those nap pods? For months, they've been used more for storage than for twenty-minute power naps.

Remember: Social media enables alternative opinions; it amplifies dissenting voices. As a result, candidates are more informed. When considering the possibility of bringing their talents and OPEN circles to your company, they don't stop at your About Us page or the flowery company description at the top of your job posting. Nor do they buy a word your recruiters are paid to tell them about how cool the company is.

They know better. The foosball and Ping-Pong tables in the break area fool no one.

As pointed out in Chapter 4, smart organizations like Taco Bell and Northrup Grumman have embraced this new reality. They deliberately, actively listen. Based on the social criticism, they act to improve. They admit their mistakes and failures. Both online and in the office, they are accountable.

We'll say this again: They deliberately, actively listen.

It is these companies that a new candidate perceives as authentic. They've shown leadership. They demonstrate a willingness to engage. Their organizational culture is continuously improving. In other words, after digital due diligence is performed, both active and passive job seekers say: *This is the kind of company I want to work for!*

The result is simple: Top talent migrates toward these companies (and away from the old-school orgs that are afraid to listen and too bureaucratic or too indifferent to change).

When your company's employer brand reaches the point where what you sell to a prospect is closely aligned with reality, building a collaborative team becomes a matter of listening to your OPEN community and your internal champions. Recruiting becomes largely a matter of mining employee referrals. Hiring becomes less about messaging, advertising, and compliance and more about picking from the best available talent for each open position.

How does your organization reach this level of authenticity?

As you know by now, your authors believe the best way to get where you want to be is to emulate those who are already there. Here are a just a few examples of companies whose employer brands are not only highly regarded but have embraced social media and use it as a platform to recruit socially enabled talent:

▶ **TOMS** | Mission-oriented TOMS is one of the first nonhierarchal organizations built on a foundation of doing social good (for each pair of shoes purchased, a free pair is provided to the underprivileged) and promoted largely through organic methods, including social media. Founded by entrepreneur Blake Mycoskie, TOMS employees, many of whom started as long-term interns, are passionate about not only the product and mission but the lifestyle that comes from being part of a team of "caring capitalists."

TOMS employees typically take to Twitter and Facebook to broadcast their devotion to the philanthropic organization, their products, and the company's customer service model. Employees also post photos and videos to Pinterest and YouTube of "shoe drops" into impoverished villages and of the benefits of their WaterForward campaign, which brings clean water to underdeveloped countries. Without a doubt, the employees of TOMS—and their use of social—are integral components of the company's success.

▶ **Whole Foods** | Whole Foods, founded in 1978 by current CEO John Mackey, is a supermarket chain that specializes in high-quality natural and organic foods. The company is well known for a commitment to sustainable food harvesting methods, humane treatment of animals, support of charitable organizations, and consumption of green energy. The company's focus on service and good corporate citizenship carries over to its employees as well. Employees at Whole Foods enjoy highly competitive wages, a personal wellness savings account, health benefits for as little as $10 per paycheck, and extraordinary employee development including access to Whole Foods Market University. There is good reason why Whole Foods routinely ranks high on *Fortune*'s Top 100 Companies to Work For list—and why the employees consistently serve as excellent ambassadors for the brand through social media.

▶ **Harley-Davidson** | Perhaps the world's most famous brand of motorcycles, Harley-Davidson was founded in the early 1900s, survived the Great Depression, and has gone on to become one of America's most notable brands—of any kind. Chief among its passionate supporters are not just customers but employees and retirees as well. Harley-Davidson builds its business by adhering to these values: Tell the truth, be fair, keep your promises, respect the individual, and encourage intellectual curiosity. The brand with the most-often tattooed logo on the planet also takes pride in treating its employees well. Similar to the comments routinely seen on Twitter and Facebook, this review from Indeed.com perhaps sums up how many of Harley-Davidson's team members feel about their employer:

*No day is "typical" . . . every day offers different opportunities and different challenges. Teamwork is key as well as the ability to embrace constant change. Co-workers are the best in the world . . . none better ever. Hardest part of job was dealing with uncertainty and the resulting employee morale changes whenever production changes occurred. The most enjoyable part of the job was seeing the faces of a wide range of motorcycle enthusiasts as they toured the factory and saw their dreams being assembled.*

Social—combined with just one disgruntled employee—can tear down your company's reputation and employer brand, sometimes in a single post.

Social—when driven by employees who are passionate about your company's mission, products, and customer service and who feel valued as contributors, as they do at TOMS, Whole Foods, and Harley-Davidson—can greatly enhance and advance your brand *organically*.

The key to being the company in that scenario? The key to being in a position to add top-notch, socially aware talent to your organization, to building your team?

Be a *really* good company to work for.

How does your organization get to this point? It starts now.

## EMULATION IS GOOD. ACTION IS BETTER.

Culture can't be a buzzword; it must be—in scalable, repeatable fashion—a core metric watched over by all stakeholders. Ideally, over time, the trolls, drama queens, and divas will be remotivated or removed (we'll talk in a bit about how attrition just might be the best friend of the social leader). But even if those who are not on board don't just go away, through active listening and engagement they will feel as though they were heard and their opinions were valued. A good company culture doesn't mean everyone gets along—work isn't a Disney movie. It means everyone feels respected and is willing to work together toward a common goal. They believe in the mission to the point that most are actively engaged. They don't just complain, they help find a solution. They don't turn to social media to complain about work or the leaders at work, they trust someone within the company enough to take their complaints there first.

That is the kind of culture you want at your organization.

That is how you'll recruit and retain top talent for your team.

## THE CRITICAL ROLE OF A COMMUNITY MANAGER

Your first hire (or next, if you've already begun hiring outside help to build your internal OPEN circle): community manager.

A good community manager is the glue that holds your organization's social presence together:

- By being consummate role models, community managers *are* the culture of their companies.

- Community managers execute with a positive, infectious, passionate attitude that drives other companies, champions, and ambassadors to the brand.

- ► They build new relationships with customers and potential team members, every day.

- ► They tell you (and HR, hiring managers, and those in the C-suite) where their attention should go, and with whom they should build or solidify relationships.

- ► They know all the right tools to use, and they live and breathe the data and reports that come out of them.

- ► They use those tools to determine what is working and what isn't and to track your company's social influence.

- ► They produce Gantt charts and reports to visualize their plans and quantify results.

- ► They dive into numbers like they're a swimming pool on a hot day.

- ► They plan social media events and overall social presence at least three months in advance.

- ► They attend conferences to promote both the brand and themselves as the chief ambassadors of the brand.

- ► They are the party everyone else wants to go to.

So where do we go to find a community manager?

In a world gone social, we don't go to Monster, Careerbuilder, or any of the big job boards or aggregators.

We go social.

Specifically, we go to the brands we respect, the ones that seem to be executing their business strategy well on social. If you've been on social for a while yourself, there may already be brands that have caught your eye. If you're still getting used to social, rely on the people in your internal OPEN circle. They know who is doing great work; they know the passionate community members.

Discover who they are. Invite them into your extraordinary network by first building an online relationship. Then buy them a cup of coffee or invite them to a Google+ Hangout. See if you think they might be a good fit before you ever mention the open opportunity at your organization.

This is how recruiting is done in the Social Age: one relationship at a time.

Just ask Justin Isaf, then of Huffington Post, who found Tim McDonald on social in a process we call "occupational matchmaking."

In April 2013, Tim shared a post on Facebook that displayed his approach to finding passion-driven work. Within that post, a Venn diagram showed three over-lapping circles labeled "what you're good at," "what you love," and "what pays well." The place where those three circles intersected perfectly was colored in red and featured another simple label that said: "#WIN."

Tim's caption for that diagram:

*I'm gradually turning red.*

Justin, who already had an OPEN relationship with Tim online, responded:

*Come to HuffPost—we'll see if we can get you closer.* ☺

Based on that one post, an already existing relationship, and a very short, unconventional interview, Tim McDonald moved to New York City to start his new career as director of community at Huffington Post Live.

No job was ever posted. No résumé was ever viewed.

Does this process work only for finding community managers? Not at all.

In early 2013, Vala Afshar, then an executive at Enterasys (which has since been purchased by Extreme Networks), was frustrated by the broken hiring process we described in Chapter 4. So, being an early adopter of social, Vala decided to try a new approach. He announced on Twitter, in less than 140 characters including the hashtag #socialcv, that he was looking for a new director of social and digital marketing—a six-figure position. He also stated that he would not accept résumés and would communicate only through Twitter.

Five hundred applications and just a few weeks later, the position went to Bilal Jaffery, who impressed Vala from the first contact and flourished during Afshar's thorough online background check. Again, no résumé exchanged hands.

When we talked to Vala and Bilal, they were thrilled with the results of this candidate sourcing/job search conducted exclusively on Twitter. Vala has gone on to repeat the process several more times and reports similar results. For his part, Bilal, who was already firmly entrenched in social and had established his online presence quite well, welcomed the chance to find an amazing job through social. He commented: "From the first moment I saw the tweet, I saw this as an amazing opportunity with a company that cared about social. This was the place for me. I was lucky to be one of the fifteen finalists, and the one to be offered the job."

Well done, Bilal. Although we doubt luck had anything to do with you and Vala connecting.

OPEN works.

## SO SOCIAL RECRUITING IS THAT EASY?

No. Not even close.

A lot goes into building your team—and into social recruiting in general.

Professional recruiters, in fact, wouldn't call the "Tim Goes to New York" and

"Vala Meets Bilal" stories "recruiting" at all. They would call that portion of the hiring process "sourcing"—the how, where, and by what means a candidate is found.

Even though Tim's joining HuffPostLive took some shortcuts and greatly reduced what is the normal time for sourcing, recruiting, and hiring a candidate, and although Vala connected through mutually beneficial relationships on Twitter, all the rest that goes into bringing on a new employee still exists. At most companies, that includes following HR's process for incoming applicants; review of career collateral; the informal online presence check discussed in Chapter 4; a multiphase interview process; background and reference checks; the offer, the counter-offer, and acceptance; and onboarding. No matter how socially enabled any organization, including yours, that process must be completed.

So, in reality, social recruiting isn't recruiting at all. It is *sourcing*. As we talk more about how to build your team around your existing culture and value proposition, we'll keep that in mind.

## BUILDING TEAMS AROUND CULTURE

Tim McDonald was a natural fit for HuffPostLive. As we've mentioned before, he is a relentless giver, a born connector, and everything his new employer needed to build an OPEN community. Perfect match, no doubt.

As you build your team, and as you fill all the open requirements HR has on hand now, your next step is to build the rest of your team around the established culture. Your goal, assuming you have forty-eight open requisitions: forty-eight Tim McDonalds.

To do that, first look inside your current operations again. Specifically, identify those who are thriving within your culture now. In each role, what skill sets—soft, technical, and professional—and personality types perform the absolute best? Who genuinely loves getting out of bed every day to come to work? Who enthusiastically mentors other team members and leads, regardless of the title on his or her business card? What type of person is not only doing the job well and playing nicely with others but serving as ambassador of your brand? Who has an existing OPEN community?

Then set out to hire more of them.

Lots more.

Hire away from those who are not doing well, who may be stuck in "how it used to be done around here." Help your team evolve, with deliberate intent to hire to the culture in place now and the culture you want your company to be known for ten years from now.

To help make and validate your potential hiring decisions, we encourage you to utilize what we feel has been significantly undervalued so far in the Social Age: assessment technology.

By no means are candidate assessments—tests designed to measure candidates' suitability for a role based on personality characteristics and aptitude—a Social Age tool. Psychometric tests like the Myers-Briggs Type Indicator (MBTI) have been around since the 1960s. And in their fifty+-year history, many have earned a poor reputation because of their inability to ultimately predict the value of one candidate over another. These tests are also regarded as easily gamed by intelligent candidates who skew their answers to "what you want to hear" versus "who I am."

However, the best forms of these tests are critical to determine not just the personality type and aptitudes of potential members of your team but how their strengths and weaknesses might affect the ability of your team to work together toward accomplishing a common goal. Two of your authors' favorites include:

► **Strengthscope** | This strengths (and, to be fair, weaknesses) assessment tool helps determine personality, performance strengths, the tasks and activities most likely to motivate a potential team member, how that candidate might best communicate and engage, and the extent to which the candidate applies those strengths in a working environment. In other words, Strengthscope helps determine the chances that the new team member you're considering has the personality and aptitude to thrive in the role you've created within your team.

► **Teamability** | Offered by the Gabriel Institute in Philadelphia, Pennsylvania, Teamability identifies and organizes the ways different types of people seek to make meaningful contributions to team activity. The technology analyzes how your team works together now and what to look for in new members to ensure that they will make a positive impact on the dynamics of the group. The results of the Teamability process have shown us that the ability to team well—in the right way, on the right team—is a critical decision point as groups change and grow. In addition, we've seen the technology improve retention, solve chronic issues among team members, and make a huge improvement in engagement, both internally and externally, with vendors, customers, and champions.

As you smartly expand your team, you will inevitably lose employees that have perhaps been with your organization for some time. When that happens, please remember this:

Attrition is *good.*

In fact, as you lead your team out of the Industrial Age, attrition may become your best friend.

Although emotionally troubling in the moment for the employee, your team, and you as a leader, the gradual reduction of a workforce through employees' leaving and not being replaced, rather than by their being laid off or fired, is a Social Age reality. Every company has dinosaurs. Not everyone who works at your organization will comprehend the change that must occur for your organization to compete well. They will, however, find work because there are going to be many companies—those without leaders like you—that will remain behind the curve, ready to post jobs on DinosaurHire.com.

One last thought on building your Social Age team: Keep time in perspective.

The Industrial Age lasted about 150 years. The assembly line portion of that era lasted almost exactly 100 years.

As we go to press in 2014, we're only about six years into the Social Age. These transitions, despite our sense of urgency, take time. Set the expectations of your team and organization accordingly.

Most important, give *yourself* time. Lead by example, knowing that good leaders—especially when systemic changes occur—are able to balance empathy with emphatic.

In Chapter 12, we'll discuss another critical element in leading your team to success in the Social Age: establishing a customer-centric focus for your organization, starting with understanding that customer service is truly a leadership issue.

CHAPTER 12

# In the Social Age, Customer Experience Comes First

*If you're not serving the customer, your job is to be serving someone who is.*

—*Jan Carlzon*

When Jan Carlzon, former CEO of SAP, said those words, social hadn't been invented yet. In fact, most of us had never heard of the Internet then. But the sentiment behind those words has never been truer than in the Social Age.

As we learned in Chapter 3, social amplifies *every* voice. Social can also make or break a brand—and often the tipping point is *customer experience*.

In a matter of a few days, social can launch an entire brand focused on delivery and service—Dollar Shave Club, for instance, a company that rode a YouTube video to nearly instant success. (Although the privately held company doesn't disclose financials, it was expected that revenue was at or near $10 million for 2013.)

Social can take a company almost no one ever heard of and make it infamous—Amy's Bakery, for example, which in 2013 suffered as the result of an epic meltdown by its owners on Facebook. (This Scottsdale, Arizona, small business soon became known as the poster child for how *not* to respond to social criticism).

Social can take a revered company—one like Ben & Jerry's—and, for the cost of one press release about a new ice cream, create an international media frenzy. (The February 2014 article on Huffington Post about the new Core ice cream products: over 800,000 Facebook likes in three days!)

Without a doubt, nothing can make or break your company's reputation faster than social.

Before we talk further about customer service in the Social Age, let's take a broad look at an important—indeed, a fundamental—principle on which all business operates but that few leaders comprehend.

## DO YOU MAKE, SELL, OR SERVE?

Think about a little business, perhaps a home-based start-up.

When there is just one founder tinkering alone in that garage, she's going to have to make whatever product her company produces and sell it herself. If she provides her customers a service, of course, she performs the service and sells it herself. This is how Ted started his first business, a language school. This is how William Carnegie weaved damask: literally in his cottage (hence, the term *cottage industry*).

Even if that founder is good at both making and selling, it has typically been difficult to do the selling and making at the same time. So when you are selling, no one is filling orders, and every time you fill an order, the sales process stops dead.

In reaction to the "do I make or do I sell?" quandary that develops, the solopreneur may find herself a partner at some point—that, or maybe cash has started to roll in and she can afford to hire someone to fill the gaps caused by her lack of bandwidth. Recruiting job done wisely and the tiny business staff doubled to two, someone is now dedicated to making what will be sold and someone is focused on selling what is made.

So things go well. Time passes; traction is gained. Bandwidth is stretched and more makers and sellers are added to the rolls, until at some point another position is added: someone to serve the makers and the sellers. Whether considered "administrative support" or "management" makes no difference: All of the roles within a business are either making, selling, or, as Jan Carlzon remarked a few decades ago, they are serving those who make or sell.

Every role in an organization, every last one, can be sorted based on its direct relationship to the customer:

► Does this person make?

► Does this person sell?

► Or does this person serve those who make or sell?

In a very small company, the answers to these questions should be obvious.

Now, step ahead ten years.

The company has grown exponentially. There are now hundreds of employees, maybe thousands. Eventually, the line that delineates who makes, who sells, and who serves is more than blurred—it is obliterated. In the sales category alone, there are many operations now involved.

Sales professionals sell, absolutely. But isn't marketing part of the sell function? Marketers don't make anything. Nor do they serve those who make. True also for advertising, and even for public relations. Thinly veiled "customer service," involving those who are primarily responsible for upsells and renewals, is also a sales function, at least when you're looking through the lens of the make, sell, or serve framework.

Phew! You still with us?

Here's where we're going with this: In the Social Age, all this changes. Everything we've accepted as truth—everything we've learned through college and the school of hard knocks—is different.

Because in the Social Age, *everyone* serves the customer.

Sales, engineering, public relations, administration, marketing—everyone has the opportunity to listen, engage, and serve. In the Social Age, internal functions that have no contact with customers do not—and perhaps should not—exist. Opportunities to serve the customer thus multiply. With each opportunity comes the chance to differentiate your brand from the competition. And with each moment of differentiation—when customers are served beyond expectations—there is the potential that those customers, already predisposed to social, are going to jump on Facebook, Twitter, or Pinterest and tell the world how well they were just served *by your brand.*

This is Jan Carlzon's vision, come to life.

Front-facing or not, everyone now has the same single function: to serve the customer. Every team member makes a difference not just to the company, but *to the customer.* Which is why . . .

## CUSTOMER SERVICE IS A LEADERSHIP ISSUE

Ted is sometimes asked how he made the transition from a focus on customer service to a focus on leadership. His standard reply:

*"What transition?"*

In 2005, when he wrote *Five-Star Customer Service,* Ted opened with a story that illustrated a culture of service: that of George Boldt, who was paid $1 million a year by William Waldorf Astor to manage the Waldorf-Astoria Hotel in New York City.

That was one hell of a lot of money for a hotel manager way back in 1893 (or today, for that matter), but after Boldt named his price and they shook on it, Astor remarked, "I would gladly have paid you more!"

It's a remarkable story involving two remarkable men: one who understood the value of unrivaled customer service; the other who lived and breathed it, and who made sure every member of his staff did as well.

Service is what customers see and feel. It is what they talk about, now more than ever.

But service doesn't happen because some trainer, armed with brownies and cans of Red Bull, motivated the staff for an afternoon in the conference room. (Indeed, that notion is almost embarrassing in its naïveté, and we still hear it—*a lot!*) Rather, customers experience terrific service because the staff shares *a passion for a culture of service*: When you pick the right people and put them in the right environment, their sincere need to delight customers is self-perpetuating.

This is what a service-first culture ensures: the perpetual delight of your customers.

That culture? It's started by a savvy leader, someone like George Boldt and Jan Carlzon, who gets it. This leader knows his or her sole responsibility is to tend to the culture, as a master gardener tends to the flowerbeds. A healthy, service-obsessed culture doesn't happen by accident—and it certainly doesn't keep going without a tremendous amount of support.

Thus, this is the only formula we've ever needed in business:

*Leadership + Culture + Service = Profits*

We've never talked to a business leader who doesn't desire profits for his or her company. Profits are any company's lifeblood; without them, the game quickly winds to an end.

Profits can come from a variety of areas, of course: monopoly, a must-have innovation, a massive sales force; mammoth economies of scale. What we've noticed about any of these advantages, however, is that they are fleeting; over time, competitors whittle away at them until yesterday's differentiator is today's me-too play.

The one area where companies can develop sustainable differentiation, especially in the Social Age: a commitment to service on an organizational scale.

Yes, we mean organizational: not just customer-facing staff, but also engineering, finance, legal, R&D, CEOs, CFOs—everyone.

You see, very few business leaders get the true value of service. Most think it's a necessary expense at best and relegate it to the basement-dwelling "customer service" organization (quotation marks to denote irony: Customer service is not a department!).

As you, the leader of your Social Age team, grasp the central role service can play in a company's success, your company will break from the pack. You can charge a premium to a discerning clientele, like Singapore Airlines, or you can attract more customers at slightly higher but still price-competitive rates, like Ace Hardware.

Show us a leader who fails to grasp this, and we'll show you—well, we'll show you most leaders. And that's a shame. It's bad for customers, which is demoralizing for staff, which is *really* bad for shareholders.

When Bruce Nordstrom was asked who trained his department store's legendary salespeople, he replied, "Their parents."

Did your parents teach *you* customer service? Did the parents of your current core team, the members of your internal OPEN community, teach *them* customer service?

As you build and expand your team, make a commitment to customer service a priority on par with passion, the willingness to mentor, and the existence of an OPEN community. Want to instill a customer-first culture in your company? Want to have that culture praised on social media by advocates, champions, and ambassadors?

Own it. Make it your focus. Lead by example.

Because customer service is—first, last, and only—a *leadership* issue.

## WHO LEADS BY EXAMPLE?

So which leaders, and which organizations, are using customer service as a true Social Age differentiator? Let's take a look at a few savvy companies that use social to strengthen their existing, customer-first business models—and that are certainly worthy of emulation.

(Pay close attention. This can take you from dinosaur to opposable thumbs in short order.)

We're going to start with Zappos, the online retailer we first discussed in Chapter 5. (What follows is why we're convinced that Zappos was just having a bad day when Ted tried to buy new shoes.)

This thirteen-year-old company does one of the most unremarkable tasks in retail: It sells shoes and clothing online.

It and 20,000 other companies, right?

*How* Zappos does it, however, is already the stuff of legend. Paramount among the company's innovations is encouraging every employee—*every single one*—to become an ambassador for the brand. Yes, Zappos offers Twitter training to every staffer. The only limiting rule? As Zappos' social media policy states:

*Be real and use good judgment.*

Really? A six-word policy on social media? Twenty-four letters?

It takes fourteen words and seventy-four characters for most companies to add the disclaimer "Tweets are my own and do not necessarily reflect my employer's opinions" to the end of their employees' Twitter profiles as insisted on by their social media policy. (What was your organization's answer to Ted's second question from Chapter 11? How many words are in *your* company's social media policy? Or should we ask how many *pages* are in it? Enough said, right?)

How does Zappos translate this tweetable policy into everyday practice? The simple answer is culture, which begins with who leads the company and who it hires. As we also discussed in Chapter 11, get the right ambassadors on board, train them within your culture with a clear focus on the mission, and they'll do the right thing.

A more detailed version goes something like this . . .

Longtime CEO Tony Hsieh realizes some things about social media that any company's leadership, from entry-level to the C-suite, would be wise to understand. For one, he knows:

*More social. Less media.*

Tony Hsieh is all about being *social* and not at all about the *media*. Broadcasting canned messages isn't social, nor does it provide good service; it's just self-serving. He doesn't want Zapponians (his staff) to be salesy or corporate. He just wants them to be who they are ("real"), and to engage folks online in an authentic manner rather than a stiff, needy, cheesy, or blatantly commission-driven way. The last thing he wants is for their tweets to read as if they've been written by a public relations committee. Or HR. Or legal. Or him.

Tony Hsieh gets the concept of OPEN.

Tony has known from the dawn of the social revolution that people love these new media tools, and he understands that his Zapponians are no exception. They're going to be online anyway, and—because it is his obsession to make it so—his team members love their jobs and the company.

So if his people love their company, and if they're going to be on social media anyway, and if his customers are also on social media . . . lightbulb! It just makes sense to let his people share their love of their company with customers present and future, online, right where they choose to spend their time. Doesn't it?

Ambassadors. Each one of them.

Tony Hsieh didn't have to be a genius to come up with this winning formula. He *did* have to be a leader who does more than just think "outside the box." Rather, his attitude is closer to "Box? What's a box?" He didn't invent a new product. He doesn't have a million patents. But he's an innovator in that he has built a company on bedrocks of morale, trust, and *service*.

This is key to leadership in a world gone social!

You don't have to be an innovator at all. Your company doesn't have to develop the proverbial better mousetrap. To build a customer-first culture—and to thrive in the Social Age—you just have to walk in Tony Hsieh's shoes for a bit. Take what he has done at Zappos, and make it your own.

By the way, Tony Hsieh believes so much in the long-term value of a customer-first culture that he pays new employees to leave, should they decide the culture isn't for them. He offers $3,000 to them to leave the company rather than work in an environment that's not for them—$3,000 to quit.

Brilliant, right?

## "DO YOU TWEET?"

As a clothing retailer, Zappos sells to the general public: It's a B2C, or business-to-consumer, company. If a B2C uses Twitter and other social media platforms to engage with customers, maybe that isn't such a hard sell to the dinosaur crowd; they might understand the potential. As we've already learned, the population of current and potential customers already engaging on social networks is now well over 2 billion (yes, billion, with a *b*). With a market that size, there's got to be return on investing at least a portion of your company's energy in social channels.

But what about B2B, or business-to-business, firms?

If your potential market is minuscule, perhaps in the thousands instead of billions, does it make any sense to spend time and resources on social? Can the Social Age enable your company to excel? This far into *A World Gone Social,* these are still completely valid questions.

So we asked Vala Afshar, the chief marketing officer of Extreme Networks—and the "Twitter sourcing specialist" from Chapter 11—for his thoughts.

Disclosure: Mark and Ted knew full well that Vala himself is quite active on Twitter. After all, that's how we met him. But we never really noticed him bragging about his company or trying to sell anything, to anyone, online. Maybe, like Mark and Ted, he tweeted mostly just to learn and engage—to develop his OPEN community rather than for work or profits?

Wrong. Vala is no fool. Vala is OPEN, but he has more than one motive in play for most things he does. Learning and engaging? Absolutely. But Vala is also online to meet potential customers—namely, the CIOs of other companies.

"When there are CIOs out there who find you interesting," he explained, "eventually they find your company interesting, too."

Food for thought? Let's hope so.

And just for the record: There's nothing phony or mercenary about Vala, so please don't take that statement out of context. As with many of the most successful people we know, Vala doesn't like CIOs and other people because it's good for business. He's good at business because he likes people.

When we caught up for an interview, Vala gave us some remarkable insight about how his organization makes use of both internal collaboration tools and social media, most notably Twitter. Rather than just explain it, Vala gave us a real-world example from earlier that week, when Enterasys hosted a Twitter chat.

During the chat, Phil Komarny, the chief information officer at Seton Hall University, and one of Vala's customers, shared this tweet:

*@ValaAfshar You have become the new standard of expectation when I work with other vendors. "Do you Tweet?" [is] one of my first questions!*

How about that?

Social media wasn't just helping Enterasys build deeper relationships with its customers. Because of how well Vala engages, he actually reset his customers' expectations for his—and his organization's—basic service. He has spoiled his clients rotten—and spoiled the idea that his customers, at some point, would jump over to other, less social, competitors.

Says Vala, "I have seen satisfied customers buy from my competition, even after they bought from my company. So I can't afford satisfied customers. I want *engaged* customers."

If you're skeptical about the notion that anyone in the C-suite is capable of consistently driving engagement through Twitter (where *does* he find the time!?), you ain't seen nothing yet.

As we learned when we talked about building a team in the Social Age, every member of Vala's team is social. But there's more . . .

Have you heard of machine-to-machine (M2M) communication? You know, that Jetsons-esque technology that has your refrigerator telling your grocer when you're out of milk? We are all the Jetsons now: That technology exists today—at Extreme Networks.

The company's equipment does M2M, but it also does one better: *M2Social.*

*More (machine) social. Less media.*

Its equipment uses Twitter, Facebook, or Chatter to report a problem even before customers have detected an issue. That report shows up on the Chatter dashboard at Extreme, accessible by everyone at the company—not just the engineers, but Vala, the CEO, and everyone else actively listening.

Vala shared a real-life example from an experience with the same customer, Seton Hall:

► A screen shot showed the equipment's report, in everyday English. Basically, it was "Help me, I'm broken."

► The engineer quickly fixed the issue remotely (the repair command showed up as simple English in the Chatter stream as well; no codes to decipher).

► On his end, Seton Hall's engineer replied that he was aware of the break (and of the prompt fix by the team at Extreme).

► Seton Hall's CIO "liked" the service, just as you would a post on Facebook.

► The CEO on Vala's end also "liked" it, which we're certain impressed both the customer and Extreme's engineer. (In the Engagement Era, instant recognition from the brass is something we could use more of, right?)

All of this happened via a social network, in plain English. As Vala says:

*The future is social, and it's already here.*

Remarkable, isn't it? Not just the technology. Not just the amazing service. Not just the social engagement. Remarkable is how the technology, service, humans, and social are all integrated, seamlessly—and intentionally.

The future *is* here.

## CAN SOCIAL SAVE A CRAPPY BRAND?

Can social save a brand that has a terrible reputation? Or that customers think so little of that their attitude is far too frequently described as "hate"?

In that environment, can one customer-focused social leader make a real difference?

Whenever we mention the word *Comcast* in speaking engagements or workshops, a pause is required to give the audience the chance to guffaw, elbow each other in the ribs, and trade horror stories. If ever a brand were capable of being hated, Comcast is it—or, at least, that's what public opinion polls show year after year, right there with AT&T, American Airlines, and Bank of America.

Why, then, do we use this firm to illustrate a tale of customer loyalty?

Let us introduce you to Frank Eliason, formerly the smiling face behind the Twitter handle @ComcastCares.

Eliason's journey from Six Sigma black belt and executive adviser to one of the world's most famous social media managers is more than interesting, especially considering the fact that he stumbled upon Twitter almost by accident.

And in so doing he transformed how businesses can—and do—use social.

The first thing Eliason did when he set up his Twitter account? He pioneered what is now standard operating procedure with any OPEN-minded customer experience team: He listened in to the comments being made about Comcast, his new employer at the time.

*More social. Less media.*

The results didn't surprise him in any way. Comcast was living up to its reputation; the situation wasn't good. What did pleasantly surprise him is what happened when he took the next logical step and started communicating with those disgruntled customers. It turns out they didn't *want* to hate their cable/Internet/phone provider, so from Eliason's first gesture on, they were convinced that Comcast genuinely wanted to help (even though there was no prior evidence to support that new position since, to that moment, no help had ever come from this company).

So that he could help them with their specific problem, Eliason invited unhappy customers to move from social to the phone or e-mail. The solutions typically came quickly and thoroughly; in the process, a relationship developed organically. There was nothing manipulative about his work, no tricks up his sleeve.

He sought to help his customers.

Without permission, process, or policy.

He just *served*—because, as a human being, he knew it was the right thing to do.

The company recognized the value Eliason provided. Comcast granted him the budget to build a small team. Before he brought team members on board, though, something interesting happened—something that illustrates the compelling power of goodwill, both goodwill earned and goodwill granted.

As you may know now, Twitter is the perfect medium for someone who literally only has thirty seconds to perform a task. You can check your phone and read a few tweets on the way from your desk to the elevator, for instance.

As soon as he woke up at five o'clock in the morning, and throughout the day until bedtime, Eliason checked what people were saying about Comcast. Weekends included. Each time a Comcast customer tweeted a problem, Eliason reached out and tried to help or asked one of the customer service reps to help. He expedited service requests that otherwise might have taken days, even a week or more, to resolve. In the process, Eliason built up a tremendous amount of goodwill among Comcast's customers on Twitter.

Then he took a Sunday off, to mark the passing of one of his daughters a few years before and to celebrate the birthday of another. As you can imagine, it was a very emotional time for Eliason. Even though one day previously, on his blog, he had explained his upcoming absence to his customers, he cringed at the thought of what might happen while he was away.

That Sunday came. And despite the promises he'd made to himself, Eliason occasionally succumbed to habit: Throughout the day he checked the activity on the Comcast tweet stream.

Eliason was stunned.

"As I expected," he said, "Sunday morning's tweets started with the usual dissatisfied customers griping about their problems with Comcast."

"Of course," he added, "a few weeks of my jumping in to help didn't change the fundamental, systemic problems, like an available service window of only nine hours for a twenty-four-hour product—that type of thing. When you want your Internet, you want it now. And you don't want to take a whole day off from work waiting for the repairman. We hadn't solved those problems."

Eliason paused. His face showed that what he was about to say still choked him up a bit.

"But very quickly that morning, some of my 'regulars' jumped in. They explained my absence and asked that people give me a break, which they did—people were very understanding. And they helped each other, too, fielding questions for another customer, that type of thing. It was just . . . great."

Did one man's tweets change the customers' impression of a previously despised company? Not nearly. We repeat: This is a business book, not a Disney movie! But look at what *did* happen.

A *community* happened. A community focused on a common mission, and maybe even a passion. A passion *for Frank Eliason*.

Because Eliason had jumped into the online discussion his customers were having, because he helped them with their problems and gave a warm, sincere face to his company, he built more goodwill and customer engagement than *any* amount of advertising could buy.

Eliason, without a budget, strategy, or approval from the legal department, went social.

Even among his peers, Frank Eliason is one man in a million, taking his place as a social legend. He was a social leader, even though for some time at Comcast he had no team and he managed no one.

A personal note about Eliason—or, rather, a personal branding note about him: Remember that we said social is tied to not only the brands of organizations but to our personal brands? Eliason is now an author, and due in large part to his pioneering work at Comcast, he landed the role of senior vice president at Citi.

Nice work, Frank.

How would your company benefit from a trailblazer like Frank Eliason? How could you follow in his footsteps to break new ground, leveraging social to wow your customers. How about a team of Eliasons, working outside current restrictive policies—without worrying about "how it's always been done"—and saving your organization a bagful of gold, and perhaps thousands of customers, one at a time?

# BUILDING A CULTURE OF SERVICE

Perhaps by now you're thinking to yourself, "You know, I'm convinced: We've gotta get us some service superstars like Vala Afshar and Frank Eliason and Tim McDonald and all of Tony's Zapponians! How do we train our people to be like that?"

Whoa there, Tiger! Remember what Bruce Nordstrom said about employees with an amazing service ethic and who trained them?

*"Their parents."* You can't train people to *care*. So what do you do instead?

Turn your company into a talent magnet: Attract the best and repel the rest.

But how? Every leader wants to attract and retain only the most talented individuals in their field, right? Don't you have to pay more if you want only the best?

Maybe. In general, we humans equate pay with respect—that is, the better employees are paid, the more they feel valued by their employer. Surely that's one of the methods VALV[E]'s Gabe Newell uses to land and keep only the best.

On the other hand . . .

On the other hand, think of a start-up. Both of your authors are immersed in that world, so we see this routinely: Many start-ups pay much less than what a person could make at a legacy corporation, yet start-ups quite frequently attract the most self-motivated superstars in the job market. Is this all a case of *deferred* pay, working for the day of the initial public offering when (if things go well—a huge "if") the first employees will cash in their stock options to become multimillionaires? Again, maybe.

But there's more . . .

For years now, motivation researchers have published study after study warning that "incentive" pay just isn't that effective at incentivizing anything.

How many years has this research and publishing been going on? The psychological researcher Abraham Maslow introduced the world to his hierarchy of needs all the way back in 1943. Pay—and the stuff we buy with it, such as food, shelter, and other needs and wants—is way down near the bottom of the list of what actually incentivizes employees. Yes, adequate pay is *necessary* to attract talent—it's a threshold issue, to start the recruiting conversation—but it is far from *sufficient*. Talented, customer-centric employees—employees who genuinely care—need more from their work than just pay, even lavish pay.

Much higher on Maslow's list of needs? Meaning. Purpose. Emotional satisfaction.

Pride.

And few things instill pride in people more than truly experiencing genuine value from their organization. Not hearing it, mind you, but actually *experiencing* the value, personally.

Which is how HCLT's CEO, Vineet Nayar, turned his company from a $700 million also-ran into a $4.7 *billion* icon, in just a few years.

In 2005, HCLT was at an inflection point. On its current trajectory, yes, it was growing, but its competitors, including the global consulting giants Genpact and Tata, were growing much faster and attracting the top talent in India and from around the world. Nayar stood at the proverbial Rubicon, with a life-or-death decision to make:

Radical transformation, or slow and painful death?

Nayar chose life, and success, and, well, HCLT doesn't have any trouble competing for the best talent any longer. The secret? It all boils down to the company's core principle, which is actually deeply embedded in all of its operational processes:

*Employees first, customers second.*

Yes, you read that right.

Nayar put his employees—most notably, those in direct contact with the customers (what he dubbed "the Value Zone")—ahead of everyone, including stockholders, management ("the Supporting Functions"), and himself as CEO (a Supporting Function).

Yes, the way employees in the Value Zone are treated comes even before the way HCLT's customers are treated. Every time.

Right about here is where our audience starts to look uncomfortable. They begin to shift in their seats. This is where the hands always go up: "If you put your employees ahead of your customers," we're asked, "doesn't that make customer service much, um, *worse?*"

Of course it does—if "employees first" means anarchy. But remember in Chapter 8, when we examined how organizations that self-manage hold employees much more accountable for tangible business results than your typical Industrial Age organization? Flat management brings with it more personal responsibility to the company and the customer, not less. Well, HCLT is not flat, but its upside-down hierarchy, with the CEO at the bottom and the workers in the Value Zone at the top, follows many of the same principles as those discussed in Chapter 8.

It isn't "Employees first, tough luck for everyone else."

Rather, "Employees first, customers second" (or EFCS, as HCLT refers to its core policy) recognizes this basic reality: Culture is 98 percent of what matters at work. Leadership? Service? Each is maybe 1 percent of the equation. Using the formula we presented earlier, modified to reflect this approach:

*Leadership (1%) + Culture (98%) + Service (1%) = Profits*
*(100% of what allows our company to stay in business)*

What most leaders might have a hard time accepting, of course, is that they have no direct impact on profits (look at where leaders are in that equation; there's a whole lot between them and the money their companies make, isn't there?). When you think of it from a different perspective, whereby all a leader *can* influence is culture, this makes a great deal of sense. Yet what is the thing most leaders focus on? What makes them scramble to make those quarterly reports look as shiny as possible? Profits. How does that make any sense?

Chase profits and watch them retreat into the distance, like one of those highway mirages on a hot summer's day that makes you squint and look again.

Here's what effective leaders in the Social Age know:

*Customer experience determines long-term profits.*

Done right, customers will love your brand well enough to stick with you through thick and thin. They'll brag about you on social so much that they'll act as a huge, ultra-effective extension of your paid sales force. They'll happily bring you their friends. Your delighted customers will grow your company—and your profits as a result.

They are OPEN Shangri-la: the brand ambassadors.

Done poorly? Even satisfactory yet uninspiring service (maybe a 6 on a scale of 0 to 10) earns you apathy—and you can no longer survive on customers who feel nothing when they think of your brand.

Remember what Vala Afshar said about merely satisfied customers walking toward a competitor for a cheaper offer? Happens all the time. Yet this is where most companies live: the indifferent middle. They compete on price to keep their market share—a sure race to the bottom. At the very least, each of those emotionally uncommitted customers represents an anchor over the side of your ship, not stopping you dead in the water perhaps, but slowing your forward progress—forcing you to spend more would-be profits on advertising to convince potential customers that you, well, aren't that bad. Not great. Just not as bad as they might expect.

Not a great value proposition, is it? An even worse business model. And pretty much the worst possible culture.

## HOW TO WIN THE CULTURE GAME

So if culture is 98 percent of what matters in business, what's a leader to do in order to craft a culture of customer delight? How do we consistently put the customer experience first?

We recommend you start here, with some tips from some of the most beloved leaders and brands we know, all of which were providing amazing customer service well before the world went social (because one day there won't be any such a thing as *"social* customer service," there will only be "customer service").

► **Put employees first** | Don't just put employees before your customers, though. As you move toward a flat management style, perhaps as an interim step place your employees before management! Flip your org chart. Refer to your management bureaucracy as the "supporting functions." Start with the very top (now bottom) of your pyramid. Over several years and numerous missteps, HCLT invented, tested, and instituted processes to reinforce this shift within the company. Vision without reinforcement isn't culture change; it's a poster on a wall that nobody reads. If you're going to change, commit to the process and bring in the help you need to get there.

► **Trust your employees** | Don't just say it; do it. What is your social media policy, for instance? How open are your books? What's your policy on remote work? What kind of decisions can your frontline employees make on their own, without asking for permission? One company we love for this type of trust is Ritz-Carlton Hotels, which allows every single employee to spend up to $2,000 on a disgruntled guest without asking anyone. What would your employees do if they had that kind of discretion? Does the very thought give you cold sweats? Trust begets trust—and you, as a leader, must make the first move. Even before the Social Age, that is how trust always worked.

► **Celebrate service** | Leverage exemplary service by putting shining examples on a pedestal; share stories of team members going above and way beyond. Nordstrom calls these "Heroics," and the company collects the most extraordinary in a newsletter it circulates to all its locations as well as via internal social media. With ease, you can do the same by investing in employee recognition collaboration tools. Jostle or Achievers are two great resources that share a common goal: the immediacy of recognition. You don't have to wait till the end of the month to publish heroic stories; appreciation happens on the fly, all day long, companywide. With either of these tools, celebrations aren't led by management; employees are empowered to recognize each other. In the days of "flat," how smart is building morale and reinforcing desired behavior from a peer-to-peer perspective?

► **Hire for a passion for service** | Bruce Nordstrom wasn't just creating a crispy sound bite when he came up with that line about parents being the providers of organic customer service training. Some people live to serve. Others, well, don't. Yes, you can train technique. But you can't make people care. You must hire those who clearly demonstrate a customer-first approach to their work.

▶ **Astonish by exceeding expectations** | When customers walk into The Container Store, they are met with the "man in the desert" approach: They don't just need a drink of water, they need an entire solution that enables them to get where they are ultimately trying to go. The Container Store believes one *great* person—the champion—is equal to three *good* people. It considers quality communication to be the core of leadership. The company lives by these and other "Foundation Principles" every time it hires a new team member or greets a customer. One of its main goals is to make customers so happy they dance inside their new home office, pantry, or walk-in closet. Yes, dancing—how's that for a Social Age metric?

▶ **Engage!** | Across the board, JetBlue gets high marks for customer experience, proactive communication, and exceeding expectations. That is its brand strategy—and it executes this well. Clearly, that execution has carried over into the company's work on social media as well. JetBlue's Twitter account is renowned for quick response times, empathetic tweets, and solution-oriented communications. When critical weather reports or air traffic control issues cause widespread delays or cancellations, JetBlue institutes an "all hands on deck" type of response whereby all available personnel go from whatever they were doing to serving stranded travelers.

Want to transform culture?
Live the culture you want to instill—online and off.
Then defend that culture as a mother bear would her cub.
In business, culture isn't everything—it's just everything that *matters*.

## BARELY SCRATCHING THE SURFACE

The incidents shared so far in this chapter illustrate what is barely the tip of a massive shift toward the customer in the Social Age—how business is done in a world gone social.

Customers are connected in a way that was unimaginable only a few years ago. They are discovering new ways of communicating with each other, sharing the best and worst treatment they experience with everyone who will listen.

Mind you, customers are only *starting* to flex their new muscles provided by social media. With examples like Zappos, Extreme Networks, and even Comcast to inspire us, who's to say what the future holds—what is in store for the organization that actively listens? What can a company that deliberately pursues an OPEN state of mind accomplish?

Not everyone, as we already know, will embrace these new models. They will do only what is mandated according to the minimum requirements of their employers. They will not find passion in their work; they will remain disengaged; they will not contribute to a positive culture within their company.

And that is terrific news for social leaders like Tony Hsieh, Vala Afshar, and Frank Eliason.

And you.

It is clear what is happening here. In the Social Age, customers do hold all the cards. The voices of employees are amplified, and the ears and eyes of potential team members are wide open.

The opportunity has become apparent.

On the one hand, there are the laggard firms that have no idea how to be social, or what it even means: the dinosaurs.

On the other hand, there are a few enterprising, savvy business leaders who get it—those who are jumping at the chance to shake up their markets. To bring the metaphor full circle, we'll refer to these bright individuals as the ones with opposable thumbs.

They are the ones not just watching the social revolution happen but serving as leaders during what can only be considered a transformational time.

All enabled by social media.

And that is an absolutely essential point: Social media in and of itself is not the story here. Social *is* the enabler, the catalyst of change. For generations, customers who have suffered through the arrogant and ignorant examples of poor customer service have been dying for a way to redress ills, to interact in a meaningful—human—way with the brands in which they choose to invest, emotionally and financially.

Social media merely gives these customers—these revolutionaries—the tools they've been hoping for, that's all.

Meanwhile, on the company side, there have always been strivers eager to shake up the status quo, to lock their existing customers in for life through deeper, more meaningful relationships, and to snatch away the customers of their more complacent rivals. Social didn't invent that desire, not nearly.

Social just made it more likely that the mission of these ambitious disrupters would succeed.

We admit, however: A portion of this may not accurately display the conviction required to make this transformation happen at your organization.

While nothing could sound simpler than building a socially enabled team, creating a top-down, customer-first culture, and hiring people you trust and then trusting your people to, as Zappos puts it, "be real and use good judgment," there's a vast gulf between *simple* (uncomplicated) and *easy* (done with little effort).

As we've mentioned throughout *A World Gone Social*, there's *nothing* easy about giving up the command-and-control method of leadership that worked so efficiently in the twentieth century and entering the Social Age. Then again, Henry Ford never took the easy route the last time one business era ended and another began. Based on the fact that you are reading this book and are ready to lead real change, neither will you.

But here's the thing: The efficiency Henry Ford and other industrialists brought to the modern workplace is no longer a differentiator. To have survived our recent, lingering recession, within the confines of what they learned during the Industrial Age, nearly all companies are more efficient to one degree or another than they've ever been before; efficiency is just table stakes in our new economy.

In the Social Age, the primary differentiator is the *human* difference. And the best possible method of showing your customers you believe in the human side of business is to treat them like humans who have already invested themselves in your brand—and who deserve your care.

To round out this chapter, and to inspire you to create impact at your company, we'll leave you with this.

When asked the secret to his company's success in the movie industry, Walt Disney said, simply:

*Do what you do so well they will want to see it again. . . .*

To inspire you to make a genuine difference to your customers, and with only the greatest respect for Mr. Disney, we'll alter those words slightly for the Social Age:

*Do what you do so well they will want to* share *it again.*

In Chapter 13, we'll bring you into the area of social that even many of the most rigid old-schoolers, assuming decent ROI exists, are willing to at least explore: social media marketing.

We'll talk about profound changes in the world of marketing in the Social Age—changes you, as a social leader, must understand. We'll also discuss both the traps of treating social media as another broadcast channel and how best to leverage social to the benefit of all stakeholders in your organization.

CHAPTER 13

# And Stop Calling Me
# "Social Media Marketing"!

*Half the money I spend on advertising is wasted;*
*the trouble is, I don't know which half.*
—*John Wanamaker*

*Social media marketing.*

Say those words, and most are apt to think of the sliver of the marketing department's budget dedicated to advertising campaigns on Facebook, flashy broadcast-style videos on YouTube, and a community manager and interns working the corporate Twitter account. Throw in some thought-provoking, cute, and/or inspirational pictures on Instagram and some infographics on Pinterest, and we have ourselves a "social media marketing" strategy.

*Wrong.*

Wrong, wrong, wrong—wrong! Not even close.

(Wow, that felt great to say.)

Your authors see this all day long, and it's, well, it's stunning, really—in a mind-numbing way.

A company gets on Twitter and sends out links to coupons or to the brand's website, or it shares news about products. And it counts Twitter followers. The company asks you to like it on Facebook, where it features gimmicks to get you to like it more. And it counts likes. The same happens on Pinterest, Instagram, Foursquare, Empire Avenue, and LinkedIn groups.

This happens not because a random person's follow, like, pin, or friend request is going to convert to a sale but because some old-schooler up the ladder, using antiquated metrics to determine ROI, is counting those follows and likes and comparing the follows and likes from this month to last month's. A downward dip is considered failure.

When "failure" occurs, big marketing dollars are spent on overpriced consultancies and some of those Madison Avenue agencies (which then outsource to the overpriced consultancies). The consultants, ninjas, gurus, and agencies promise to deliver social campaigns destined to go viral.

But they don't.

(Well, unless you're Old Spice—which nailed it.)

So we're back to counting follows and likes, and broadcasting instead of engaging, and pretty soon someone says, "Social isn't working for us."

That, to most old-schoolers, is considered social media marketing.

They are measuring the wrong things.

They are judging success by the wrong metrics.

So what is marketing in the Social Age, if it isn't "social media marketing"? If likes and follows don't really count or convert? And if you have a better chance of getting hit by a bus *on* Madison Avenue than having a campaign *from* Madison Avenue go viral?

## SOCIAL MEDIA MARKETING IS . . . MARKETING

Until the qualifier at the front of "social media marketing" (SMM) is removed—which, we understand, won't happen until we're a bit further into the Social Age—it may be best to think of the process of using social and digital media to market your brand's products and services as . . .

Marketing (M).

And, like any other endeavor, marketing starts with a plan.

A company we advise struggled consistently with this idea. Social, it thought, was different. There was no media buy. No agency or schedule. No scripts, proofs, or comps. The concept of marketing online was well outside this company's comfort zone.

The reality was, though, that most of those items they wanted to check off their marketing to-do list existed on social.

▶ **Media buy** | With every marketing plan, decisions must be made on where to invest the resources, where to get the biggest bang for the buck. Television, print, radio, direct mail, billboards—many choices existed for the savvy Industrial Age marketer. Today, those choices are replaced, or augmented, with just as many choices on the social side: Facebook, Twitter, Pinterest, and so on. Rule No. 3 from Chapter 5, "Meet customers where they are now," has never been more important than in the Social Age. A more-than-obvious example: If your brand wants to attract Millennials to an urban-themed event downtown, you probably wouldn't waste a whole lot of marketing dollars on a rural newspaper, right?

► **No agency** | SMM is the hot new toy, so the number of agencies—both traditional and those that specialize in social—is staggering. When making a service bureau decision, remember these points: (1) There is almost nothing an agency can do for you that a small, customer-first team can't do in-house (and, let's face it, your agency is going to do a very poor job of serving your customers); and (2) as occurs often in the traditional agency model, the agency is going to outsource your SMM to a small house that specializes in social—and add up to a 300 percent markup. If you're concerned about ROI from social (or know a dinosaur CEO who is), a traditional agency may not be the best way to go.

► **No schedule** | Wrong! Deciding the best time of day to post, tweet, blog, and promote your brand is one of the most critical decisions you'll make. Just as you wouldn't normally run a television commercial for an early-bird dinner special after the restaurant has closed for the night, you should schedule your social media presence when most of the demographic you want to attract is online. (We'll discuss the tools that help make these decisions in Chapter 14.)

► **No scripts, proofs, or comps** | The most important aspect of a planned marketing campaign on social—just like any other marketing campaign—is relevant copy that draws an emotional response and a clear call to action. With one very important distinction, social is certainly no different. In traditional marketing, your copy and call to action may be transactional in nature and based on a sense of urgency, convenience, or price. On social, your copy is most likely going to be designed to drive traffic to a website, build credibility, and be far more conversational—engaging—in tone. To accomplish that, as for any other marketing campaign, the goals must be clear, the expectations must be set, and the copy scripted, and proofed, accordingly.

As you can see, there are far more commonalities between traditional marketing and SMM. And—just like traditional marketing—it all starts with a plan that serves your goals (as well as your OPEN community, customers, and potential customers) well.

One major difference we must emphasize here, and throughout this chapter: *Social media is not a digital megaphone.*

*More social. Less media.*

As we've learned throughout *A World Gone Social,* your task of leading your team into the Social Age focuses around engagement, building relationships, service of your current and potential customers, and expansion of your OPEN community.

To do that, trust must be established and then nourished so it thrives and deepens over time. In the Social Age more than ever in the history of business, when you lose trust, it ain't coming back in time to save your brand.

## TRUST IS THE NEW CURRENCY

Most of us grew up with advertisements broadcasting at us (yes, *at*, like an attack), so by now we're completely immune. We don't even notice. Sure, we laugh at a Super Bowl ad—yet we completely disregard, *or never even notice*, whatever brand the ad is shilling.

In the Social Age, broadcasting at our "friends" and "followers" is the opposite of trust. We expect more. We expect a brand to earn our trust through consistent quality, providing value beyond the product we ordered, for doing business with integrity—and, as we've learned throughout *A World Gone Social*—for doing something because it was *the right thing to do* versus adhering to some decades-old service policy.

As in real-life, person-to-person relationships, trust must be earned.

And that's where social comes in.

In the Social Age, word of mouth is what connected consumers listen to; it is what they believe. Really, that's what confuses so many broadcast marketers: Social isn't a new set of marketing channels to add to the list of old ones. Social is word of mouth on steroids, and then grown exponentially.

Social media = word of mouth. Full stop.

Word of mouth. Advocacy. Trust. Whatever name you give it, the principle is the same.

In the Social Age, it's how you build loyalty and increase market share.

But is trust *really* how we make our purchasing decisions?

## A NONTRUST STORY

Once upon a time, Ted had AT&T cell phone service—not because he trusted AT&T, but because way back when he and his wife, Jane, bought their first iPhones, AT&T and Verizon were the only two carriers (decision point: near-monopoly).

Ted's employer at the time also had a 20 percent off deal with AT&T (decision point: price).

So off he went to the Apple store, where Ted was offered two choices, and he chose the most discounted of the two (decision point: price).

Then Ted moved to a new neighborhood and quickly discovered that everyone in his area had to make calls outside their homes if they had AT&T. (True story, it's still that way today, four years later.)

Ted called AT&T, from his front yard. AT&T said it knew of no such problem, but if he liked, they made a signal-booster he could buy for about $100. Ted knew better and made the choice to leave AT&T (decision point: mistrust, compounded by obvious conflict of interest).

Ted asked his neighbors what carrier they had and if their cell phones worked *inside* their home. The neighbors had Verizon. He thought Verizon worked fine. Jane asked another neighbor. Verizon again.

Ted turned to Twitter:

*In Naples, Florida, who do you trust for good cell coverage?*

Verizon, again.

Ted and Jane signed up with Verizon (decision point: trust—of his neighbors and followers, not of either brand).

Haven't you lived a similar story?

Think about many of your recent purchases. Chances are, you bought a specific brand because a friend, either in person or through a post on Facebook or Twitter, displayed trust in that brand. For big-ticket items, didn't you hop online to read reviews from objective fellow consumers (albeit complete strangers) before you bought? The same pattern repeats itself with just about every other purchase:

► We read amateur reviews before buying books on Amazon, which smartly features its own thorough reviews.

► We look for opinions on Yelp before going to a new restaurant.

► We check Rotten Tomatoes to see what others think before seeing a movie.

► We peruse ratings on TripAdvisor, Expedia, or Kayak before reserving a hotel room (decision point: trust, with cost usually thrown in on the hotels, of course).

And besides all of the sites that supply these anonymous reviews, people also go online to discover what the influencers in their OPEN communities have to say. They flock to niche, tech, and "mommy" bloggers to read what they have to say (so much so that many brands court these opinion makers so they'll write (or vlog) favorably about their products.

What's "vlog?" That stands for "video blog," which folks have been doing for years, including now-bestselling author Gary Vaynerchuck, who took to promoting his parents' wine store through vlogging back in the early Web 1.0 days, before the

Social Age was even under way. Back then, and several bestselling books ago, Gary felt he was not a strong writer; blogging did not come naturally to him. Instead, he set up an inexpensive camera in his office and tasted the different wine sold in his family's store, uploading his episodes to YouTube. Good, bad, or indifferent, his audience got it straight from Gary, and they loved him for it—Gary's energy is contagious, and his unscripted presentations were a refreshing change from the utterly biased broadcast ads available on TV from wine companies themselves (wine buying decision point: trust).

Opinion perceived as objective commentary, whether it is in written form on a blog, in video form on a vlog on YouTube, or via photo with a link on Pinterest, the trick is . . . no tricks. In the Social Age, real people trust other real people. Marketing, controlled messaging, advertising—or any canned, biased, Industrial Age presentation of the brand—is no longer as relevant to consumers connected by social.

Smart companies have already caught on.

For instance, when Virgin Airlines wanted to introduce new flights to Toronto, it was socially savvy enough to fill a plane with bloggers and social media influencers active in the travel space. In hopes that those bloggers and early adopters of social would tell their fan base about the experience, the company rolled out the red carpet treatment. And the bloggers blogged, and the social influencers tweeted and posted. A new segment of Virgin was launched, complete with testimonials from real and trusted people (albeit with champagne and caviar hangovers).

(Decision point for next purchase of airline tickets to Toronto *or anywhere else Virgin flies*: trust.)

## THE POWER OF CONTENT

Virgin's creative use of bloggers is only the tip of the iceberg when it comes to content marketing. In fact, saying "content is king" is more than a cliché, it is a Social Age cold, hard fact.

Some industries will always benefit from Industrial Age broadcast advertising. Everyone buys ketchup, for example, so a captivating television commercial, *especially when combined with a clever Facebook campaign,* can pay off.

Another example: Infomercials may sell ShamWows by the millions to insomniacs late at night, but connected consumers and businesspeople who are responsible for making good, well-researched business decisions are a different audience. They don't take kindly to being yelled *at*—and, from our experience, it seems they rarely impulse buy, no matter how many "But wait, there's more!" pitches are thrown in their direction, and no matter how sexy the accent of the person screaming at them. They buy smart from people they trust; they think long term.

Yet thousands of organizations, when they saw the power of social media, simply took their traditional selling model and went to broadcast on social. And failed. Miserably.

Why doesn't this old-school selling process work in the Social Age?

First, because not many enterprises sell ketchup. Or ShamWows. Nor do small, innovative companies pushing a new technology, purpose-driven niche businesses trying to gain traction, or B2Bs with a finite list of potential customers. This model never really did work for these organizations (although many tried).

Second, this approach simply doesn't work with socially enabled buyers. They don't fall for infomercials disguised as content; they know when a blog has been developed as yet another broadcasting channel to help the company rather than the reader. They know better, and they do not like to be *sold at*. No trust develops. In fact, socially aware consumers will then reach out to their OPEN community and let the world know how they disliked the experience with the brand.

This is the opposite of *selling*.

In a world gone social, this is *repelling*.

(We advise firms on this for a living, and we've seen blogs—and blogging strategies—in which the misuse of content marketing makes us shudder in disbelief.)

## HOW CONTENT MARKETING REALLY WORKS

Unlike the broadcast marketing we all grew up with in the Industrial Age, organizations in the Social Age build trust and credibility through content marketing. Done right, here's how it works:

1. A company provides information (content) and thus establishes credibility and expertise in its field.

2. Through that credibility—and a distinct lack of active selling—trust is established.

3. Once trust is established, and with a light touch (softly, gently, *professionally*), the company introduces the solutions it provides to fix the challenges faced by the reader.

Easy? No.

Effective? *Yes!*

Just ask global IT services and software giant SAP. As it entered the Social Age, the company realized it faced many of the challenges discussed so far in this chapter:

► A finite number of potential buyers

► Well-informed, connected customers

► The need to provide value (and, in the process, dutifully avoid a sales pitch)

► The necessity to build long-term, mutually beneficial relationships

► The desire to generate trust and build credibility

SAP's solution: Start a blog.

And not just any blog but a blog that adds extreme value to the leaders and potential leaders from within the IT industry who might, someday, buy from SAP. Which means SAP's Business Innovation blog isn't just an ordinary platform for an SAP engineer to drone on about his cool new product or how an SAP customer benefited from an SAP product sold by a great SAP sales team. No selling. No pitches or accented screams of "But wait, there's more!"

The savvy marketer behind SAP's Business Innovation blog is Michael Brenner, VP of marketing and content strategy for the entire brand, globally. He started the blog a couple of years ago with the mandate to establish SAP as a trusted source for thought leadership in an area relevant to SAP's customers and (more important) to *potential* customers.

The first wise decision he made?

Don't just offer another source of IT information—that's been done, *a lot.*

In fact, many of the publishing giants that serve the information technology industry—which combined to generate $3.7 trillion in revenue in 2013 alone—make a living doing just that. There was no way any little team Brenner assembled was going to be able to go up against *Information Week,* CIO.com, *CIO Insight, Computer World*—you get the idea.

Besides, even if they *were* downright saintly about it and followed every unwritten rule of OPEN, who would consider SAP to be unbiased when writing about the IT scene? Reporting on any of its products unfavorably would undermine the company's own position, of course. But not being objective would cause massive distrust.

But what about another topic near and dear to every CIO and his or her peers and boss as well—innovation?

Brenner saw enough of an opening in that arena. And he went for it.

That decision considerably broadened the topics SAP could offer on the blog. After all, innovation isn't just products and services. Innovation is exploring new ways of doing things. And that goes well beyond the topic of IT.

So Brenner and his team set out to provide value to those interested in everything that falls under the huge umbrella that covers innovation. Not just products and technology solutions but value in the form of expert advice on business trends and objective examination of case studies. The blog also featured inspiration on critical issues such as leadership, employee engagement, customer engagement, company culture, and even social media's role in how business is done in the twenty-first century.

For SAP's customers and potential customers, Brenner generated nearly instant trust—and immediate credibility.

We first interviewed Brenner for this book in the middle of 2013, so we checked in with him one last time before going to print in 2014. This is just a small part of what he told us:

> *Our 2013 final numbers were off the charts. 400% growth in users. 4,000% growth in conversions and we maintained high engagement and a strong and quantifiable ROI. 2013 was a great year!*

Conversions?

Those are blog readers who are converted from mere readers into buyers of SAP services. Remember, that's the point.

Content marketing isn't a public service; it's a savvy marketing channel. A *very* savvy channel, because it's based on providing value up front, building reputation and trust, and from there—finally—turning members of OPEN into customers.

As Gary Vaynerchuck puts it in his third book, content marketing is "Jab, Jab, Jab, Right Hook." As Gary explained on *The Human Side*, Ted's TV show, that means "Give, Give, Give, then Ask." Gary's area of expertise is marketing via social media, and with more than 1 million followers on Twitter and a thriving social media agency, he knows what he's talking about:

1. Give a bunch.

2. Provide value plenty.

3. Earn the right to ask for the sale.

4. Ask.

That is how content marketing works—when it works well.

Michael Brenner and his staff are relentless givers. From the content they feature, they provide value multiple times each day. That value is an invitation to join the community and, in many cases, SAP's OPEN circles. When mutually beneficial relationships have been built, the "ask" seems natural.

From there, a sale is almost inevitable, isn't it?

Just a few years into its existence, SAP's blog is returning measurable ROI—the

Holy Grail of marketing, something that need no longer be a crapshoot as it was for John Wanamaker. With this measurable success in hand, these days Brenner and his staff do more than write their own content and curate posts from other blogs. Today, you'll find original guest posts on the site as well, a savvy move that has led to even more readership, more engagement, and more trust.

Today, SAP's Business Innovation blog is a standard-bearer for enterprise-level blogs. It features original content from in-house contributors as well as curating the best posts from many related blogs. It is consistent, promotes effectively via social media (where SAP's official Twitter account, for instance, bears the photo of Lindsey LaManna, the person tweeting for the company, rather than a logo), and—most important—it adds value to the lives and work of its readers.

That is how business is done in a world gone social.

## CONTENT MARKETING WORTHY OF EMULATION

SAP isn't the only company using content marketing to great benefit. Six years into the Social Age, companies from mom-and-pop shops to government organizations and legacy corporations are providing valuable content that not only leads to trust in the brand but expands their OPEN communities, creates customers for life, and generates sales.

Let's take a look at some of those worthy of emulation as you lead your organization toward content marketing:

- ► **Duct Tape Marketing** | One of our favorite blogs, period. Founded by author and entrepreneur John Jantsch, this site excels at unique, valuable content on all things entrepreneurial. Featuring posts by Jantsch and guest contributors from within his OPEN community, this blog gives, gives, gives . . . and then, very subtly, *asks.*

- ► **Brazen Careerist** | Brazen Careerist was a very early entry not just in the career space, but in the social space. The community launched in 2007 has had plenty of starts and stops. But one thing has been more than consistent: its blog. Now called Brazen Life, the site features content on a wide variety of career- and work-related topics—and is the go-to resource for young professionals.

- ► **HootSuite** | In all fairness, the HootSuite blog, HootSource, isn't a stand-alone content marketing site; it benefits greatly from a strong community of HootSuite users and a marketing team that clearly gets—and implements— the very best of what social brings. They deliberately build communities and foster ambassador-quality relationships, making the job of Matt Foulger (curator and sole contributor to HootSource) much easier.

▶ **Gov.uk** | A revered content marketing site . . . for government? Yes, Gov.uk accomplished this unprecedented, and certainly unexpected, goal. By covering topics directly related to government and administration, the site renowned for simplicity is setting the bar high for similar sites. (Are you listening, Mr. President?)

▶ **CEO.com** | You don't have to think too hard to figure out who the target audience is for this blog: CEOs (and those who aspire to be among them some day). The blog is amazingly useful for leaders, with a nice emphasis on social leadership. And who owns CEO.com? Domo, a company that sells CEO dashboards—a tool made for leaders, that displays critical data points all in one place.

▶ **CMO.com** | This site, by Adobe, follows the same model as CEO.com: Create a one-stop resource for your target audience—in this case, chief marketing officers, who are actually a larger purchaser of Adobe's IT analytics services than CIOs.

Want to know the quickest way to find out the best possible blogging emulation point for your business?

1. Read your competitors' blogs.

2. Look at your industry's best blogs.

3. Make a note of the best design elements and content marketing aspects.

4. Using subject matter experts within and outside your team, build your blog!

## CAN YOU CAPITALIZE ON CM WITHOUT A BLOG?

If you run a large organization, hiring five or ten staffers to create a blog for you makes a lot of sense. If you have long-standing relationships with influential bloggers, and if you treat them with nothing but respect and gratitude, maybe you, too, can create a stellar blog like that of SAP, Duct Tape Marketing, or Brazen.

There are other ways to skin the content cat, though—ways that can bring you many of the benefits of a solid content marketing presence without making a Fortune 500–sized investment.

How *else* do you gain some of the benefits of content marketing *without* starting—or before starting—a corporate blog to rival HootSource and CEO.com?

Other than guest-blogging on other industry sites while you get your feet wet and develop mentor relationships with fellow bloggers, one highly effective option is to sponsor a popular blog with a theme in line with your marketing ambitions and brand identity. If you're a consumer products company selling to a largely female-head-of-household audience, then sponsoring a mommy blog or working with Pinterest on a campaign makes great sense. If our friend Vala Afshar, CMO of Extreme Networks—a decidedly B2B company—chose to sponsor a mommy blog, or foray too far into Pinterest, his CEO would have every right to get concerned.

Where does a large B2B company buy a sponsorship package to get the word out?

Our Friend Tom Mendoza, vice chairman at NetApp, brought this to our attention a while back when discussing his own (excellent) posts and short videos on Forbes.com (one of the more successful paper-turned-digital magazines). If you go to Forbes, under the BrandVoice umbrella you'll discover some branded posts and videos with a brand's name followed by "Voice" (NetAppVoice and Northwestern MutualVoice, for example).

It turns out, these are paid sponsorship packages, where a company like NetApp or Northwestern Mutual buys media slots for its employees to post blogs or videos just as if they were bloggers on Forbes.

In this model, Forbes sells valuable space on its site. The customer gets to draw on Forbes's brand and reputation. Since much of the content is quite good (doubtful Forbes would allow a sales-toned, digital megaphone piece to use the BrandVoice product unwisely), the reader derives significant value.

In this model: reputation, credibility, engagement, and value.

Brilliant—and a terrific way to amplify your voice even before your organization starts its own blog.

Although, note that this need not be an either/or proposition. Despite the success of SAP's blog, and to draw more new readers into SAP's OPEN circles, the company also has an SAPVoice presence, which Michael Brenner tells us really knocks it out of the park at times.

BrandVoice isn't the only content marketing game in town, however.

For a less committed way of participating in content marketing, you can look to IBM's Midsize Business strategy.

To gain credibility and a brand presence on established niche blogs, IBM purchases sponsorship of posts that cater to the audience they're out to reach. To be clear: IBM staff are *not* writing the content—and the post is not about an IBM product, or IBM at all for that matter. IBM sponsors posts the blogger was going to write anyway. At the bottom of those posts appears a note of sponsorship, a link to an IBM site, and perhaps the IBM logo.

We discovered this when our friend Anthony Iannarino took on the subject on his respected site thesalesblog.com. Twice a month, Iannarino features a post that doesn't really talk about IBM at all. Rather, these posts provide the same great sales-related wisdom he shares with his audience pretty much every day. By sponsoring these posts, IBM benefits—similar to the way Forbes's BrandVoice works—by being associated with a respected blogger. In a sense, the bloggers' OPEN community, at least for that post, is now part of IBM's OPEN constellation.

Again, this is brilliant execution of the content marketing model—without the commitment of a full-blown blogging and editorial team.

## IF YOU WRITE A BLOG, AND NO ONE READS IT . . .

. . . Does it make a sound?

Here's the one thing all bloggers feel as they begin their digital journey:

*Hello, anyone out there?*

Your organization will likely experience this hollow feeling as you take on the role of content marketers. The quickest way to make sure this period in your blog's development helps it become a go-to resource in your industry?

*Really* good content.

The second best way?

Deliberate sharing of the content, first from your accounts and then from those in your OPEN community. For that purpose, there is no end to the number of tools available to you:

► Twitterfeed, FeedBlitz, and NetworkedBlogs, for example, monitor your blog's RSS (Rich Site Summary, often called by its nickname, "Really Simple Syndication") to automatically publish frequently updated information from your blog (posts, updates, etc.) to Twitter, Facebook, Google+, LinkedIn, and your e-mail subscriber list (more on the issue of subscriber lists a bit later). These tools work quite simply, as the nickname implies: A new blog post publishes on your site; within a few minutes the blog post is tweeted, posted, and shared to the social networks you established as feeds during setup. We strongly encourage your team to use these feed mechanisms to promote your blogs as soon as they go live.

► For what Mark refers to as "scheduled spontaneity," Buffer, HootSuite, and

TweetDeck are easy to use and (at free or nearly free) affordable tools for scheduling promotional tweets in advance. This enables your team to tweet across many time zones in 24/7 mode, and it keeps your OPEN communities consistently aware of your content. These tools also allow you to schedule tweets for content other than your blog posts, so your brand avoids the perception that it is a spammer (we recommend that your tweets and posts be 50 percent about your brand and 50 percent everyone else's content).

► Blog-sharing platforms and aggregators such as Triberr, StumbleUpon, Digg, and Reddit allow your team to share your relevant posts. Triberr shares by engaging in mini-tribes (think of them as small OPEN circles) where you share the content of the members in your tribe, and they share yours. StumbleUpon, Digg, and Reddit are blogging aggregators that allow you to share your content as long as you also share the content of others (a 5:1 ratio—five shares of everyone else's content to every one of yours—is considered acceptable on aggregation sites).

► Of course, sharing buttons are a mandatory element on your blogging site. You simply must make it easy for members of your OPEN circles to share your content or most won't share—defeating much of your purpose. Three of our favorite sharing button plug-ins (apps that work directly with the most popular blogging sites like WordPress) are Socialize, GetSocial, and ShareThis.

► Another must: a subscriber button on your website that enables readers to sign up for your newsletters, receive notice of special content or offers, get updates from your organization, and more. As a starting point, both MailChimp and Constant Contact are simple, easy-to-use tools for collecting, managing, and e-mailing to subscriber databases.

## SCHEDULE—BUT NEVER FAIL TO ENGAGE

Scheduling is a welcome tool on social media, for many reasons. However, scheduling tweets and posts and then not answering the questions that come your way, failing to acknowledge comments, and "broadcasting" instead of engaging is not an acceptable trap to fall into. You don't want your brand to come across as arrogant, out of touch with the OPEN community you're trying to foster, and you don't want to seem like an RSS feed rather than social in any way—a trait that makes you eminently easy to ignore. At all times, be aware that in direct response to your outgoing tweets, scheduled or not, *humans* are listening, answering, and asking. As a social leader, your role is to make sure the entire team is working under the phrasing Mark and Ted first heard from Steven Levy, a social media–adept recruiter out of New York:

*You have two ears and one mouth— use them proportionately.*

## SHOW SOME FACE

Much of the advice in this chapter so far has centered around the idea that social is all text-based, faceless engagement. Obviously, this isn't true—unless your strategy doesn't deliberately include an effort to reveal your team as humans worthy of caring about or of building a mutually beneficial relationship with.

We strongly encourage you to present your team members' faces as the "face of your brand." Let their smiles get out in front, as if to say, "This is a very good brand, but mostly I like buying from Tracy" and "I really enjoy this blog; Bobby really gets what it's like to walk in my shoes."

Whenever possible, personalize!

*More social. Less media.*

How? How do you attach a face to a brand?

Start simply: Twitter pics, posts on Facebook that feature your team at work, uploads to Instagram, and team pics that demonstrate your positive, customer-first culture. Each of these provides a welcome distraction from all the text-based tweets and posts. They make people—your customers, potential customers, applicants, vendors, and champions—smile. And what better can anyone say about your brand, regardless of your industry or primary product, that is any better than "Those guys make me smile!"?

Of course, all of this humanity in your social efforts means you need to treat your employees well. If your customers come to love them and they leave to work for your competition—well, make that the kind of concern that keeps your rivals up at night, not you.

## TAKE "PERSONAL" TO THE NEXT LEVEL

How do customers, champions—and even competitors—know when your community has reached a tipping point? When your "marketing," as we discussed in Chapter 6, has become more about what advocates say about you (testimonials) than what *you* say about you (advertising)?

It's when you launch your own media channels via social: a Twitter chat perhaps, or maybe a Google+ Hangout featured on YouTube, or a podcast that features passionate voices from your brand.

Driven by a hashtag (as mentioned in Chapter 10), Twitter chats typically last sixty minutes and occur once per week on a day of the week and at a time established by your team. Biweekly and monthly Twitter chats are also relatively popular. While they must be facilitated with a great deal of care, Twitter chats are an outstanding method of connecting members of your OPEN community to each other and to the brand.

Google+ Hangouts—where a passionate facilitator from your organization (perhaps you or your community manager) and a guest expert tackle a topic relevant to your community, customers, and potential customers—are also highly effective. Recorded like a television news interview, these twenty-five- to sixty-minute "shows" are uploaded to YouTube, where they can be watched when it's convenient for your community members. They also provide great video-based content, which, when done well, exposes significant numbers of viewers to your brand.

Podcasts—typically also interviews between an influencer at your brand and a guest expert—are recorded and featured on many popular channels, including iTunes and Stitcher. The most successful podcasts seem to be promoted weekly and run between twenty-five and fifty-five minutes. Especially among technology-aware members of your community, podcasts are extremely popular.

When your team is ready—usually defined by a significant amount of traction gained for your primary product and significant growth of your OPEN circles—take personal to another level and greatly increase your brand's social presence.

## THE SOCIAL SANITY CHECK

*Experience is simply the name we give our mistakes.*

—*Oscar Wilde*

No matter what level of success you achieve on social, there is always room for a mistake. Often, several mistakes.

Your authors are frequently told that the best advice they offer is to perform what they call a "social sanity check." In other words, is your organization's presence on social media as good as you think it is, or even as good as it could be?

If you're already on social, take a look at the ten points that make up the social sanity check. If you haven't jumped into social quite yet, keep this for future reference. Without any doubt, you'll be happy you did:

► **Social Sanity Check No. 1: Maintain consistent profiles** | Does every profile on *every* site include your most up-to-date branding message on your company? Use the same logo and images? The same color schemes and fonts? When members or potential members of your OPEN communities find you, they should instantly recognize you based on the brand image already in their heads.

▶ **Social Sanity Check No. 2: Serve your niche** | How far, since you originally forayed into social, have you strayed from your original plan? How well are you serving the niche you are known for now? Often on social, we try way too hard to be everything to everyone. Resist the temptation. Retain your subject matter expertise. Serve your niche well.

▶ **Social Sanity Check No. 3: Respond promptly on social** | How long is it taking you to respond to a question posed on Facebook? To respond to a tweet or DM on Twitter? To respond to a comment on the blog or an inquiry on your LinkedIn group? By the standards set by today's connected consumer, anything more than an hour or two is likely to be considered unacceptable. Twenty-four hours is stretching it. Two or three days? Well, that is dinosaur territory.

▶ **Social Sanity Check No. 4: Send tweets that support blog posts** | Your team and contributors work very hard to post high-quality content consistently on the blog. How well are you rewarding that hard work? How many tweets were sent out for every blog post? How engaging were those tweets? Want to kill content marketing? Fail to promote. (This goes for sharing content on sites like LinkedIn for B2Bs and Facebook for B2Cs as well.)

▶ **Social Sanity Check No. 5: Engage** | Are you truly engaging, or are you broadcasting? Compared to your promotional tweets and posts, how many of your tweets ask a provocative question, share a value-added blog post from another source, comment on an industry news item, or deliberately inspire or make someone smile? By all means, schedule your promotional tweets. But also remember to schedule some time for spontaneity and non-product-related engagement.

▶ **Social Sanity Check No. 6: Monitor keywords, hashtags, and branded terms** | How often are the keywords that are important to your industry monitored? How closely do you watch over your hashtags and other branded terms? Even the largest enterprises have been found to be more than complacent when it came to hashtags getting hijacked.

▶ **Social Sanity Check No. 7: Be willing problem solvers** | Throughout your online presence, do you take advantage of opportunities to turn a challenge into a victory for your brand? Do you see complainers as drama queens and trolls, or as a chance to listen? Do you own a problem reported to you on social until it's resolved? Want to impress a connected consumer with a problem in the Social Age? Own the problem.

► **Social Sanity Check No. 8: Keep mobile in mind** | As technologies change, we tend to sit back and assume everything is okay, that all our sites, images, and posts look good everywhere. And then we find out that our blog isn't rendering correctly on an Android device or the logo on our Twitter account, the one we've used for months, is not representing the brand well on a tablet. With the world moving rapidly from desktops to mobile, you routinely want to check your presence on every media-enabled device; you're sure to catch something that could otherwise be a gut punch to your brand.

► **Social Sanity Check No. 9: Keep your competitors close** | There are those who tell you not to worry about your competitors. They say, "We can't control what anyone else does; we just do the best we can." If you hear that in the Social Age, look for beady eyes and scaly skin, because there's a dinosaur in front of you. At all times, keep an eye on the social movements of your competitors.

► **Social Sanity Check No. 10: Avoid automessaging** | If you ever, ever, *ever* feel the need to communicate to those in your OPEN community via automessaging of any kind, at any time, it is time to reevaluate your social strategy. It may even be time to realize that if your team needs (or chooses) to speak through canned messages and auto-DMs, maybe you don't belong on social yet. We agree: You were not— *you are not*—ready. Hire someone who is. Quickly.

This last point—refusing to use automessaging at all costs—is worth examining a little more closely.

## BANK OF AMERICA'S EPIC AUTOMESSAGE FAIL

In September 2013, Mark Hamilton wrote an anti-foreclosure statement on the sidewalk in front of a Bank of America branch. Apparently alerted about his chalk abuse of the sidewalk by employees of the bank, New York police told him to leave. From his @darthmarkh Twitter handle, he tweeted:

*Just got chased away by #NYPD 4 "obstructing sidewalk."*

A supporter of Hamilton's, Steve Timmis (@stevetimmis) responded via Twitter (note the use of the @bankofamerica Twitter handle):

*@darthmarkh @CyMadD0x @bankofamerica looks like you were really causing an obstruction*

Regrettably, Bank of America's automessaging picked up the use of the bank's global Twitter handle and sent the following autotweet from @BofA_Help:

*Hi Mr. Timmis, I work for Bank of America. What happened? Anything I can do to help? ^sa*

(That "^sa" typically indicates the staffer using the Twitter handle at that moment (perhaps Sarah Adams or Steve Anatole); in addition to being able to track communication, this practice is supposed to, ironically, help the brand appear more human.)

About then, what appears to be a less-than-objective person on Twitter with the handle @OccupyLA got involved:

*@BofA_help @stevetimmis you can help by stop stealing people's houses!!!!*

In response to which, Bank of America sent out the following tweets:

*@OccupyLA We'd be happy to review your account with you to discuss any concerns. Please let us know if need assistance. ^sa*

*@stevetimmis We'd be happy to review your account with you to discuss any concerns. Please let us know if need assistance. ^sa*

About that same time, several other "heartfelt" tweets went out to some other people from the @BofA_Help Twitter account (text inside brackets implies the fields used in the automessages):

*@<TwitterHandle> We'd be happy to review your account with you to discuss any concerns. Please let us know if need assistance. ^sa*

*Hi <Salutation LastName>, I work for Bank of America. What happened? Anything I can do to help? ^sa*

The only conclusion that could be drawn, as noted by many tweets throughout the flare-up, was that the Bank of America Twitter account was run exclusively through autobots; a human was nowhere near this tragic use of social. The bank—rather than answering the tweets in an engaging manner as consumers of the Social Age demand—simply reinforced the perception of the company as faceless, uncaring autocrats.

As they say on Twitter: #epicfail.

## RESPECTED RESOURCES

Before we leave this chapter, a full disclosure moment . . .

As you may have noticed, there isn't any talk in this chapter about what some experts would consider basic aspects of SMM—Facebook and Twitter ads and campaigns, for example. There is a good reason for that: It isn't within your authors' collective wheelhouse.

We build content. We build relationships. And we leverage the power of social. A lot.

But Mark has never bought a Facebook ad. Ted has never spent a penny with Twitter or LinkedIn. Our social techniques are organic and self-contained; as a result, neither of us has ever spent significant money with a social network or an agency.

So, while we can tell you how to build and lead your own socially aware team with a customer-first mentality and how to build your OPEN circles ad infinitum, we can't tell you how much it will cost to buy your way to an effective social presence. It's not the way we think, or work.

We do, however, have many resources and consultancies from the social advertising space within our personal and business OPEN circles. We learn from them with every interaction and we trust them—and their reputations—to do right by you as you explore social advertising. Some examples:

▶ **Dr. Roshan Khan of SocialRankMedia.com** | Rosh has always been a tremendous help to Mark and the YouTern team whenever a question arises. A class act and a relentless giver.

▶ **SocialMediaExaminer.com** | A blog with a million answers. If these guys haven't discussed it, you don't need to know it.

▶ **Moz** | These guys came in at the very beginning of the Social Age and have witnessed every plus and minus since. They get it—and they share.

## DOES SOCIAL MEDIA MARKETING ACTUALLY *WORK*?

In a different era, the answer to that question would be similar to the remark that appears at the beginning of this chapter, made by a frustrated John Wanamaker in the nineteenth century: Half of our money is most likely wasted, but who knows which half?

Social, however, is not the only technology to advance since the Social Age began; analytics—the collection of data from blogs and social media platforms to help steer decisions—has advanced as well. Today, savvy companies can measure *both* halves of their advertising/marketing spend down to the very last interaction online. Indeed, the more such interactions, the better, because the information they generate—the data we need to make decisions—is priceless.

Come with us now to Chapter 14, as we explore the modern-day alchemy not only available but infinitely usable to measure the ROI of our interactions in the Social Age. We'll also bring the power of social full circle.

Most important, we'll explain that power in such a way that not only will even a *herd* of dinosaurs get it, but, from the moment that lightbulb above their heads begins to burn bright, they'll fully embrace the Social Age.

# CHAPTER 14

# Investing in Social: Is What You See Real?

*A strategic inflection point is a time in the life of the business when its*
*fundamentals are about to change. They are full-scale changes in the*
*way business is conducted, so that simply adopting new technology*
*or fighting the competition as you used to may be insufficient.*
—Andy Grove, CEO, Intel

When you're as immersed in social as we are, and so many business leaders—leaders of brands that would benefit greatly from an effective presence on social—haven't yet dabbled, you get the following question a lot.

## WHAT IS THE ROI ON SOCIAL MEDIA?

Ugh.

Now, what we'd really like to say is basically what an exasperated Gary Vaynerchuck blurted out several years ago during a pitch meeting when some old-school leaders kept pestering him with that exact question:

*What's the ROI on your mother?*

Go, Gary!

We'd like to jump in with one or two of our own, such as:

*"What's the ROI on being relevant to your target consumers?"*

Or even:

*"What's the ROI on still being in business ten years from now?"*

That's what we'd *like* to say, because we feel that we are at a strategic inflection point, right now, and we feel strongly about the need for most organizations to be deeply immersed in social.

Instead, we understand the pressure most every early adopter of social media is under to justify his or her activity—or even existence—on social. Despite data from Hotspex Market Research for Syncapse that shows the average value of a Facebook fan increased 28 percent (to $174.17) from 2010 to early 2013, we get how adding what is perceived by many as another overhead unit with no direct profits attached is counterintuitive.

We grasp that sticker shock occurs when a business leader sees the price tag that comes with some social media management software (SMMS; software that manages, monitors, and measures multiple social media accounts such as Facebook, Twitter, and YouTube, often across multiple departments and business units) required by that "overhead" unit. And we appreciate how hard it may be for executives to go "all in" when they don't completely understand the process themselves.

Consider these statistics, as compiled by Digital Marketing Depot and Altimeter Group:

► Across many locations and multiple departments (sales, HR, marketing, product management, customer service, etc.) the average enterprise manages 178 different social media accounts.

► 56 percent of enterprise leaders were unable to tie social media activity to desired business outcomes.

► Even among those using the best available SMMS, just one-third of executives stated they were able to accurately measure the financial impact of social media.

Is it any wonder that the ROI questions come up so often? And why it is important, no matter how exasperating it is at times, for us to continue this important conversation?

## WHAT IS THE ROI ON YOUR MOTHER?

Since Gary uttered the "mother" line in 2011, advances in analytics, including those within SMMS, have more than kept pace with developments in social. In addition to the more established organizations already in the space, many start-ups have jumped in to fill the need for quality data reporting and near-real-time predictive analysis—and have received hundreds of millions in funding to help realize their dream.

From basic (Google Analytics, HootSuite, and Sprout Social) to enterprise level (Salesforce's Marketing Cloud, Sprinklr, and Argyle), analytics tools now make measuring and reporting key social metrics a painless process. SMMS interfaces with all major social media accounts; Facebook, Twitter, and LinkedIn are standard; Google+ is now managed by many solutions. In addition, some track less-known U.S. social networks and major international sites such as China's Renren. The largest systems also monitor activity on Reddit and Yelp.

Understanding the need to standardize data collection across multiple networks and platforms, several networks—including LinkedIn, Twitter, and Google+—did their part and launched certified marketing developer programs to normalize data sharing with SMMS vendors and facilitators.

Thanks to collaboration between SMMS providers, the social networks, third-party developers, and SMMS customers, we are able to determine frequency of engagement, the types of posts our community responds to best, who our champions and ambassadors may be, and a brand's perceived influence. We are also able to track the effectiveness of specific social campaigns and how our customers and prospective customers view our brands and products (in other words, "customer sentiment").

SMMS also manages a variety of social media functions across all social accounts including:

- ▶ Listening and monitoring tools
- ▶ Work flow and task management
- ▶ Reporting of mentions by influencers noted as "key"
- ▶ Analysis of your competitor's accounts

Does your organization need SMMS?

You just might. Do you have multiple accounts across many departments and locations? Do you have a blog? Is the majority of your staff customer-facing? If yes, are they already using social, or will they be? Do you have someone on your team to learn and monitor the SMMS, or will you have time? Can you reasonably expect the decision makers to fund SMMS—most often offered as SaaS (software as a service)? Is federal regulation such as equal opportunity laws an issue?

Even if the answer to all these questions is yes, you may be able to invest a much smaller amount in SMMS provided by HootSuite, Engage121, or uberVU.

## BUT DOES SMMS MEASURE ROI?

Unfortunately, the metric those in the C-Suite are most accustomed to using—financial return on investment—is one of the most difficult metrics to track in social. In social, especially in the area of recruiting, engagement, and community building, it is much more difficult to assign a direct expense number to a campaign and compare those expenses to the income directly generated from the campaign.

And that may be okay—or need to be okay.

Why?

First and foremost: Marketing, although technically an expense on your organization's profit-and-loss (P&L) statement, has always been a *long-term investment* in your company. A company that can't afford to market its business shouldn't be in business. Social media marketing (SMM) is no different, because ultimately it is just "M" (marketing, remember?).

Second: We must stop confusing marketing with advertising. We simply can't assign a pure number to social media as we can with digital advertising efforts such as a point-per-click banner ad, opens of an e-mail, or the click of a Google campaign link.

Perhaps most important: The old-schoolers who insist we develop an accurate ROI based on direct expenses versus direct income generated must stop applying an Industrial Age process to winning in the Social Age—which is tantamount to asking Henry Ford how much hay would be consumed by one of his early Model Ts.

As Andy Grove from Intel said about strategic inflection points:

*They are full-scale changes in the way business is conducted...*

When talking ROI, we must embrace this philosophy. We must change mindset.

And yet here we are, living square in the Social Age and being measured by Industrial Age leaders, using what has been—up to now—industry-standard techniques.

So how do we remedy this?

Over the next ten years, how do we reconcile the simplicity of the way social is likely to be judged versus its actual impact on our organization—and not just on dollars?

## THE SOCIAL CIRCLE OF LIFE

At this point, it is important to discuss the entire IT milieu that exists as we go to press in 2014. Even more important—for many reasons, including getting past the attempt to measure social's impact this quarter by revenue generated—we must understand where that environment is heading over the next few years.

Social is big. If you're still reading, you get that now.

But you can't talk about social—or issues like overall ROI—without also talking about the technologies that have intersected with social media to cause what we call the "Social Circle of Life."

As this discussion continues, you'll see two trends here.

First: Each of these relatively new business components is understood by only a handful of old-school leaders (it is our job—and now yours—to help them understand).

Second (and this is an incredibly important lesson to ponder): It is essential to know that your business, if it hasn't already, *will* incorporate every one of these technologies into your daily operations. You'll just use them as part of your daily routine, as you do your smartphone and/or tablet today.

You will. Or your successor will.

You can't stop the Social Circle of Life.

The circle is made up of the following components:

- ► Social
- ► Mobile
- ► The cloud
- ► Big data
- ► Analytics

Let's talk about each component, and its position in the Social Circle of Life.

(Before we do, let us warn you: This will take a while to explain. Stick with us, because we're working up to something big you won't want to—no, *you can't*—miss.)

## MOBILE IS A FAIT ACCOMPLI

Remember in Chapter 2, when we told you that, as of January 2014, 58 percent of Americans are now using smartphones? As if that isn't a huge enough increase in the use of mobile technology, note that comScore reported that the sales of computing tablets like the iPad are increasing year over year at a rate of 75 percent. Now, factor in that, according to Nielson, time spent on mobile apps is increasing by 100 percent every year.

It goes without saying (but we're going to say it anyway): If you're leading a business right now, you need to be cognizant of the impact of mobile computing. Sell to Millennials, where the use of mobile to reach apps and social networks is far greater? Operate in overseas markets, especially in the rapidly developing world that is engaging, communicating, and buying with a smartphone already? Your stakes just quadrupled.

Why? Because Millennials and consumers in the emergent areas of our world have zoomed right past old-world, desktop-dependent websites and computing habits and into mobile technologies.

And it isn't just them. Where our youngest generations and these countries are today—with most connected to the Web through their smartphones rather than via home-based computing—is where *every human on the planet* will be as soon as we cut the cord from our desktops and laptops (yes, pun absolutely intended).

As of now, your organization has an itty-bitty window to jump into mobile in a big way; a sliver of opportunity remains that allows you to catch up to the many organizations already there. When that window closes, your company will officially be a laggard.

History usually doesn't look favorably on laggards. The future never does.

Even if you don't want to accept that theory as possible, even probable, consider this: The term *smartphone*, although a catchy marketing play, is a terrible misnomer.

Today's cell phone is barely a phone at all. A smartphone is more like a small computer. We use them to text and e-mail, interact on social sites, check prices while we shop in brick-and-mortar stores, make online purchases, play games, read, take and share photos and videos, and much more. In the Social Age, the actual *phone* function is just one of the hundreds of features available on handheld devices.

And all of that is just the first stop on the Social Circle of Life. Next stop . . .

## THE CLOUD

Remember when cloud computing was new?

Ted remembers the day the cloud hit our collective consciousness. At the time, he was working with enterprise CIOs and their teams, trying to help them explain the cloud to their C-level peers and their boards. Then, during the 2011 Super Bowl, Microsoft ran some fluffy ads on the cloud. That next Monday, the phone rang off the hook; Ted's team could not keep up with demand. CEOs had watched the ads and wanted the cloud for their companies, *stat!*

Back then, many were still afraid of the cloud—not that there was anything to be afraid of, or even that it was radically different. They just didn't get it.

(Maybe that describes someone you work with now?)

The fact is that the cloud isn't all that scary or complicated. When you are traveling and access money from your bank account using another bank's ATM, the network that enables that is in the cloud—and has been for more than a generation now.

That isn't scary, right?

Well, for those who are misguidedly insecure about security and privacy issues and who still want the slick software box that holds the CD-ROM and the 240-page user's manual, this part may be scary enough to start a dinosaur stampede.

Many suppliers of software products we use for work and life—including 100 percent of the SMMS vendors we researched for this book—exclusively offer cloud-based solutions. Their SaaS doesn't sit on your hard drive. It lives, breathes, and stores data in the cloud. If you want to use an application like Salesforce, for instance, you have no choice. You must go to the cloud; Salesforce offers no other options.

Mobile. Cloud. Mobile clouds.

(That, friends, is just the necessary background on mobile and the cloud. Now strap in while we discuss how big data and analytics get involved, and create a whole new way of doing business in this still-new Social Age of ours.)

## BIG DATA

Is there more to big data than just big hype?

Depending on who you ask, big data can seem like nothing more than a big bunch of buzzword-driven propaganda. On the surface, it may seem that big data is the last thing any business leader needs. Seriously: If there's one thing that kills decision making and hobbles organizational success, it's devout bureaucrats who find it much safer to put off a decision for another six months while legions of MBAs gather *yet more* information that will tell them what they want to hear: that their decision is foolproof.

But not so fast.

Rather than being a killer of decision makers everywhere, as it might seem, big data helps bring *real* change to the Social Age. And not just to business. With big data, not only can we spot business trends as they form, we can conduct research in days instead of decades, identify potential challenges to food and water supplies before they happen, and prevent certain diseases.

Big data is . . . *big.*

Big data is often thought of as the exponential growth and availability of data, both structured and unstructured, for anyone equipped to listen (and, as we've learned, more and more businesses are actively listening). Despite its large and complex foundation (data is collected in petabytes; data is measured in hundreds of millions of "collisions" per second), big data is ultimately a relatively simple process that organizations of any size, in any industry, can leverage.

To understand how all this applies in *A World Gone Social,* let's look at where this data originates and social's role in how this all works.

Every time anyone visits a social network—and most every time we click that "I accept terms of use" button on the websites or social networks we visit—data is collected. Service bureaus, brokers, and enterprises collect that public data, often from our mobile devices and stored in the cloud, and package it for business, government, and global uses. (Sound creepy? We're with you.)

From there, organizations like yours use that data to enable cost and time reductions, develop new products (as well as refine current product offerings), spot trends among massive numbers of consumers by any demographic, discover how best to build digital relationships, and, yes, make smarter, and faster, business decisions.

Bottom line: Big data = big bucks.

(Now we complete the Social Circle of Life and finally, through use of analytics, understand the true impact of social—for those who insist on demonstrable-ROI-or-bust, that is.)

## MAKING THE TURN: ANALYTICS

Analytics is modern-day alchemy. But it isn't new.

MBAs have been doing analysis on data since the first days of the Industrial Age. Back in the Victorian Age, fictional Bob Cratchit used a slide rule to perform "analytics" for his employer, Ebenezer Scrooge. Scribes did it for King Tut.

Ah, but they didn't have an IBM supercomputer working for them, did they? Whereas medieval alchemists were never truly able to turn iron into gold, with Social Age analytics, your company can turn big data into *huge* competitive advantages.

Using megacomputing power, business leaders can sort through your staff's efforts on social and see for themselves what strategies and resources are bearing fruit—and which might feel good or come with a lot of sound and fury but signify nothing.

Remember in Chapter 13, when SAP's Michael Brenner said his global content marketing team was already showing solid ROI? He also told us this:

> *SAP is a data-driven company. We measure outcomes. If our thought leadership and content efforts weren't paying off in actual increased sales that we could track, we [the team behind the Business Innovation blog] wouldn't have lasted long.*

Long story short? SAP uses analytics, combined with careful tracking of every aspect of the company's business model (website visits, subscriber lists, white paper downloads, technology and sales inquiries, and much more), to do what John Wanamaker could only dream of: Tell them how *both* portions of their marketing dollars are paying off. Exactly how. Exactly where. As logic would dictate, they then invest more in the most successful areas and back off in those that aren't performing as well.

Simple, right?

Yet so few organizations have the data in hand to make these kinds of decisions. They guess. Or they follow someone else's tired old "best practices." Or they hire another consultancy.

SAP gets it. SAP knows how business is done in a world gone social.

## SAP IS NOT ALONE

While we were researching this book, we came across IBM's intention to turn all 400,000+ of its employees into social advocates for the brand.

More than 400,000 focused brand ambassadors.

A huge internal OPEN community, about to be set loose on the world.

*More social. Less media.*

Without another word, IBM had our attention.

Think about the progress made here—and in such a short time. Despite its place in the technology sector, IBM is considered by many to be about as old-school as they come. And yet it's not just embracing social, IBM is giving it a 400,000-person-strong bear hug.

(Give us a minute while we enjoy that visual—a proud moment for sure.)

But hold on, some of our readers are doubtless thinking this just can't be . . . it just can't happen. Maybe you're wondering how IBM could possibly trust *all* of its employees to represent the brand online without initiating at least intermittent moments of branding disaster.

"Get them all on social?" you may be thinking. "Not us. No way."

Before we get into the firm's mission of mass brand ambassadorship via social, let's address how we can see this happening at IBM:

▶ By definition, IBMers are considered smart. Isn't that their reputation? Isn't it a company full of highly educated contributors?

▶ Those educated and (it is assumed) emotionally intelligent contributors can be trained, in small groups by Social Age leaders. Not only will they accept the training, they will consider it a welcome career development benefit.

▶ As we learned by attending IBM Connect in Orlando in 2014, IBM is changing the way it thinks, acts, and operates. It operates under Douglas McGregor's Theory Y: that people are inherently trustworthy and are eager to do well by the company. (SAP, with 60,000 employees, is striving for the same thing: creating 60,000 brand ambassadors. Zappos, with 1,500 employees, has actually been doing this for years now; rare is the non-social Zapponian.)

► By creating an internal OPEN community, and by centralizing the content sharing—and by hand-picking what each IBM brand ambassador should share—IBM is leaving the actual social sharing up to each individual; no one will share something they aren't comfortable with.

► Shareable branding is delivered through a tool called the Social Advocator, developed by Expion. This content marketing optimization platform empowers brands like IBM to manage the social marketing efforts of their internal ambassadors. The platform listens, monitors, and records what is working for whom, what is not working, and, for that matter, *who* is not working: which employees, regardless of title, actually have the most engaged OPEN communities on social (the answer is often revealing, and maybe—just maybe—will in time prove to be hierarchy-flattening, as star performers are identified regardless of their rank within the company hierarchy or the title on their business card).

► Finally, here's the way we see this bold adventure from IBM: This is the very definition of a mutually beneficial, OPEN community. With each share, the personal brand of the IBMer will grow, as will the IBM brand. The team member and the IBM brand, several times a day, will be intrinsically orbiting in the same OPEN constellation. Nearly instant credibility is established, relationships are developed, sales are made, and service is delivered in a sincere, *human* manner.

*More social. Less media.*

Now, we understand that the execution of this massively OPEN community (which we've been calling "MOPEN" ever since we fell in love with IBM's social model), like every other aspect of social, won't be without challenges, obstacles, and detractors. Not every IBMer will buy into this purely social ambassadorship. (Remember–and this applies even to IBM: "Attrition will be your best friend.")

Think, though, of the potential impact. Even if just 50 percent of all IBMers embrace OPEN in this fashion, IBM will have a 200,000-strong network of independent ambassadors sharing value-added, non-salesy content with customers, potential customers, vendors, friends, bloggers, influencers, and champions.

More than impressive.

That's a whole lot of people saying good things about your company all over the Web.

## THE CIRCLE IS COMPLETE

And yet that isn't IBM's *"Why."*

When we learned the *real* "Why," we were floored. We knew right then that IBM fully understands the value that [Social + Mobile + Cloud + Big Data + Analytics] provides a brand fully immersed in the Social Age.

Let's say that again:

*SOCIAL + MOBILE + CLOUD + BIG DATA + ANALYTICS = Social Age SUCCESS*

Here's how IBM's Ethan McCarty explained IBM's view, which we paraphrase here: Every time IBM ambassadors initiate a social media interaction, anywhere on the Web, they *shake off data* that IBM collects and analyzes.

"Shake off data" . . . like a dog shaking off water after a swim. Each droplet is a data point, and it's incredibly valuable to a savvy company like IBM.

That's a lot of data to gather, isn't it?

Some might call it . . . *big data.*

We call it the Social Age.

And in the Social Age, companies like IBM and SAP take all this data and do what? What is the next logical step?

All this knowledge now goes full circle back into social—and into nearly every other aspect of a socially aware business. Companies that harness this power now:

► Know exactly what content worked and what fell flat

► Engage with those already talking about the brand: bloggers, influencers, and organic brand ambassadors

► Know—and can target—the advocates of their competitors

► Have perhaps millions of contacts that may become mutually beneficial relationships

► Take objective input to their product development and advertising teams so they know what their customers like and don't like—and even how to improve

► Reach out to passive and active job seekers: talent ready to make a career change that is already, the data shows, passionate about the brand

► Seek collaboration and strategic partnerships with closely aligned brands, purpose-driven nonprofits—even competitors

The list goes on and on . . . and on.

After all, this is the Social Circle of Life, and all of this new work via social media and mobile—all these new contacts and data points—is stored in the cloud. Companies starving for business intelligence pull it into big data. Analytics tools process the data; reports and predictive analytics are generated. Action is taken.

And the circle is complete, again.

This all happens over and over, millions of times per day.

And the companies that leverage this immense power, that embrace the Social Circle of Life, win. This is how business is done in a world gone social.

## LEVERAGING THE SOCIAL CIRCLE OF LIFE

It may seem obvious that legacy organizations—and especially technology companies like IBM and SAP—would be able to leverage big data and every other stage of the Social Circle of Life.

But how does a start-up, nonprofit organization, or even a small to medium business take full advantage? How do those with smaller teams and budgets, and those without a data scientist in-house, benefit from big data?

As more data-focused businesses leap in to fill the gap between the data haves and the data have-nots, smaller organizations can, with relative ease, jump into big data:

► **Data brokers** | The brokers we briefly mentioned earlier in this chapter— including companies like Acxiom, Rapleaf, Datalogix, Epsilon, and Spokeo— provide data and custom data-based projects at what most consider a reasonable cost.

► **Kaggle** | This data gamification company positions itself as leader in solving business challenges through predictive analytics. Smaller organizations flock to Kaggle to specify the data challenge in front of them, and then dozens— perhaps hundreds—of data manipulators take on the challenge, competition style. Yes, Kaggle uses the crowdsourcing power of OPEN to find solution-oriented collaborators for its clients.

► **Factual** | While its focus has shifted toward "local" big data, this start-up actually began as the "wiki of databases." Anyone can add to or create new data on Factual, which also provides application programming interfaces (APIs) so everyone can both manipulate and visualize the data they need to target the right customers, test a product offering, or perhaps even know which ad to place on the right side of someone's Facebook page once the person logs in.

As big data and the Social Circle of Life grow exponentially, so will the service bureaus built to support the business needs of those that don't have in-house resources that support the need for data-intensive analytics. Big data, even the most skeptical of experts agree, isn't exclusive to big companies. Everyone will benefit. Everyone wins.

Unless you're on the sidelines, not ready to play the game.

## SOCIAL IS THE FIRST WAVE

Way back in the beginning of *A World Gone Social,* we talked about how social media was similar to the asteroid that slammed into Earth, killing off the dinosaurs that had dominated right up to the point impact occurred. From that cataclysmic change came a new balance of power, a new voice. The turf-protecting, message-controlling autocrats—those who, like the dinosaurs before them, didn't adapt to our new business climate—we said, are doomed to extinction.

And now we understand why. We can now see why social, and the petabytes (that is, 1 million gigabytes) of data points created from social every day, is where we need to be now.

For many, social is a place of rebirth.

And yet, in the Social Age, the use of social networks constitutes just the first wave of change.

It is when social media joins with the other elements of the Social Circle of Life that we begin to see the bigger picture. This is what moves social media from the warm and fuzzy "we're building relationships" and "Social has no ROI" stage straight into the change agent we've been talking about since you—physically, digitally, or audibly—opened the front cover of this book.

This realization alone will help you take even the most stubborn old-schoolers, the elders of the dinosaur tribe, and help them see the light.

One small warning—something we've learned as we've watched dinosaurs evolve into evangelists: Get the Kool-Aid ready. Because when you're done explaining social *this* way—and they really start to get how the social Circle of Life works—copious amounts of social Kool-Aid will be consumed; even the most-heavily defended Industrial Age fortresses will come down.

Walking among the ruins, herds of smiling dinosaurs with bright orange mustaches, compliments of all that Kool-Aid, staring up at a light . . .

That light?

A new dawn.

The Social Age.

This is not just change for change's sake. This change has occurred as the result of insurmountable market pressure.

And even the dinosaurs should get it: Commit, or face certain obsolescence. Perhaps extinction.

That's the future that we're already living in.

In that future, should we be investing in social? Is what we see now real? Will these trends continue? Or are the dinosaurs right? Will social media go the way of eight-track tapes, newspaper classified ads, and Blockbuster?

Here's the thing . . .

Considering how far this technology has come in the six years since the Social Age dawned, we can anticipate that what the most sophisticated analytics are telling us today from all of our social interactions is nothing—*nothing!*—compared to what analytics will enable us to accomplish just a few years from now.

Think back six years.

Wasn't a lot of life laughably simple compared to today? Wasn't technology a shadow of what we presently have at our fingertips? Six years ago, neither of your authors had smartphones. Now, we can't imagine going more than an hour without checking our Twitter feeds, OPEN circles, and e-mails, and communicating with our families. All from the palms of our hands.

Life would not be the same. Just six years later, we are not the same.

A bit less than six years after this book is published, it will be 2020.

Hard to imagine what's in store, isn't it?

Hard to comprehend what the Social Age will bring us six years from now. Or what we—as one planet-sized OPEN community of relentless givers—can bring to the Social Age. Coincidentally, that's what the final chapter in this book is all about. Join us now as we discuss the future of business in a world that has gone—and will continue to be—social.

# CHAPTER 15

# The Future of Business in a World Gone Social

*Maybe you were going to fall off that razor's edge before, but not today.*
*Today, we're going to jump.*

—*Tamora Pierce*

Let's begin this chapter with an important confession:

*No one knows what the future of social, or its impact on business, will really*
*be. No one—yet—understands its full potential.*

In our experience, those who claim they *do* know are likely trying to sell you something. And they probably bill themselves as "ninjas" or "gurus." Proceed with caution. Because they don't know what the future holds in store.

We don't know. You don't know.

## A SOCIAL WISH LIST

Yet we do have our hopes, or at least we know what we'd like to see happen as the Social Age matures. On our wish list is as follows:

► Removal of the digital borders between major networking sites. Development of tools that allow cross-platform communication can't be that difficult.

► Further standardization of reporting from social networks so SMMS and predictive analytics could work far more seamlessly.

► Interface tools between web browsers and social that would serve as B2C engagement tools and lead generation ("@mattszimmer Thanks for visiting @ REISeattle.com today! Did you find the tent you needed? How can we help?").

► SMMS tools that take us, aggressively yet graciously, from active listening to engagement to actionable intelligence. (Who do we reach out to first, next, and why?)

▶ More cost-effective analytics solutions to ensure the little guys have the same access to big data as enterprise organizations.

And, based on the impact we've seen already from social, we have some educated guesses—both positive and negative in nature—about where the Social Age may take us next. Here are our thoughts. (Let's see if any of this actually happens in the next decade or so.)

## OPEN COLLABORATION WILL BECOME THE NORM

There are some who will say our position on building a customer-centric culture—starting with putting employees first so they can serve the customer well—may be a little too warm and fuzzy. Some will say it just can't work because employees are too lazy and customers too apathetic. Furthermore, they'll say, we just can't trust our employees and customers enough.

To those dinosaurs, we say: You ain't seen nothing yet.

First, let's just state that if employees seem lazy and customers apathetic, it's because that brand has not yet properly engaged their hearts and imaginations; they are still not emotionally invested. (Anyone who thinks a large group of people can't become emotionally invested or driven by a mission should visit a little site called Wikipedia: Every word on that website, with its zillions of topics and countless contributors, is put there by a volunteer.)

With that out of the way, let's review what happens when both customers and employees are actively engaged: high loyalty and maximum effort. In the Social Age, then, it's a brand's responsibility to create that culture. And, as we've seen, when that culture exists, magic happens.

Which is why OPEN collaboration will become the norm. Customers and employees will go out of their way to actively make a product better. They will engage on social; despite constrictive "primary responsibilities," they will cowork in person. They will provide input on features they find lacking or missing. They will act like a 2-billion-strong focus group. And companies—some perhaps for the first time ever—will actively listen.

And it doesn't stop there. Once a company gets used to listening, more magic happens. With mutually beneficial relationships established, organizations will learn to ask—they'll ask good questions, and they'll ask for help. And companies that really get it will ask before a product is even fully developed. Customers and employees will collaborate to design the products they sell and buy.

Admittedly, this particular wish list item is a softball pitched right over the plate—pretty easy for us to hit a home run with this one.

But let's take it a step further . . .

What if a shoe manufacturer floated a challenge to members of its OPEN circles to invent a whole new material or an entirely new design? One that would make Ted's new Topo Athletic shoes seem ho-hum? And then what if the manufacturer let the crowd decide which design wins? What if it gamified this process and repeated it once a year, or once a quarter? What kind of really funky, or revolutionarily functional, new shoes would consumers design?

What kind of buzz would that create?

What kind of market share would this company steal from today's incumbents?

Tapping the creative juices of your current customers? That remains a largely unexplored vista. Not only is OPEN collaboration a trend we can predict for the near future, it is one we see playing out to very good results for the most socially savvy companies. The only question is: Who will be perceived as social collaboration innovators—and who will be perceived as me-toos and also-rans?

## CONSUMERISM IN 3D

Social isn't the only technology to thrive in our twenty-first century. Three-dimensional printers, for instance, are certainly making headlines. Their potential blows us and millions of others away. Still, for many, 3D printing seems a little . . . out there.

And yet there is Easton LaChappelle, 17 years old and using only information available online, readily available parts (including fishing line), and a borrowed 3D printer, creating a prosthetic arm capable of utilizing brain waves to control arm and hand function—for less than $500.

So what if we didn't need an arm that talked to our brain? What if we just needed a cane? Or shoes? Or a leash for the dog so we could put on the shoes, grab the cane, and take the pooch for a walk?

As we go to press with *A World Gone Social,* you can buy a 3D printer on eBay for about $500—less than what most of us might pay for a tablet computer or a television for the bedroom. So imagine that in just a few years everyone needs a 3D printer like we need our smartphones now.

Why?

3D consumerism.

Imagine this scenario: A person announces on Twitter that she's been invited to an event-to-die-for . . . tonight. Trouble is, she needs a dress. An amazing dress. Now. A friend sees the dilemma and sends her a link to a little dress she saw last night in a Facebook post. She follows the link—and loves the dress! She provides the innovative clothing company her perfect size via MeasureMe, a universal sizing web app by GGIS, as well as a color swatch from the clutch she'll be clutching at the event. She pays for the dress, clicks a button, and goes to take a bubble bath, thinking of what an amazing evening it will be.

When she comes out of the bathroom, she walks straight to her 3D printer. There, exactly as she ordered it, is a brand-new dress.

Hey, it could happen. (The printing of the dress has happened. When Ted was looking for real-world applications of 3D printing for a speaking engagement, he discovered a dress created entirely on a 3D printer!)

If a dress is possible, how many other products that you spot online could be created at home? Someone on Pinterest might say, for example, "You have to see this vase!" only to have the connected consumers within that OPEN circle say, "Oh, nice!"—and before they can cut flowers from the garden, there is the vase. That person then takes a picture, posts it back on Pinterest, saying, "Thanks for the recommendation—here's mine!"

We believe 3D consumerism will be a major disrupter in the Social Age, that customers will go from social to order to creation—all in the comfort of their own homes. Where today we go to Facebook to share intangible experiences with our friends, tomorrow we will be drawn to make-it-yourself sites with intuitive open-source code for us to manipulate a product to our liking, then create, and share, in near real time.

We're so sure, we'll bet you a pair of shoes—which we'll produce on a 3D printer.

## DIGITAL SHARECROPPING WILL BECOME A GLOBAL ISSUE

We can't remember exactly where we first heard the term *digital sharecropping*. Mark believes it was back in 2010 when YouTern was considering moving a job board function to what amounted to a plug-in on Facebook. The term stuck with us. And the longer the Social Age is upon us, the more this concept rears its butt-ugly head.

This threat to your organization derives its name from the days after the Civil War when the poorest of farmers made a living by working and improving land owned by someone else and yet had no say in how that land was utilized, bought, or sold. Despite their investment of sweat and elbow grease, the farmer had no control, no power. If the landlord ended the agreement with the sharecropper, for any reason, the farmer was left with nothing.

Similarly, digital sharecropping is when your brand (a portion of your site, your online presence, perhaps even your business/revenue model) sits primarily on platforms owned and controlled by someone else. And by "someone else," we mean social networks, WordPress, LinkedIn, and eBay. Not that Twitter or anyone else is diabolical by nature. They're not—or, at least, we don't believe them to be.

However, with a quick change in their terms and conditions, their privacy policy, or the function of an API (an application programming interface a company releases to the public so that other developers can design products powered by its technology), your model—your social media presence—could be threatened. As we've already seen, many start-ups and service bureaus (including tools recommended here in this chapter) have had to change their operations dramatically after their "landlords" made a decision that directly impacted them.

Specifically, Facebook's pay-to-play model now forces brands to purchase sponsored posts in order for all those who "like" your page to see your content. Twitter's frequent changes to its terms and conditions and APIs and Google's constant redesign of the page rank algorithm are likewise concerning.

As entrepreneur, author and speaker Jim Rohn says:

*If you don't design your own plan, chances are you'll fall into someone else's plan. And guess what they have planned for you? Not much.*

As you plan the Social Age version of your organization, and especially your marketing plan, be aware of the current tendency toward digital sharecropping. Wherever possible, own your domain names. Drive your OPEN community to that URL with original content (blogs, video, and podcasts). Build custom mobile apps. And rather than customizing your Facebook page ad nauseam, build your intellectual property on a sustainable platform you control.

## SOCIAL MEDIA FATIGUE WILL BECOME A REAL ISSUE

There is no doubt that, as we become more adept at and more reliant on social media, *social media fatigue,* a term we first heard used by social recruiter Steve Levy, will become increasingly common. Especially among early adopters who, just a few years into the Social Age (and despite their understanding of the inherent value of social media), are perhaps starting to feel like enough is enough.

For root causes of their burnout, they point to tweets from divas, trolls, and drama queens; to narcissistic Twitter chats; to organizations with no clue how to create an authentic online brand; and, most exhausting, the self-promoters who are far more concerned with ego than integrity.

So how can you strike a balance between creating a consistent, respected online brand and suffering from social media fatigue?

Try incorporating these steps into your social strategy.

First, don't allow yourself or your brand to contribute negativity and noise to the social stream. In other words: "Think twice; press Send once."

Second, deliberately be a relentless giver. When tweeting compelling content, wishing a colleague good luck before a speaking gig, serving as an ambassador for a brand that has earned your respect, or helping a worthy cause spread the word via your OPEN community, not only do you use your influence to assist others, you greatly enhance your personal brand within a larger network.

Next, avoid the social echo chamber. When you find yourself posting the same perspective—even the same words—over and over again, when you realize you've stopped contributing original thought to a conversation, you are suffering from social media fatigue. At this point, it is not only time to step away, it is time to unplug.

Finally, set out to meet someone amazing, every day, online. This step alone helps you avoid—or at least significantly reduce the effects of—social media fatigue.

The early adopters of social media have discovered that balance is the key to combating social media fatigue. We recognize that a deeply personal relationship and genuine influence occur far more often when you hear the other people's voices, when you see their body language, when you look into their eyes. After all, 140 characters offer little insight into another person's soul. Pick up the phone. Arrange a Skype call. Buy a cup of coffee.

*More social. Less media.*

Regardless of any further predictions we, or you, might have—and despite any disagreement about the likelihood of the items on this wish list happening relatively soon—one thing we can all agree on when it comes to the future of social is this: Social media must self-regulate so it remains a safe haven for what might be 5 billion users within the next couple decades. We simply must ensure that social does not become the field where trolls and contrarians meet for battle. Emotional intelligence must be the expected norm. Perhaps even more important, social cannot become a hunting ground for predators far too anxious to separate the weak from the rest of the herd.

We all must feel safe. We all must have a voice.

## SOCIAL CHAOS WILL REIGN

And yet, chaos will remain consistent.

Chaos theory tells us that in complex systems we can't predict outcomes the way we can with more straightforward problems such as, say, an apple falling from a tree. Weather operates under the law of chaos. Stuck in a freak rainstorm without an umbrella? Don't get mad at the meteorologists. They're trying. Blame chaos.

The thing is, in a world gone social, business is ruled by chaos.

Sure, by understanding the Social Circle of Life and enabling analytics, we can anticipate some of the inevitable changes and leverage the opportunities presented. But the reality is that the future will do what the future does.

So what's the trick to leading during this chaos?

Own it! Anticipate the chaos. Deal with it head-on, quickly consider the data available to you, turn on a dime, and *go!*

Sound difficult? Think of the alternative. Schedule a meeting to discuss *if* the organization should turn, why it is or isn't turning *already,* and who is actually responsible for it *not* turning. That established, assemble a task force to decide who *will* make it turn, then determine in which direction the organization *should* go and for *how long.*

All the while, the competition has already adapted, made their decisions, executed their pivots . . . and moved on.

Chaos is inevitable. Leading in the Social Age is all about building an organization that, empowered by engagement and collaboration, thrives within that chaos. Don't shield yourself from change.

*Lead the change your competitors dread.*

That is how you will survive—and thrive—in a world gone social.

## THE REBEL HERETICS

In the sixteenth century, Copernicus, referred to as the "father of astronomy," proclaimed that the Sun did not revolve around Earth, as was commonly believed. Understanding this to go against the church doctrine of the time, and perhaps worried about being labeled a heretic, Copernicus quietly advanced his theory until he died in 1543.

Eventually, the church labeled the Copernican view of the universe as heresy. Punishment for those labeled as heretics ranged from excommunication to the death penalty and eternal damnation.

For almost a century after the death of Copernicus, the scientific community, mostly quietly, widely accepted the science behind his theory; the Sun was indeed the center of the universe.

Galileo, the father of modern astronomy, was not quiet.

He continued to speak what he knew to be true: that the way we were taught to think and act was wrong. Subsequently, he was tried and convicted by the church and labeled a heretic. Galileo spent the last decade of his life under arrest. No matter how strongly he believed in his version of the truth, he was prohibited from ever speaking of it again.

We all know change must come. We deserve more. By ushering in a new wave of leadership—leadership for the Social Age—we can do better.

Because we now know that, no matter how appropriate it was at one time, the way we've been taught to think and act as leaders is wrong; we must become rebels. We must embrace our role as heretics.

Because the best social leaders—those who institute real change—are Rebel Heretics.

Your role as a social leader—a Rebel Heretic—is to determine *how* you will bring change to your organization, industry, and the communities that support your mission. Using *A World Gone Social* as a field guide—or perhaps a compass—you must:

▶ Become hyperaware that social is both a force for good and an amplifier of bad. Be capable of looking inward for potential trouble spots while exploring new ways to extend your reach.

▶ Provide your customers and potential customers the voice they deserve while enabling them to organically grow into a series of OPEN communities and intersecting constellations. Enable them to become your boldest advocates.

▶ Through effective recruiting (and through your new best friend, attrition), hire toward the culture you want to see in your organization ten years from now. Above all else, build a socially aware, customer-first environment.

▶ Respect employees so they come to work every day feeling like the mature, responsible adults you deliberately hired. Enable these highly talented individuals to offer up their personal OPEN circles to your brand, refer their friends, and become actively engaged brand ambassadors.

▶ Through active listening, deliberately engage with customers and those you want to be customers: current and potential employees, vendors, influencers—even your competitors. At every opportunity, build mutually beneficial relationships.

▶ Tap into the unrelenting power of OPEN, making both your personal brand and the brand of your organization into a social powerhouse, to build reputations as relentless givers and no-reciprocation-required connectors.

▶ Turn nano—*get nimble*—so you can compete effectively with those that will be coming after your customers, and your market share.

▶ Over time, democratize the workplace. No matter what path you take—flat,

Holacracy, or turning the org chart upside down—dismantle the costly and calcified hierarchy and bureaucracy that hold your organization back.

► Bring up, right alongside you, any dinosaurs who may be lagging behind— C-suite executives, middle managers, members of your board, perhaps—so that embracing the Social Age becomes a top-down imperative at your organization.

► Consistently earn your relevance with the customers and communities you serve by coupling the power of content marketing and audience engagement to your overall business strategy.

► Master technology within the Social Circle of Life. Make thorough use of analytics, both forensic and predictive, to bring sense to all the data your social employees are "shaking off" as they go about their daily engagement.

► Most important, you must become a "Blue Unicorn"—the true social leader who sets the example for active listening, engagement, and unqualified service to your customers.

While you are doing that, here's what your dinosaur-led competition is asking:

*How do we protect ourselves from this change? How do we maintain our position . . . the status quo? How do we hold on to what we have?*

In the Social Age, guess who wins—who doesn't just survive, but *thrives?*

As we've said throughout *A World Gone Social,* this won't be easy. And only the bold will succeed.

You must be bold enough to be different, to wear your "Rebel Heretic" label like a badge of honor. You must be bold enough to be passionate about your role and the mission of bringing those you lead—whether it be a team of 6 or 600,000—into the Social Age. You must be bold enough to ask the tough questions, listen to the answers, and learn from what you hear.

Most essential, you cannot enter the Social Age as just another isomorphic "me too" player, doing only what is expected under the banner of "best practices" (which by definition means you aren't likely to be considered better than anyone else with that same mindset).

You must be bold enough to be yourself. While the advice within *A World Gone Social* is meant to be thorough, it is intentionally *not* a step-by-step "how to" book. Every situation, every organization, has different goals and priorities. Your job is to apply all this advice at your pace, within your style. Make it your own!

Determine what makes you stand out. Why do others love working with you?

What are you really, really good at? What do you do that makes people smile? What about your personality makes them want to follow you?

*Find that. Bottle that. Sell that.*

Be yourself. Be different.

*Change happens only as the result of insurmountable market pressure.*

The primary purpose of this last chapter in *A World Gone Social* is to talk about the future—how social might continue to impact our business world as we move deeper into the Social Age.

If this Law of Change holds true—if change does come only as the result of insurmountable market pressure—then we can't talk about that future without talking about you.

*You* are the future of social. You are—or will soon become—a member of a small community of passionate leaders, change makers, and social catalysts.

Together, we will become *insurmountable* pressure. A force of change.

Are you ready to lead your team *into the Social Age*?

# THIS IS NOT THE FINAL THOUGHT
## ON *A WORLD GONE SOCIAL*

We hope you've enjoyed reading *A World Gone Social*. More important, we hope the thoughts shared, during what has been a passion project for us, ignite passion in you. The best-case scenario: You are now ready to lead your team, or your organization, into the Social Age.

Yet we know this is only a book—and books are static, aren't they? Books are resources, certainly, and a great way to get a conversation started, but they aren't *social* resources. In a way, to this point this book has served the same role as Industrial Age broadcast media: For the last 200+ pages we've been talking *at* you, not *with* you.

For the Rebel Heretics this book inspires, we want there to be a place or two where we build an OPEN community of social leaders. A place to continue the conversation around not just surviving the Social Age, but thriving.

That is why we've established AWorldGoneSocial.com. There, we provide a forum for blog posts, videos, and podcasts—not just from the two of us but from all Rebel Heretics and Blue Unicorns. We feature social leaders willing to share what has worked (and what has *not* worked!) for them while they built a socially enabled team, created a customer-first culture, or collaborated to build an entire constellation of OPEN circles.

The site also presents insights from respected thought leaders in the social space as well as advocates, champions, and brand ambassadors actively moving their mission forward through social. And, of course, we share the stories of your fellow social leaders as they travel around the Social Circle of Life.

We also invite you to join the Rebel Heretics LinkedIn group, where we join the Switch and Shift community to talk about leadership, engagement, culture, customer experience, and every other aspect of the human side of business.

Most important, we want to hear from you.

As you know by now, both your authors spend more than a little time on Twitter. Reach out to @tedcoine and @MarkSBabbitt. Introduce yourself. Ask us questions. Invite us to join your OPEN circles. Tell us your thoughts on how best to grow as leaders in a world gone social.

We'll be thrilled to engage with you.

See you on AWorldGoneSocial.com, in our LinkedIn group, and on Twitter!

# References

## Chapter 1: Welcome to the Social Age

Stan Phelps. *What's Your Purple Goldfish? How to Win Customers and Influence Word of Mouth.* (Cary, NC: 9 Inch Marketing, 2012).

Tim Nudd. "How a Fan Post on Panera's Facebook Page Got Half a Million Likes." August 14, 2012. Accessed August 5, 2013. http://www.adweek.com/adfreak/how-fan-post -paneras-facebook-page-got-half-million-likes-142716.

## Chapter 2: The Customer Holds All the Cards

"United Breaks Guitars." Wikipedia. Last updated February 27, 2014. Last accessed March 1, 2014. http://en.wikipedia.org/wiki/United_Breaks_Guitars.

Pete Cashmore. "Southwest Tweets, Blogs Apology to Kevin Smith." Mashable. February 10, 2010. Accessed July 12, 2013. http://mashable.com/2010/02/14/southwest -kevin-smith/.

Elizabeth Dias. "The 22-Year-Old Who Led the Charge Against Bank of America." Time.com. November 7, 2011. Accessed July 11, 2013. http://content.time.com/time/nation/ article/0,8599,2098715,00.html.

"The Web at 25 in the U.S." Pew Research Center. February 27, 2014. Accessed March 4, 2014. http://www.pewinternet.org/files/2014/02/PIP_25th-anniversary-of-the -Web_0227141.pdf.

"One In Every 5 People in the World Own a Smartphone, One in Every 17 Own a Tablet." BI Intelligence. December 13, 2013. Accessed January 2, 2014. http://www .businessinsider.com/smartphone-and-tablet-penetration-2013–10#ixzz30oFwxRYe.

"Forecast: PCs, Ultramobiles, and Mobile Phones, Worldwide, 2010–2017, 4Q13 Update." Gartner. December 18, 2013. Accessed January 2, 2014. https://www.gartner.com/ doc/2639615.

Tim Mak. "Bank of America CEO Brian Moynihan: 'A right to make a profit.' " Politico .com. October 6, 2011. Accessed July 14, 2013. http://www.politico.com/news/ stories/1011/65297.html#ixzz30oQa7MVJ.

Jake Horowitz. "Thanks to Change.org Petition, Verizon Cancels $2 Convenience Fee." PolicyMic. December 31, 2011. Accessed July 14, 2013. http://www.policymic.com/ articles/3127/thanks-to-change-org-petition-verizon-cancels-2-convenience-fee.

## Chapter 3: The Social Employee: Good, Bad, and Way Past Ugly

Casey St. Clair. "Target: Take the High Road and Save Thanksgiving." Accessed January 15, 2013. http://www.change.org/petitions/target-take-the-high-road-and -save-thanksgiving.

"Target Talks Thanksgiving and Black Friday." November 14, 2012. Accessed January 13, 2013. http://abullseyeview.com/2012/11/target-talks-thanksgiving-and-black-friday/.

Emanuella Grinberg. "Retail Employees Fight 'Black Friday creep'" November 15, 2012. Accessed January 15, 2013. http://www.cnn.com/2012/11/15/living/black -friday-thanksgiving/.

Matt Brownell. "Target Responds to Backlash Over Thanksgiving Night Black Friday Sale." November 16, 2012. Accessed January 14, 2013. http://www.dailyfinance .com/2012/11/16/target-responds-to-backlash-over-thanksgiving-night-black-friday/.

Cavan Sieczkowski ."Lindsey Stone, Plymouth Woman, Takes Photo at Arlington National Cemetery, Causes Facebook Fury." Huffington Post. November 20, 2012. Accessed August 1, 2013. http://www.huffingtonpost.com/2012/11/20/lindsey-stone-facebook -photo-arlington-national-cemetery-unpaid-leave_n_2166842.html.

David Griner. "Justine Sacco Fired by IAC for 'Hope I Don't Get AIDS' Tweet." Adweek. December 21, 2013. Accessed January 2, 2014. http://www.adweek.com/adfreak/justine -sacco-fired-iac-hope-i-dont-get-aids-tweet-154639.

Meredith Bennett-Smith. "Pax Dickinson, Business Insider CTO, Forced to Resign After Offensive Tweets Discovered." Huffington Post. September 10, 2013. Accessed October 24, 2014. http://www.huffingtonpost.com/2013/09/10/pax-dickinson-fired-business -insider-tweets_n_3900548.html.

Susan Adams. "Don't Fire an Employee and Leave Them in Charge of the Corporate Twitter Account." Forbes. February 1, 2013. Accessed January 4, 2014. http://www.forbes .com/sites/susanadams/2013/02/01/dont-fire-an-employee-and-leave-them-in -charge-of-the-corporate-twitter-account.

Pete Pachal. "StubHub Twitter Account Posts Vulgar Tweet, Then Deletes It." Mashable. October 5, 2012. Accessed January 4, 2014. http://mashable.com/2012/10/05/ stubhub-tweet/.

## Chapter 4: The Evolution of Social Recruiting

Matt Adler. "Redefining Social Recruiting for 2011." Metashift. March 8, 2011. Accessed July 21, 2013. http://www.metashift.co.uk/blog/2011/03/08/redefining-social -recruiting-for-2011.

Kimberly Kasper. "The 2013 Social Recruiting Survey Results Are Here." Jobvite. September 5, 2013. Accessed July 21, 2013. http://blog.jobvite.com/2013/09/ 2013jobvitesocialrecruitingsurvey/.

"2013 North American Social Recruiting Activity Report." Bullhorn. April 2013. Last accessed July 21, 2013. http://www.bullhorn.com/sites/default/files/ 2013NASRActivityReportFINAL.pdf.

"Jobvite Social Recruiting Survey Finds Over 90% of Employers Will Use Social Recruiting. Jobvite. July 9, 2012. Last accessed July 21, 2013. http://recruiting.jobvite.com/ company/press-releases/2012/jobvite-social-recruiting-survey-2012.

"You Won't Believe Who Is Tops in Social Recruiting." HR Daily News. May 21, 2013. Accessed July 21, 2013. http://hrnewsdaily.com/tops-social-media-recruiting/.

John Zappe. "The ROI of Social Media: Branding, Not So Much for Sourcing." SourceCon. April 16, 2013. Last accessed July 22, 2013. http://www.sourcecon.com/news/ 2013/04/16/the-roi-of-social-media-branding-not-so-much-for-sourcing/.

## Chapter 5: The Engagement Era

"State of Engagement: Unveiling the Latest Employee Engagement Research." Modern Survey. December 2013. Last accessed March 1, 2014. http://www.modernsurvey.com/wp-content/uploads/2013/12/The-State-of-Engagement-Report-Fall-2013.pdf.

Ted Coiné. *Spoil 'em Rotten!: Five-Star Customer Delight in Action.* (Bloomington, IN: iUniverse, 2007).

Becky Robinson. "The Story of the Shoes: How @topoathletic Won My Heart." December 21, 2013. Accessed January 10, 2013. http://weavinginfluence.com/social-media/the-story-of-the-shoes-how-topoathletic-won-my-heart.

## Chapter 6: It Takes a Community

Michael Port. *Book Yourself Solid: The Fastest, Easiest, and Most Reliable System for Getting More Clients Than You Can Handle Even if You Hate Marketing and Selling.* (Hoboken, NJ: John Wiley & Sons, 2010).

## Chapter 7: The Death of Large

Renee Montagne. "1 Man Does It Faster, Cheaper Than Big Pharma." NPR. June 27, 2011. Accessed November 11, 2014. http://www.npr.org/2011/06/27/137441972/1-man-does-it-fast-cheaper-than-big-pharma.

Seth Godin. "Bat Boy Syndrome" Seth Godin's blog. February 4, 2014. Accessed March 1, 2014. http://sethgodin.typepad.com/seths_blog/2014/02/bat-boy-syndrome.html.

## Chapter 8: Flat: The New Black?

"Self Management." MorningStarCo.com. Accessed February 1, 2013. http://morningstarco.com/index.cgi?Page=Self-Management.

Spencer Johnson. *Who Moved My Cheese? An Amazing Way to Deal with Change in Your Work and in Your Life.* (New York: Putnam, 1998).

Rick Wartzman. "If Self-Management Is Such a Great Idea, Why Aren't More Companies Doing It?" September 25, 2012. Accessed October 25, 2013. http://www.forbes.com/sites/drucker/2012/09/25/self-management-a-great-idea/.

Malcolm Gladwell. *The Tipping Point: How Little Things Can Make a Big Difference.* (New York: Little, Brown, 2002).

Jason Fried. "Why I Run a Flat Company." Inc. April 1, 2011. Accessed March 1, 2013. http://www.inc.com/magazine/20110401/jason-fried-why-i-run-a-flat-company.html.

Ricardo Semler. Maverick! The Success Story Behind the World's Most Unusual Workplace. (New York: Warner Books, 1993).

## Chapter 9: The OPEN Challenge
## (Ordinary People, Extraordinary Network)

Adam Grant. *Give and Take.* (New York: Viking Books, 2013).

James Surowiecki. *The Wisdom of Crowds.* (New York: Anchor Books, 2004).

David Burkus. *The Myths of Creativity.* (New York: John Wiley & Sons, 2013).

"The State of Independence in America." MBO Partners. September 2013. Accessed

December 7, 2013. http://info.mbopartners.com/rs/mbo/images/2013-MBO
_Partners_State_of_Independence_Report.pdf.

Ian Greenleigh. *The Social Media Side Door: How to Bypass the Gatekeepers to Gain Greater Access and Influence.* (New York: McGraw-Hill, 2013).

## Chapter 10: The Social Leader: A Blue Unicorn?

Kurt Wagner. "70% of Fortune 500 CEOs Aren't Using Social Media." Mashable. August 7, 2013. Accessed January 10, 2014. http://mashable.com/2013/08/07/fortune-500 -ceos-social-media/.

Ann Charles. "2012 CEO, Social Media & Leadership Survey." BRANDfog. January 2013. Accessed November 10, 2013. http://www.brandfog.com/CEOSocialMediaSurvey/ BRANDfog_2012_CEO_Survey.pdf.

Tom Peters. *In Search of Excellence.* (New York: HarperCollins, 1982).

## Chapter 11: Building a World-Class Team for the Social Age

Gary Flood. "Facebook Ranks Top 'Enterprise' Collaboration Platform." Information Week. May 20, 2013. Accessed January 12, 2014. http://www.informationweek.com/ applications/facebook-ranks-top-enterprise-collaboration-platform/d/d-id/1110033.

"Doing Business with Harley-Davidson: Company History and Background." Harley-Davidson Supplier Network. December 1999. Last accessed March 1, 2014. https://www.h-dsn.com/genbus/PublicDocServlet?docID=18&docExt=p.

Review of Harley-Davidson. Indeed.com. September 22, 2012. Accessed March 1, 2014. http://www.indeed.com/cmp/Harley—davidson/reviews?start=20&lang=en.

## Chapter 12: In the Social Age, Customer Experience Comes First

"Ben & Jerry's Nails It with New Core Ice Cream Flavors." Huffington Post. February 25, 2014. Accessed March 2, 2014. http://www.huffingtonpost.com/2014/02/25/ben -jerrys-core-ice-cream_n_4854680.html.

Ted Coiné. *Five-Star Customer Service.* (Lincoln, NE: iUniverse, 2005).

Robert Spector and Patrick D. McCarthy. *The Nordstrom Way to Customer Service Excellence.* (Hoboken, NJ: John Wiley & Sons, 2005).

Linda Dishman. "Corporate Social Media Policies: The Good, the Mediocre, and the Ugly." (FastCompany.com. July 2010. Accessed May 4, 2010. http://www.fastcompany .com/1668368/corporate-social-media-policies-good-mediocre-and-ugly.

Vineet Nayar. "Employees First, Customers Second: Turning Conventional Management Upside Down." HBR Press. June 8, 2010. Accessed February 1, 2014. http://hbr.org/ product/employees-first-customers-second-turning-conventio/an/12330-HBK-ENG.

"Walt Disney Quotes." Source of Insight. April 8, 2013. Accessed January 10, 2014. http://sourcesofinsight.com/walt-disney-quotes/.

## Chapter 13: And Stop Calling Me "Social Media Marketing"

"John Wanamaker." Wikipedia. Last modified April 11, 2014. Accessed May 5, 2014. http://en.wikipedia.org/wiki9/John_Wanamaker.

Gary Vaynerchuck. *Jab, Jab, Jab, Right Hook: How to Tell Your Story in a Noisy Social World.* (New York: HarperCollins, 2013).

## Chapter 14: Investing in Social: Is What You See Real?

"The Value of a Facebook Fan 2013: Revisiting Consumer Brand Currency in Social Media." Hotspex/Syncapse. April 2013. Accessed February 15, 2014. http://www.purplewifi .net/wp-content/uploads/2013/04/Syncapse_Value_of_a_Fan_Report_2013.pdf.

"A Strategy for Managing Social Media Proliferation." Altimeter Group. January 5, 2012. Accessed January 12, 2014. http://www.slideshare.net/jeremiah_owyang/smms -report-010412finaldraft.

"Enterprise Social Media Manangement Software 2013: A Marketer's Guide." Digital Marketing Depot. April 2013. Accessed January 12, 2014. http://downloads .digitalmarketingdepot.com/rs/thirddoormedia/images/MIR_1305_EntSocMd13 .pdf?mkt_tok=3RkMMJWWfF9wsRons63LZKXonjHpfsX77%2BksUa%2BwlMI %2F0ER3fOvrPUfGjI4DTsNnI%2BSLDwEYGJlv6SgFTbLCMbpx37gNXxU%3D.

John H. Sheridan. "Andy Grove: Building an Information Age Legacy." IndustryWeek. December 21, 2004. Accessed January 12, 2014. http://www.industryweek.com/ companies-amp-executives/1997-technology-leader-yearandy-grove-building -information-age-legacy.

## Chapter 15: The Future of Business in a World Gone Social

Tamora Pierce. *Bloodhounds*. (New York: Random House, 2009).

Jim Rohn. BrainyQuotes. Accessed March 14, 2014. http://www.brainyquote.com/quotes/ authors/j/jim_rohn.html.

# Index